Re-Visioning Methods and Approaches in the Study of Religion

Contents

Section - III

Prof. Rev. Dr. T. Swami Raju

institutions today work for promoting interfaith dialogue for understanding of religions, religious harmony and peaceful coexistence of religions.

Rev. Dr. Raju who though was born Hindu, the family chose to follow Christ immediately after few months of his birth. Rev. Dr. Raju vividly describes in his autobiography the healing and life-giving touch of Christ Jesus to him brought the family to follow Christ. His writings speak volumes of how religious communities interact among each other and make their faith experience proclamatory to other communities. Rev. Dr. Raju's parent's 'testimony' and his own faith encounters made him what he is today. Nevertheless, he has never given up his passion to study Hindu Religious Traditions, particularly the popular religious traditions and practices that are very much prevalent in faith communities. Therefore, to him interfaith dialogue takes place in most informal ways in communities.

His personal encounter of Christ is both scholastic and experiential. For him academic approach to the study of religions rather strengthens the personal faith, for one cannot journey academically without encountering in personal ways. Faith and reason go hand in hand for students of religions. His writings also encroach the field of biblical studies and Christian theology. His one volume bible commentary in Telugu language reflects his commitment to his faith that his parents embraced, and contributions to the church at large by reading the scripture from interreligious perspective. His students have contributed articles in the book. As students of religions they too are deeply committed to scientific study of religions. How does one view faiths and beliefs in today's context? How does the religions find relevance in modern and postmodern world? In what ways religions respond to various contemporary challenges? The rise of religious fundamentalism, communalism, terrorism in the name of religions, ecological issues, the religious nationalism and the exhibition of religions in public and marketplaces are few that need immediate attention in the study of religions. The geo-political situation and the societal expectations make the study much more complex and at times critical. As budding scholars and the future teachers of religions in theological institutions they give us the hope that they are committed to make study of religions move forward to the next level. They further reiterate that the only way to study religions is to study from the perspectives of faith communities.

This volume is an additional wealth of resources particularly for students of theology who want to learn more about religions of the people. Such writings and many more in related areas must be encouraged from scholars and researchers alike to make academic community to understand the role of religions in society.

Kolkata
September 11th 2019

Rev. Dr. Santanu K. Patro, Registrar
Senate of Serampore College (University)

Editorial

It is an honour and privilege to present this festschrift in commemoration of the life and contributions of Prof. Rev. Dr. Swami Raju Tadivaka in theological education on his 60th birthday. Sir Swami Raju, as we know him, is an exemplary teacher. His life is a testimony of humility, sincerity and dedication. He is a man of God who begins and ends every endeavor with prayers. His contribution in the academic scholarship, especially in the field of religion, under the Senate of Serampore College (University) is commendable. He is also an active promoter of the ministry of interfaith relations.

Re-Visioning Methods and Approaches in the Study of Religion: Essays in Honour of Swami Raju Tadivaka is a collection of 20 articles on the issues, methods and approaches in the study of religion. The book maintains that the study of religion is dynamic. The modern science of religion developed in the second part of the 19th century. The applied methods and approaches in the study of religion during this period were the product of the day. Overtime, the changes in contexts and emerging prospects in the study of religion necessitated a critical appraisal of the erstwhile modern science of religion. The contributors of these articles have attempted to appraise the methods and approaches in the contemporary study of religion, especially in formulating the theoretical frameworks of religious plurality and interfaith dialogue.

The editors would like to express our sincere thanks to Swami Raju sir for the privilege as editors of the book and to all the contributors for your efforts and co-operation without which this book would not have seen the light of day.

Pranay Bin, Aorenla Longchar and Pamhor Thumra

1

Understanding Religion(s)— Is A Particular Faith A Handicap?

Eric J. Lott

Given the vast range of the world's many religions, seeking to understand religion's essence seems an endless task. Even finding an acceptable *definition* of 'religion' is far from straightforward. Simple assumptions often prove unfounded. And in theological circles (in the West at least) for over a century influential voices have often attempted to depict true Christian faith as somehow beyond 'religion'. In the 1930s Hendrick Kraemer, following the lead given by Barthian theologians in Europe, gave this position prominence within missiological circles. Faith in Christ is thought to rise categorically above all other religious systems, taking us to a different order of human experience. (See his *The Christian Message in a Non-Christian World* 1938). Then, in the 1970s and 80s there was even a move among certain theologians to develop 'religionless theology', as the most authentic form of modern faith.

In reality, this attempt to place Christian faith as something *beyond religion* seriously distorts that faith. The very opposite can be argued: it is by exposure to a wide range of religious traditions that the true function of theology is appreciated. Or, in the words of the nineteenth century religious studies pioneer, Max Mueller, 'To know only *one* religion, is to know none'.

And we may well ask just how this claim for a religion-transcending position for Christian faith differs from crude fundamentalism. It is the testimony of many, myself included, that their faith, even their faith in Christ has been greatly enriched by their exploring of the religious experience of traditions very different from their own. In itself, then, Christian faith is not somehow beyond the realm of 'mere religion'.

The title of this brief essay, however, puts the issue differently. And before responding more directly to the question raised in that title, we shall look briefly at the key features of 'Religion'. I make no apology for turning here to the work of my early guru, Ninian Smart, who in the late 1950s introduced me to the wider—indeed almost limitless—world of 'Religions'. It was Smart who proposed six essential, and still pertinent, 'dimensions' of this vast area of human experience.

While these six can be listed separately, in reality they are interdependent, relating organically to each other. They are differing ways in which human experience, or seek to engage with, that which is perceived as *Sacred Power*. Thus, there is the experience of sacred *act*, sacred *story*, sacred *belief-system*, sacred *community* and a set of *life-values* derived from this sacred life-view. Together these give varieties of lived experience of that which is seen as the sacred centre of our human world.

And the negative side of this is the sense of being *impure*—especially if somehow separated from the source of purity. (We might think here of the fear of Hindu people in earlier times that travel abroad, away from holy Mother Bharat, entailed loss of purity, a tainting pollution that required special washing away with water from some holy source. Christians belonging to certain sects feel similar nervousness—'Will we become polluted if we are in any way separated from the community of the saved'?). Purity and impurity can thus be seen as key categories in traditional religious experience.

Now to the five key 'dimensions' of the Sacred:

i. First, the sacred *act* is found in a vast range of differing forms of ritual that religious people engage in and find to be meaningful at some deeper level of their being. More monotheistic religious traditions—Judaism, Christianity, Islam—may ridicule what appears to them to be 'vain idolatry', but the fact is that vastly more people do find meaning (even if not articulated) in the various sacred acts in which communally they engage in: national festivals, community pilgrimages, family rituals and suchlike.
ii. Then, there is the sacred *story*. Tales with mythic status are told and retold—and thus probably find slightly different forms through the centuries as a community's circumstances change. While some scholars will claim, 'In the beginning was the sacred *act*', others will see the *story* as having this primal position—especially stories relating to the community's origins, or perhaps creation's origins.

iii. Thirdly, there are *belief-systems*, though *systematic* expression of religious belief may be minimal, especially in primal traditions. Clearly mythic story and faith-system overlap at times. Few traditions have the credal orthodoxy of Christian history—the consequences of which many would see as a sad blot on the life of the Church. Whether found in credal form or not, whether even consciously articulated or not, all religious communities have assumptions about the way things are that form a body of beliefs.

iv. A focus on 'orthodoxy' links us with the fourth dimension of religious life, belief in a sacred *community*. Many Christians, for example, are part of a worshiping group that each week declares its faith in a 'holy, catholic and apostolic church'. No doubt there are numerous religions (e.g. some forms of Buddhist and Hindu tradition) in which the individual is eventually to aim at a state of being that transcends community relationship A similar goal seems common in modern 'westernised' spiritualties too. Quite large numbers today seek refuge in a yogic experience of 'aloneness', free of all limiting entanglements with the outside world.

v. Finally, there are *ethical life-values* that are equally part of the religious world-view. In the Judaic, Christian and Muslim traditions, for example, such life-values, even held as 'commandments', are clearly prominent. While less obvious, in Eastern religious traditions too the life-values taught as essential to the tradition are made very clear, as we see, for example, very clearly in the *Bhagavad Gita*. It is in more 'primal' communities that personal and social ethical values seem less clear-cut, less held in common by all.

vi. For example, I recall from my early years in India—in a very rural community in Telangana—at a crowded and very popular fair, seeing a father displaying his son of 9-10 years old that he had whipped to the point where the skin of his back was deeply lined with bleeding lash-marks. And this was nothing to do with the need for children to be obedient. It was shown as a mark of deep devotion to his deity. But, even in the modern world, when mothers from certain regions of the globe believe it their duty to have the clitoral parts of their daughters cut away, critical questions are quite rightly raised. What is seen as the right way to some is regarded as dangerously un-ethical, even un-human, by others.

It should again be stressed that this analysis of the key dimensions or facets of what can be regarded as 'religious' life can be termed a 'phenomenological' stance on the subject (ignoring the way in which at times this term has been used in a highly specialist manner). The above analysis also reckons with the fact that we have to do with a multiplicity of different *religions* (in the plural), rather than with *Religion per se.* In other words such an approach takes seriously both the variations found between different traditions, as well as the commonalities.

Nor does such a view of religious life make any normative theological judgements, or raise questions concerning the reality or unreality of any aspect of religious life. It is essentially *descriptive* not prescriptive. And this is a position that theologians have invariably found very difficult to maintain, even if they desired so to do. Beginning with a theologically based view of what religion *should be* often makes it difficult to have an *unprejudiced* view of what religion actually is.

Briefly, then, let us look at the question of whether a particular faith *necessarily* makes the understanding of the religious experience of others problematic. Or, are there actually *advantages* in being a believer of some sort? Does faith of any kind actually enable *greater sensitivity* in understanding the belief-system of others?

It could be argued that once there has been experience of the sacred dimension of our life in this world, provided this experience is not immediately hedged in by hard-line doctrine of what such an experience *ought* to be (as can happen all to easily within fundamentalist communities), left to mature within the person or group of persons having the experience, it is far more likely to result in an inclusive rather than an exclusive life-attitude, even when this entails relating to other people of faith.

This will especially be the case when at the heart of the conversion experience there is a message of divine Love. Love is essentially *inclusive* rather than exclusive. Thus, when a preacher such as John Wesley, who was so gripped by the conviction that he too was wonderfully loved by God, Love that knows no bounds, he declared himself happy to shake the hands of (i.e. be in fellowship with) anyone, Muslim or any other, who is similarly sure of God's love.

Finally, to take this a small step further, the experience of divine Love within one's own tradition, is also able to make us more sensitive to, more able to appreciate and to communicate with people whose faith-tradition happens to be other than our own. We are then more able to explore the inner meaning of their religious life. I am personally convinced that, if there has been anything of value in the vast amount of engaging with thc faith of others that has been part of the 65 years of my life-ministry, it is because of an early conviction (in tune with my Methodist heritage) that divine Love is ultimate. It is this essentially *religious* experience that leads on to finding God at work in an endless range of life situations.

2

Challenges of the Plurality of Scriptures and Responses

Israel Selvanayagam

Shattering our Convictions and Challenging our Knowledge

How wonderful to have a scripture, the only scripture holy and truly revealing that has appeal to the whole of humanity! We cherish, revere, read it devotionally and get guidance for day to day living. However, we are suddenly struck with questions about clear application as we encounter contradictions and factual inconsistencies. Because of this situation, new sects emerge within each religious tradition, and each develops a particular line of interpretation, seeking cardinal truths as doctrines and attractive structures. There have been many conflicts over scriptural interpretation. There have been different viewpoints on translating the scripture from the original which is believed to be holy. We have martyrs of scriptural translations and revisions. While we had enough of these for wounded memories of our history, a new challenge erupted with more questions.

Frederick Max Müller (1823-1900), celebrated as the pioneer of the modern scientific study of religion, an Anglo-Saxon genius based in the University of Oxford, initiated a project of translating the world's scriptures by Oriental scholars, being himself both a translator and the chief editor. The project resulted in the fifty volumes of the *Sacred Books of the East* produced over the span of 32 years (1879-1910).[1] With detailed textual notes the work proved to be outstanding and impressive. Although, Müller's definition of religion and his proposals for the study of religion have been surpassed by new theories, there is nothing to replace these translations of the world's scriptures from classical languages. Western scholars must have found them overwhelming and not many had the courage and humility to use their contents in their biblical and theological scholarship. However, Müller's philological dictum 'he who knows one knows none' continued to be echoing in the scholarly world.

Müller in his long Preface of 41 pages to the first volume points out in passing some of his key assumptions about the sacred books. He notes the general attitude of those scholars who had 'devoted their life either to the editing of the original texts or to the careful interpretation of some of the sacred books'. Identifying himself with these scholars, he nevertheless criticises their inclination 'after they have disinterred from a heap of rubbish some solitary fragments of pure gold, to exhibit these treasures only then to display all the refuse from which they had to extract them'. He speaks disparagingly about their 'joy of finding one or two fragrant fruits or flowers' but gladly forgetting 'the brambles and thorns that had to be thrown aside' in 'the bewildering forest of the sacred literature of the East'. For him now the time had come when the study of religions of humankind 'must be approached in a different, in a less enthusiastic, and more discriminating, in fact, in a more scholar-like spirit'. Müller looked for truth, the whole truth, and if it must be told, he observed that, 'however radiant the dawn of religious thought, it is not without its dark clouds, its chilling colds, its noxious vapours'. In the way of facing the problem of completeness, he confesses that he himself discovered how the Sacred Books of the East 'by the side of so much that is fresh, natural, simple, beautiful, and true, contain so much that is not only unmeaning, artificial, silly, but even hideous and repellent'.

Students of religion of any religious persuasion and adherence have something to learn from Max Müller. An honest student, however, would straight away ask one penetrating question which is very significant for Christians: are the cases of 'solitary fragments of pure gold in a heap of rubbish'; 'fragrant fruits or flowers in the midst of brambles and thorns'; 'the radiant truth within dark clouds and chilling colds and noxious vapours'; and 'so much that is fresh, natural, simple, beautiful and true but mixed with unmeaning, artificial, silly, hideous and repellent' not applicable to the Bible also? How do we account for the unending genealogies, complex

1 *The Sacred Book of the East*, translated by various Oriental Scholars and edited by F. Max Müller (Oxford: Clarendon Press, 50 volumes [1879-1910]). Now available as an eBook.

prescriptions on rituals, the tales of terror and the ambiguous characters of some of the great figures mentioned in the Bible? Müller did not seem to be aware of this question, although in passing he mentions as a positive thing that the Old Testament has been kept distinct from the Talmud, and the New Testament from spurious gospels and the records of the wrangling of the early Councils. He seems to think that the process of the canonisation of the Judeo-Christian Scriptures saved them from the perplexing mixture of good and bad and 'the wild confusion of sublime truth with vulgar stupidity that meets us in the pages of the Veda, the Avesta, and the Tripiṭaka'. Additionally, the following scriptures are also translated: the Upanishads, sacred laws of the Aryans, sacred books of China (including the texts of Confucianism), Phalvi texts (from middle Iran), the Quran, institutes of Vishnu, Bhagavad Gita and its extended books, Buddhist Suttas, Dhammapada, the Satapatha Brahmana, Jaina Sutras, Saddharma-Pundarikas (Lotus of the True Law)—some of them in more than one part and volume.

Max Müller was interested in the Indian scriptures written in Sanskrit and Pali languages which he considered classics. Later there were more works of translation from regional yet classical languages. Some of them have the marks of a more empathetic approach with theological openness. For example, G.U. Pope (1820-1907), an Anglican missionary to South India, in the course of learning the Tamil language came across the most popular devotional text of the Tamil Saiva tradition which he found fascinating. The melting appeal of the 'Sacred Utterance' (*Tiruvacakam)* of the poet-saint Manikkavacakar was so proverbial as to be claimed that those who do not melt to the sacred utterance cannot melt to any utterance. Pope translated the text of fifty-one hymns of varying lengths into English and saw its publication in Oxford (1900) by the same publisher. As he notes in his preface, his experience as a translator taught him 'that to get even a glimpse of the thought of a real poet, the student must often go down into the depths, must use every means to put himself in sympathy with his author, must learn to think and feel with him, and so—it may be—at last come to understand him.'[2] He advocated that his fellow missionaries 'should take pains to know accurately the feelings and convictions of those for whom, and in the midst of whom, they work'. He called for a recognition of aspects of the divine truth in different religious experiences.

What was the purpose of translating and editing the sacred books of the east? Some have suggested that it was part of mastering the classic languages and scriptures in order to demonstrate the intellectual power of Britain in the colonies. But, it cannot be generalised as the result of such a committed and hard work enriched the scholarship of histories, cultures and thought forms.

2 *Thiruvasagam, The Sacred Utterance* (Oxford: Clarendon Press, 1900), xi.

Interestingly, Müller betrays his allegiance with the Christian theologians and missionaries of his day when he noted that 'the interest which the Sacred Books of the East of all religions possess in the eyes of the theologian, and more particularly, of the missionary, to whom an accurate knowledge of them is *as indispensable as the knowledge of the enemy's country is to a general*'[3] (italics added). Thus, the spirit of the militant missionary triumphalism of the day did not spare even an 'objective' scholar like Müller.

Where there is interest to know and understand other scriptures, the attitude of 'knowing the enemy' continues to remain in many Christian circles today. At the same time it should be mentioned that the *Sacred Books of the East* in the libraries of the West, including those of the theological institutions, have assumed the character of ancient materials deserving a place in the Archives: one can notice in the UK many pages of these books have yet to be cut open! Their style of language now appears to be somewhat archaic. At the same time new translations of some of them and of other documents flow into bookshops and specialist libraries. This is true of *Tiruvacakam* and other Tamil Saiva and Vaishnava texts also. Their publication is often carried out with a new missionary zeal on the part of the 'enemy'. Perhaps an awareness of them would save those who still share the cultural prejudice and ignorance of Thomas Macaulay who went to India in 1834 as the English Governor General and who wrote saying that no Orientalist would deny 'that a single shelf of a good European library was worth the whole native literature of India and Arabia.'[4] Such judgement may be shared by some scholars today, but no Indian Christian who wants to be guided by true knowledge may ever subscribe to it. Also some Eastern scholars have rightly claimed that when their ancient scriptures appeared, some of the European countries including Britain were not yet on the world map!

Although not himself having visited India, Müller several times expressed the view that a 'reformation' within Hinduism needed to occur, comparable to the Christian Reformation. In his view, 'if there is one thing which a comparative study of religions places in the clearest light, it is the inevitable decay to which every religion is exposed'. 'Whenever we can trace back a religion to its first beginnings', he added, 'we find it free from many blemishes that affected it in its later states'. He used his links with the reform movement Brahmo Samaj to encourage such a reformation on the lines pioneered by Ram Mohan Roy. Müller believed that the Brahmos would engender an Indian form of Christianity and that they were in practice without

3 Müller, *The Sacred Book of the East*, ix.

4 Quoted, Kenneth Cracknell, *Towards a New Relationship – Christians and People of Other Faiths* (London: Epworth Press, 1986), 22.

denominational divisions. This would in turn with the support of education cause the disappearance of superstition and idolatry in Hindu India.

Additional Sacred Books

To be sure, Müller's project of translating and editing the 'classical' scriptural texts of the East did not exhaust the importance of the other classical and non-classical texts. In the Hindu religious traditions, for example, there are the great epics—Ramayana and Mahabharata, encyclopaedic in nature, whose stories are rich sources for inspiration, guidance and devotional expression, to the respective major 'incarnations', Rama and Krishna. Müller's SBE (Sacred Book of the East) included the Bhagavad Gita which was originally a part of the Mahabharata. The law books, the epics and the earliest texts of the six metaphysical visions are said to have been produced between the 2nd century BCE and 2nd century CE. Then came the major Puranas (ancient lore). They contain stories of creation and dissolution, and genealogies of gods, sages and dynasties. The 18 Mahapuranas (c. 6-9 cent. BCE) are classified into three, each one extolling the glory and miraculous acts of the constituents of Tirumurti—Brahma, Siva and Vishnu, who had both sectarian characteristics as well as claims of supremacy. There are 18 Upapuranas or secondary or sub-puranas. They deal with different deities of which the most prominent is the goddess, whose sacred acts are particularly celebrated in the Devi Matyamikam. The most down-to-earth forms of the puranas are the Sthala Puranas (local myths), and every temple has a local myth which tells the story of its significance, god-connection, sacred sports, rituals, pilgrimage and so on.

The bhakti elements are evident in some of the puranas of which most important is the Bhagavata Purana. It describes stories with poetic embellishment about Krishna's frolics with the women of a shepherd community, the paradigms of true devotion. The Hare Krishna movement has taken this purana as their central text apart from the Gita. Further, a flood of bhakti literature appeared in the vernacular. For example, the Saiva saints produced 12 canonical texts, and the Vashana saints a compendium of 4,000 verses. These texts combine the puranic stories of the descents of gods and goddesses and their miraculous acts, their own experience of encountering them, and heart-melting devotion and theology. These texts are the primary scriptures for the systematic theologies or philosophies of their respective traditions.

The Sanskrit Ramayana was later reworked and translated into Tamil by Kambar (c. 1180-1250) and into Hindi by Tulsidas (1511-1623).While keeping the core story of Ramayana, they enriched it with local stories and expressions and they are often referred to in public speeches for noble ideas. They inspired the Marathi poets such as Mirabai and several Tamil poets as well as secular thinkers.

The Agamas ('that which came down', or tradition) are a collection of scriptures of several Hindu devotional schools. Their origin has yet to be identified, though evidently they were written over several centuries. They describe cosmology, epistemology, philosophical doctrines, and precepts on meditation and other practices. They classify yoga into different kinds (karma, jnana, bhakti, etc.). They contain mantras, prescriptions for temple construction, deity worship and ways to attain the six-fold desires of the devotees. These canonical texts are in Sanskrit and also selectively in Tamil and Grantha (Sanskritised form) scripts. The three main branches of the Agama texts are Saiva, Vaishnava, and Shakta. The Agamic traditions are sometimes called Tantras (esoteric, describing creative acts of sex) although the term Tantra is used specifically to refer to Shakta (Sakti) Agamas. The Agama literature is voluminous, and includes 28 Saiva Agamas, 77 Shakta Agamas (also called Tantras), and 108 Vaishnava Agamas (also called Pancharatra Samhitas), and numerous Upa-Agamas. The Vaishnava Agamas are found into two main schools—Pancharatra and Vaikhanasas. Today, to understand what happens in and around a Hindu temple one has to read the agamas of the particular sect or tradition.

It is significant to note that new religious movements emerged with new scriptures and their translations. Most remarkable is the Sikh scripture of Adigranth (the first book). This was the early compilation of teachings, prayers, lyrics, etc. by Guru Arjan Dev, the fifth Sikh Guru, in 1604. The tenth Guru Gobind Singh added prayers and lyrics to the first compilation of the Granth during the period 1704 to 1706. Then in 1708, before he died, Guru Gobind Singh affirmed the Adi Granth as the perpetual Guru of the Sikhs and it came to be known as the Sri Guru Granth Sahib. No other scripture takes such a central place as this scripture in the worship, devotion and moral teaching in the Sikh community. Though simple, as its parts were composed and compiled in the context of Hindu-Muslim conflict, the generosity of accommodation has found expression in having taken some Hindu lyrics and prayers as well.

The Baha'i religion emerged in mid-19th century Persia. Its founder Bahahullah (1817-1892), a follower of Bab ('gate' or 'door') Sayyid Ali Muhamed Shirazi who had claimed to be a messenger of God. After he was executed, the disciple claimed to be the messianic figure promised by Bab. Bahahullah was succeeded by his son. Bab's letters written to various individuals, including some heads of state, along with the works of the two successors have been collected and assembled into a canon of Baha'i scripture. Baha'i religion is all-embracing as it accepts all the earlier figures such as Moses, Buddha, Jesus and Mohammed and their teachings. All have been brought to the essence of the equal worth of all religions and the unity and equality of all people. But, the Baha'is have their own identity with gathering and rituals and they are enthusiastic to spread their religion around the world.

Besides, there is a division between primary scriptures and secondary scriptures. The writings of charismatic leaders also assume the role of the scripture in the lives of their followers or fans. Texts with common human appeal have come to assume the role of a scripture. For instance, Thirukkural by the ancient Tamil sage Thiruvalluvar (in the early centuries of the common era) is called and used as the scripture of the Tamils, and its 1,330 couplets exhort in cryptic manner in almost all areas of human life. It is quoted by persons of all religions and of no religion, and Christian speakers and preachers are no exemption.

Responses

When the knowledge of scriptures all over the world came to be known first through the English language and then in other languages, it appeared to shake the foundations. The historical-textual studies of the Bible revealed extra-textual influence or resemblance with it. Particularly, certain rituals, laws and proverbs found connections with those of Egypt and neighbouring countries. As recorded in the Hebrew Bible, the leadership model was taught to Moses by his father-in-law, a priest from Midian. And there are resemblances of Israelite kingship, priesthood, temple and ritual sacrifice with the neighbouring countries. Leave alone the external evidence shown from archaeological excavations, there are hints which raise questions of the origins of a text. For example, the Nazareth Manifesto which is a quote of Is. 61:1-2 replaces the words 'to proclaim the year of the Lord's favour and the day of vengeance of our God' with 'to proclaim the year of the Lord' (Lk. 4:18-19). What is the reason for this significant change? Jesus in his Sermon on the Mount said, 'You have heard ... Love your neighbour and hate your enemy' (Mt. 5:43). It is not clear where was it said. Paul quotes what Jesus himself had said: 'It is more blessed to give than to receive' (Acts 20:35). We do not have the original version! Many more instances can be cited, and these make us think about the difficulty of understanding the nature and development of the Christian scripture.

Scientific and higher criticism of the Bible became popular and, in reaction, a new movement emerged and its influence on Christian thinking is considerable. The word 'fundamentalism' originated in the USA in the 1920s. The background was the following. In 1909 two wealthy Christian laymen 'set aside a large sum of money for issuing twelve volumes that would set forth the fundamentals of the Christian faith, and which were to be sent free to ministers of the gospel, missionaries, Sunday School superintendents, and others engaged in aggressive Christian work throughout the English speaking world. A committee of men who were known to be sound in the faith was chosen to have oversight of the publication of these volumes.' Twelve volumes were brought out according to the original plan between 1910 and 1915. 'Some of the volumes were sent to 300,000 ministers and missionaries and other workers in different parts of the world.' The common title of the twelve booklets was *The Fundamentals: A Testimony to the Truth*. Later editions have been produced in different combinations.[5] The arguments were supported by selection of favourite verses. Fundamentalist preachers followed this pattern of selecting favourites—authoritarian and comforting verses that would attract masses. Slogans such as 'Jesus is the crown', 'the only way' and 'the only name for salvation' were popularized with emotional manipulation.

Islamic fundamentalism, to a great extent, resembles the style and content of Christian fundamentalism. Accordingly, what the Quran says is the only truth, Mohammed is the climax of the prophets, and the Islamic way of life is perfect. Any claim of interruption or interpolation is stoutly denied. There is considerable scholarship about the Quran, but the basic beliefs are not challenged. In order to embarrass Christians and even anger the fundamentalists there are enthusiastic Muslims who publish leaflets about the defects of the Bible—the factual inconsistencies, the immoral life of prophets like Dawood (David), and the horrible death of Jesus on the cross which would have never happened as he was the last but one perfect prophet of God Almighty. Worse and more dangerous are the militant movements of Muslims who raise a tyrant against modern western culture and its domination. On the contrary, the same Quran has inspired Muslim saints. Now there is a movement within the Islamic world that stresses love as the essence and on which they can have dialogue with Christians and others.

Reacting to the criticism of the multifarious and even dubious character of the Hindu scriptures by others, Hindus (often without worrying about the contextual meaning) repeat certain verses such as the following: 'The truth is one and the wise call it differently' (Rig Veda); 'whichever way people pursue they come to me' (Krishna in the Gita).

There are different ways by which the Vedantic schools prioritized and interpreted the primary texts, and their hermeneutics itself is not easy to follow. In the modern period Ram Mohan Roy found the Upanishads to affirm the oneness of the God-head, introduce simple forms of ritual and denounce idol worship and superstitions. Most remarkably, it was Swami Dayananda Sarasvati (1824-1883), the founder of the Arya Samaj (watershed for Hindu revival) who boldly initiated a new approach with the watchword

5 The 1917 edition was issued by ***The Bible Institute of Los Angeles*** and reprinted in 1993 by Baker Books, Grand Rapids, MI. The website on the topic has adapted from this edition of four volumes and listed under each volume the individual totaling 90 topics. Cf. I. Selvanayagam, *Being Evangelical and Dialogical* (Delhi: ISPCK, 2012), chapter 13.

'back to the Vedas'. 'Dayananda's vision of Vedic Hinduism rejected most of the major elements of the Hindu religion: idolatry, polytheism, the puranas, priestly privilege, popular rituals, and deities. Dayananda's religion was monotheistic, open to all, rationalistic, and compatible with modern science. It was in addition the true faith. Not only did he reject popular Hinduism but also all other religions, Buddhism, Christianity, Islam, Zoroastrianism, for these too were false beliefs, since only Vedic Hinduism contained the truth.'[6] Here we need to clarify that when Dayananda went back to the Veda he selected only the samhita part of the Vedas, hymns of praise with simple rituals of offering hospitality to gods as well as humans. It is puzzling that he claimed monotheism while Vedic deities are so many!Yet he turned the corner by declaring all the post Vedic (i.e., post-samhita) texts as invalid. He denounced the great war of antiquity recorded in Mahabharata which, in his view, 'had led to a loss of correct Vedic knowledge, which in turn began a lengthy process of decline among the Hindus'.

Dayananda's denouncement of all the 'Hindu scriptures' except the samhita part of the Vedas provides a new avenue for students of Hinduism to explore the full implications of his approach. Most notably, the Bhagavad Gita is part of the Mahabharata. It represents two figures in opposition in the field of the fluid dharma, and finally the Brahminic dharma wins while assimilating some gods, values and virtues from outside.[7] When the Muslims came to India with one Holy Quran and the Christians one Holy Bible that challenged Hindus as they had no such holy book to handle for devotion and guidance. M.K. Gandhi happened to see a copy of the Gita in English translated by a British civil officer. The book, handy and concise, woke him up and he projected it as the Hindu Bible with the cardinal message on un-harming, self-control and doing one's duty without expecting the fruits. Of course, Gandhi read it as a Vaishnava devotee, not a student of comparative religion or scriptural hermeneutics! But political Hinduism used the book and Gandhi's excitement about it as a tool for asserting dignity and pride and countering the challenges of the fundamentalist Christians and Muslims.

Scriptural Interpretation and the Political Power

The history of the formation and final authorisation of every scripture reveals the play of political power even if councils have done preparatory debates and reflections. This is true of the reaffirmation and interpretation of a particular scripture as well. We cite a recent example in India. India's former External

6 Kenneth W. Jones, "The Arya Samaj in British India, 1875-1947," in *Religion in Modern India*, edited by Robert D. Baird (Delhi: Manohar, 1981), 28.

7 See S. Israel, "Asoka and Arjuna as Counterfigures Standing on the Field of Dharma: A Historical-Hermeneutical Perspective," *History of Religions*, (Aug. 1992), 59-75.

Affairs Minister Sushma Swaraj (1952-2019), addressing a crowd with some passion and with claims of personal discovery, has suggested we 'make the Gita (our) national scripture.'[8] Interestingly, a couple of years ago (2011-12), in the heat of a controversy over the Russian translation of the Bhagavad Gita, one of her predecessors, S.M. Krishna, declared that the Gita was India's national book! Within scholarly and interreligious circles, this was regarded as an insensitive declaration, since as a specifically Vaishnava scripture the Gita cannot represent even the multi-scriptural and multi-traditional Hindu community, leave alone the non-Hindu communities in secular India. At the beginning of September (2014), during his visit to Japan, Prime Minister Narendra Modi presented two copies of the Gita to the Japanese government, saying that there could be no greater gift from India. He did the same when he met the US President at the end of the month. The peculiar tolerance of the Indian religious community was evident as there was no hue and cry about such events.

The Bhagavad Gita is part of the great epic Mahabharata (denounced by Dayananda) which in traditional classification of Hindu scriptures falls under 'secondary scripture'. It became a primary scripture in the hands of the cardinal exponents of Vedanta, and their interpretations differed from one another. Moreover, the Gita was not as simple and straightforward as Gandhi wanted it to be. For example, with reference to the virtue of non-harming (*ahimsa*) occurring four times in passing, Gandhi claimed that the ideal of non-harming was the Gita's quintessence, but for an objective reader its central message is to fight and kill in order to restore an ancient dharma. Also scholarship has exposed several instances showing that Gandhi was not immune and categorical to the ideal of non-harming.[9]

Those who read the Gita with new eyes, recognizing historical realities, will find in it a struggle to synthesize different strands of religious thought of its time. Does it really synthesize all the strands? Can it provide a framework for the distinctive religious visions and traditions of all the religious communities of India? How can the reaffirmation of the Vedic ritual as indispensable at all times and all stages of life as well as of the creation of four castes be synthesized with the transcendence of bhakti? Obviously much depends on what we mean by synthesis. But, at the same time, there are some striking insights in the Gita which can have an appeal to all engaging readers. The profoundest of them seems to be that 'having fixed one's mind on God one has to do one's duty without worrying about the rewards' (although in its context

8 *The Hindu,* 8 December 2014, 12.

9 See I. Selvanayagam, "Gandhi's Interpretation of Ahimsa: A Re-View," in *Enhancing Our Home: Re-Reading and Re-Living Gandhian Thought*, edited by Johnson J. Puthenpurackal (Bengaluru: Asian Trading Corporation (with Association of Christian Philosophers in India, 2016), 56-75.

duty is the caste duty of a warrior and the rewards is the horrible consequences of killing in war). Here meditative mind-control (jnana-yoga), concentration on God (bhakti) and action (karma) are brought together to form a harmonious commitment. If taken out of the context, this insight is fascinating to anyone who takes religious life or spirituality seriously. It may call for a new seriousness and commitment to work for 'cleaning India' in all spheres as we struggle with some burning issues of 'national shame'. Sushma's claim that the Gita has answers to everybody's problems needs to be tested against these challenges by groups of different religions and of no religion with a spirit of dialogue characterized by commitment and openness.

Proposing one text like the Gita as India's national book or scripture is not only insensitive but unfortunately also exposes ignorance. We are not in a position to know the percentage of people in this country for whom the Vaishnava text Gita is actually the scripture because our census does not count the population with reference to the particular tradition/sect to which individuals belong. We hear from teachers of the Krishna/Vishnu cult again and again that Siva is inferior to Vishnu while for the Saivites do not subscribe any scripture that does not extol the supremacy of Siva. The puranic stories of the conflict between Vishnu and Siva are repeatedly referred to in the bhakti texts of these sects. Further, Vishnu takes *avatars* but Siva does not as it would involve the Supreme having to go through the process of karma-samsara. In fact one wishes that the Shiva bhaktas would come forward to make a response to Sushma Swaraj's declaration, unless they identify with her for Hindu political solidarity. Further, it is understandable that in reaction to Swaraj's declaration of the Gita as India's national scripture with the ever-ready support of the Hindutva ranks, many leaders and thinkers reminded her of the secular fabric of the nation. They pointed out that the Indian Constitution is our scripture. What is made most clear is that India's is a constitutional nationalism, and the preamble of the constitution provides the finest vision and statement of our common identity, shared values and collective aspiration. As it stands now, it is certain that any scripture that does not conform to it will lose its validity.

Proper Christian Approach to the Plurality of the Scriptures

The Bible is held to be normative for Christian life; it follows that it is overwhelming to take note of the number of scriptures we have listed above. However, its normative role is perceived differently by different persons and church bodies. For example, the original Methodist Society affirmed that 'All which we are taught of God to observe, even in his written Word, is the only rule, and the sufficient rule, both of our faith and practice.' The Anglican affirmation that the Bible is the 'supreme and decisive standard of faith' and that it 'contains all that is necessary for our salvation' is shared by united churches such as the Church of South India. Significantly, one of

CSI's constitutional bases gives the right to every member to contextually interpret the scripture. But, massive study and sharing is required to identify the primacy of scripture over tradition, reason and experience; what are the implications of being normative when we have a peculiar scripture which contains extreme stories ranging from barbarian acts of rape, butchery, murder, etc., to the supreme acts of love; when we say it contains all that is sufficient for our salvation how do we understand salvation? Is there any criteria for contextual interpretation? Our committed, critical and sensible approach to our scriptures may influence other religious communities' approach to theirs. Of course, maintaining division on the basis of selected or sectarian views of the scriptures will confuse them. Those who have experience of relationship and dialogue with people of other religions are convinced that the denominational and sectarian divisions created by political influences, doctrinal rigidities and petty issues of structures and familiar practices cause ridicule of the credibility of the one Holy Bible. In other words, if people of the present denominations develop a generosity of the spirit, clarity of though and warm mind-set for sharing the core message of the Bible, they work for achieving the long-delayed organic union which alone validates the Bible as one and holy.

We have no convincing answer to the question 'Why did God or the sacred power reveal or allow to emerge such a plurality of scriptures with such contradiction?' What is fairly clear is that there is no scripture without human contribution and with a simple and systematic message. In the case of every scripture there was a process of formation, and there may be clues to identify decisive moments, original intent and deviation. However, in spite of all imperfections and blemishes, scriptures do reflect the transcendence and sacred awareness of human life. They have given the communities that own them identity and guidance for a liturgical, spiritual and moral life. Today, if there is an open mind, one can see them as complex repositories containing exemplary models, creative experiments, and inspiring teaching applicable to common humanity. This need not affect the core vision and ideals of a particular scripture. Such a reasoning will stimulate Christians to reread the Bible with certain parameters collectively prepared by the church.

Our master Jesus in his approach to his own scriptures applied the four principles of rejection, revision, selection and reflection.[10] By doing this he restored the core vision and experience of the Hebrew community that God's primary revelation was that he was in solidarity with victims of injustice and oppression, as he was moved by a community groaning in slavery. Using human leaders, he liberated them, made a covenant with them, and gave

10 See I. Selvanayagam, *Relating to People of Other Faiths: Insights from the Bible* (Thiruvilla: Christava Sahitya Samithi, BTTBPSA, 2004), 37.

them guidelines for worship and commandments for practising justice, mercy and love. When they went astray, he raised prophets who called people to return to their creator and renew their life and focus on their sacred duty of seeking the lost on the margins, heal their wounds and restore their God-given dignity. Jesus did exactly this, though he became a multi-faceted figure and the changing perceptions of his person, from a prophet to embodiment of the eternal Word or Son of the Triune God provide the greatest example of growing towards perceptions. Without telling the whole story and process but presenting him as a super-figure who fell from heaven distorts what actually happened. Further, Jesus and his followers experimented with a servant-style leadership and their teachings had the grades of great, greater and greatest, the last being the twin love for God and for our fellow humans. In order to restore the initial credibility of the Jesus movement and the church, it is indispensable for the present church to reform in every aspect, based on the biblical insights distinguishing faith from familiarity and recovering the core insight of the power and authority of love and servanthood.

Moving away from a sense of identity, claims of divine inspiration and ritual sermons and fancible interpretations, it is suggested that the word 'insights' helps to handle the Bible with passion and sustained engagement.[11] Quoting from other scriptures may be enriching our message: e.g. 'only the ignorant say that Siva and love are inseparable' (Thirumular); 'just as a boneless body is dried by sun, so a loveless person by the law of righteousness' (Thiruvalluvar); 'in the name of God (Allah), all Merciful and most Compassionate'—the opening words of every chapter of the Quran; 'highest is the truth, higher still is truthful living' (Adhigrandh). Studies of cross-scriptural themes may complement or supplement the biblical insights or clarify the differences.[12] Reading the scriptures together in the local context will be most profitable. Loud monologues are no longer effective to communicate, but dialogue does facilitate mutual communication. In fact, fundamentalist preachers inflict the greatest damage to interreligious relationship and block the way to recapture the core insights of the Bible and reforming the church accordingly. Using these preachers for their pietistic enthusiasm without insisting on proper training to understand the Bible and present its insights properly, is failing in

---

11 For some detail, see I. Selvanayagam, "Identity, Inspiration, Interpretation and Insights: The Significance of the Christian Scripture in the Midst of Scriptures", in *Bible Speaks Today* (Essays in honour of Gnana Robinson, ed. by Daniel Jones Muthunayagam (Delhi: ISPCK for UTC Bangalore, 2000), 224-241.

12 E.g. see S. Gangadharan & Israel Selvanayagam, "The Communion of Saints: Christian and Tamil Saiva Perspectives," *Hindu Christian Studies Bulletin* 5 (1992), 13-19; *Voices from the Margin*, edited by R. S. Sugirtharajah (Orbis/SPCK, 1995), 381-393; *Kristu Bhakti and Krishna Bhakti: A Christian-Hindu Dialogue Contributing to Comparative Theology* (New Delhi: Christian World Imprints, 2017).

the fundamental duty on the part of church leaders. Let sterile and superficial piety not fool us. Also, we must have truth and love in our heart to appreciate the 'great faith' of people from other religions or secular movements who perform remarkable acts of transformation which go well with the biblical insights. Jesus did appreciate such people!

Finally, in India, formal Protestant theological education started in 1910 based in the Senate of Serampore College (University) and today about 55 theological institutions all over India are affiliated to it. Even since the start, study of other religions and scriptures has been an important component in the curriculum of theological education and ministerial training. But, its impact on the practice of ministry and mission seems to be almost nil. This is mainly because the study is often aimed at obtaining a paper qualification, and candidates are expected to return to the churches with the same kind of 'faith' they had come with. Teachers of Religions in these institutions are placed in an invidious position. Compared to Religions professors in other universities here and in the West (where their particular religious commitment is no requirement), they have no prestige, position and fatty financial remuneration. But, they have double-sided pressure – on the one hand to present other religions and their scriptures truthfully without falling into the trap of bearing false witness against them, and on the other to be faithful to the churches where they preach and in the seminary train their candidates to be good pastors and evangelists. If a comprehensive balance is not maintained they may end up with spiritual schizophrenia! Yet some of them have maintained this balance exceptionally well through hard work and commitment to truth. Brother Swami Raju is certainly one of them who deserves appreciation, admiration and applause!

3

Towards A Feminist Theological Methodology for India

Santanu K. Patro

Introduction

The paper intends to attempt a 'methodological exploration' into the Feminist Studies in India. But, before one attempts to propose, it is necessary to understand the ground reality of India. In a multi-religious, multi-ethnic and multi-cultural contexts such as India, what would be our approach to Feminist methodology? Should we have to limit Feminist methodology only to Christians, which constitute less than 3% of the population? How inclusive is methodological perspectives of Feminist Theology in doing theology among the Hindus, Muslims, Jain, Buddhist, Sikh women. What is the a priori methodological commitment towards our neighbouring sisters? Is there a possibility to construct an inclusive feminist theology? The paper does not attempt an answer, nor tries to provide any answers rather it provokes a group of serious researchers to evolve methodological resources for the purpose of higher academic research by developing critical tools of scientific analyses. As theologians and budding research scholars, we know theology cannot be done in isolation. I take the position, first and foremost, that religious pluralism is a 'God-given' gift to the Indians. Poverty and marginalisation of sections of people are human-made catastrophe. Therefore, equally we prioritise the 'essentialism'. The minimum definition of essentialism is that every entity has a set of attributes that are necessary to its identity and function.

The study has twofold objectives to achieve: (i) To find direction to integrate Women's Studies into the theological curricula as an interdisciplinary approach. (ii) To promote it as an independent branch of study within the broader framework of the academic curricula. In order to achieve both, the study needs to re-look at already constructed theories, reformulate methods, methodologies and epistemology.

Let me sound a word of caution. I am a man interested in studying feminism. I have a personal and historical reasons for such an interest. I am particularly interested in theory and methodology. The limit to such scholarship is that I do not experience the way women experience, yet I am committed to listen. At the same time, I am not a conformist. You may further notice as you read this paper, I am not talking about specifically on Feminist Theology. I am convinced that Indian Feminism has to be distinct and provide alternative if it were to serve all women. One cannot do Feminist Theology ignoring nearly 97% women who do not profess the same faith.

Feminism

The term 'feminism' has many different usage and its meanings are often contested. The generic use of Feminism was more about politics. In the West the demand for universal suffrage for women in the late 19th century, led by the women were identified as feminist. Feminism is also coming to be known by distinguishing ideas and beliefs from that of historically specific feminist movement. "The First International Women's Conference held in Paris in 1892 that the term, following the French term *féministe*, was used regularly in English for a belief in and advocacy of equal rights for women based on the idea of the equality of the sexes."[1] Gerda Lerner in her book, *The Creation of Patriarchy* (1979) she points to a 'monumental neglect' by the historians to write "men's History." She gave a clarion call to reconstruct "women's History' by isolating traditional history that has obscured women.[2]

The Waves

It is important to briefly view history of women's movements in history in last two centuries which serves as precursor to the contemporary feminist movements, thoughts and theorisation. Generally, scholars identify three 'Waves' beginning from the later part of 19th century.

The "First Wave" is primarily attributed to a political right movement led by women and also by some men, from the mid-19th century until the passage of Nineteenth Amendment in 1920 in the US allowing women suffrage. The "Second Wave" moves beyond political rights to fight for equality in

1 "Feminism," in *Stanford Dictionary of Philosophy* (Stanford, 2016).

2 Gerda Lerner, *Creation of Patriarchy* (Oxford: New York, 1987), 1ff. and p.168 ff.

education, in workplace and at home. This resulted in the quality of women as the first and second were primarily concerned of white women. It had strong racial undertone. The "Third Wave" critiqued the Second Wave feminism for its lack of attention to the differences among women due to race, ethnicity, class, nationality, religion, caste. Many attribute Third Wave provided the space to look through the lenses of other women. Women, across the board, are marginalised because of their gender.

Our interest for the purpose of study is on methodology. The French Feminist, Simone de Beauvoir's work titled *The Second Sex* (1952) has provided the generations of Feminist thinkers to articulate and propose theorisation of Feminism. My interest for this paper is not to go deeper into the history of Feminist methodology rather to concentrate on the development of methodologies in past 50 years which will give a glimpse of women's activism. Let me in brief outline the methodological approaches to Feminism in last 50 years.

Methodological Approaches to Feminism

Liberal Feminism

Liberal Feminism emphasises on equality, freedom, justice and dignity of women. They are enshrined in liberal democracy, and understands the discrimination of women is political and social. One presupposes in Liberal Feminism that the separation of private with that of public is essential for women. The traditional assignation of women in private promotes inequality and prejudices freedom. Liberal Feminism is heavily dependent on the construction of Western liberalism that were developed during the time of enlightenment. Liberal Feminism produced white, middle class and heterosexual scholarship and interpreted them as part of women's empowerment. Such universalism is generalisation on a perceived notion biased and developed by one section of women and thrust on others ignoring differences in race, class, caste, nationality, ethnicity.

Post-Liberal Feminism

Since the liberal democracies and Western thoughts had disconnect with academia due to strong detached scholarships; the Feminist looked for an alternative in the 1980s. It attempted to be non-white, non-English, indigenous, immigrant, and different sexual orientations. It was primarily concerned with working class and marginalised women. Women in general became both subject and object of not only of their gender but also of their social, political, economic, religious status and stratifications, including class, caste and gender. It identified women, particularly in India, as thrice oppressed—

gender, caste, class. They are strongly embedded in powerlessness even after achieving women suffrage.

Postmodern Feminism

Taking the cue from the post liberal, Postmodern feminism rejects universality. There is no fixed worldview or rigid *theoria* for feminism. It affirms epistemological diversities. Feminism has to take seriously the diversity of culture, people, social construct, political and economic conditioning. Women are suffering from sexualised dominance not merely because of their gender but because of their attributed fixed identities. There is a need for women to be resisters to counter subordination that are produced and based on fixed identity.

Deconstruction of dominant narratives by "multi narratives" and "local discourses" and making the body as a site of meaning[3] are the job of the poststructuralists. All texts, including the canonical and authoritative texts are subjected to rereading and reinterpretation. It is through them recovery is accentuated. In other words, rereading and reinterpretation provide recovery or discovery of meanings in the context. Jacques Derrida advocates the development of the ethical relationship to the other in order to engage the otherness to challenge power by multifaceted means.[4]

Methodology

There is a subtle difference between methods and methodology. Methods refer to the techniques of gathering data and methodology is a theoretical framework. Methodology chooses an existing paradigm or takes multiple paradigms. The multiple paradigms when chosen, the researchers may use all but in most cases applying select paradigmatic components that are suitable to research. In the process, a researcher may come up with his/her epistemology. Methodology involves choosing a theoretical framework in which researcher defines the problem or makes problem statements. Researcher further employs methods, such as field study, empirical research etc. to obtain knowledge to analyse on the basis of the theoretical framework. The question is who does the research? On whom do we research? Feminist methodology is praxiological for the simple reason that a researcher though undertakes the research, it is not purely for his/her academic interest. It must produce desired results whom we research, like in any other social research. But the uniqueness of feminist study is that women are in the centre of research. If the women in question are

3 P. Cheah, D. Fraser and J. Grbich, eds., *Thinking through the Body of the Law* (Sydney: Allen & Unwin, 1996), 35ff.

4 For example, J. Derrida, *Margins of Philosophy*, translated by Alan Bass (Chicago: University of Chicago Press, 1982).

interviewed and field research are undertaken, yet it is for them the research is meant. Therefore, it becomes praxiological.

Specific to India, gender oppression must also include all other forms of oppressions. One cannot isolate such oppression though the forms and manifestations of oppressions are different. The target victims are women. Feminism must seek justice and equality in all spheres and they cannot be considered in fragmented manners in methodologies.

Maithreyi Krishnaraj says "it is now fashionable to use "gender" to mean "women", whereas technically speaking, gender merely means a term that denotes whether a person is male or female. (…) Originally, the term was invented by feminists to distinguish between the socially constructed human male/female from the biological sex difference."[5] Feminist theory often reduces gender to sex. This loses the sight of social construction and control of women as gender. Gender is a social institution. It has dynamic social processes and such processes are controlled by the social institutions.

Methodology must seek three broad areas to engage in feminism: i) the visibility of women is important to bring women to the fore. Women, hitherto, went unrecognised and often were unnoticed in the readings. ii) There are issues and concerns which are which to women as gender, particularly the social constructs. iii) Women face systemic injustice and inequality.[6]

There are several other categories that are important in doing feminist methodology. Mary Margaret Fonow and Judith A. Cook in their book, *Beyond Methodology,* emphasises four themes: reflexivity, spontaneity, creativity and improvisation in the selection of both topic and method. (pp. 1-19) In her *Handbook of Feminist Research*, Sharlene Hesse-Biber (2007, pp. 16-17) "describes feminists' research in a similar way: It asks new questions, 'going beyond correcting gender bias in dominant research studies'; centralizes issues of power, authority, ethics, and reflexivity in the practice of research; and is typically conducted at the margins of traditional disciplines."[7]

In any research, one needs perspective, and for feminist research the focus may not be always gender, it may be a woman question and it may be done by anyone including men who are interested and committed to feminism. Sandra Harding writes that feminist theorists must approach discussion method of gathering the evidence, use methodology that analyses methods of data gathering and have the epistemological conviction to present the

---

5 Maithreyi Krishnaraj, "Methodological Concerns," in *Economic and Political Weekly* xlv/44 (October, 2010), 43.

6 Krishnaraj, "Methodological Concerns," in *Economic and Political Weekly*: 45.

7 Quoted in "Feminist Theory and Research," http://www.sagepub.com/sites/default/files/upm-binaries/45934_chap ter_1.pdf, 3.

facts.[8] In other word, Harding says when one goes into researching, dialogue with women is a must because women question is always at the centre of doing research. Techniques of data gathering is nothing but making women the subject of research. Methodology emerges out of experience and context. It is here feminist methodology becomes doing methodology. Epistemology carries the conviction of truth of fact but does not make absolute truth claims. Knowledge as experience only outlines the facts that might appear to some as true but to others they may be mere knowledge. Epistemology of hermeneutics provides plausibility of facts, thereby, it appears truth. The danger to 'Feminist Theology' is when attempt is made to truth claims. One must refrain from absolutizing one's research.

Normative and Descriptive Approaches

> In many of its forms, feminism seems to involve at least two groups of claims, one normative and the other descriptive. The normative claims concern how women ought (or ought not) to be viewed and treated and draw on a background conception of justice or broad moral position; the descriptive claims concern how women are, as a matter of fact, viewed and treated, alleging that they are not being treated in accordance with the standards of justice or morality invoked in the normative claims. Together the normative and descriptive claims provide reasons for working to change the way things are; hence, feminism is not just an intellectual but also a political movement.[9]

Examples of Normative and Descriptive approaches:

> i. (Normative) Men and women are entitled to equal rights and respect.
> ii. (Descriptive) Women are currently disadvantaged with respect to rights and respect, compared with men [...in such and such respects and due to such and such conditions...].
>
> On this account, that women and men ought to have equal rights and respect is the normative claim; and that women are denied equal rights and respect functions here as the descriptive claim.[10]

Many of thc Feminists do seem to disagree with such categorisations. Rather they would prefer to run over the other as the woman questions are not limited to neither normative and nor descriptive models alone, rather

8 Sandra Harding, *The Science Question in Feminism* (Columbia: University of Columbia, 1986), 19.

9 "Feminism," in *Stanford Dictionary of Philosophy.*

10 "Feminism," in *Stanford Dictionary of Philosophy.*

they need to use both to bring the woman question to the fore. Between the methodology and method, epistemology plays a key role. The knowledge and experience should go hand in hand and they cannot be segregated as normative and descriptive respectively.

More and more Feminists are of the convictions that the research methodology cannot have single philosophical or political indoctrination. In the same way, it is not necessary that all woman researchers should pick up research topics related to only feminism. Scholarship, in such a case, would be limited to be focussed by women's experience thus indoctrinating experience alone is necessary.

Locating Feminist Studies in the Context of India

Feminism in India emerged first as movement, then as an interdisciplinary study well before it was established as an autonomous discipline in the University curricula. Hence praxis element cannot be ignored; in fact, it is the strength of the discipline. Without praxis, the discipline will lose its purpose in advancing the cause for which the discipline is established. It is truer with feminist theology. As theology of liberation it cannot ignore the praxiological dimensions. In other words, feminist methodology must locate in the ethos, pathos, struggles and celebrations of women's movements, thereby giving leverage to the academic discipline.

Over the years the Department of Women's studies (Gender, Feminist) in India has taken rather an interesting turn, thanks to the women's movements that have contributed largely to the emergence of it as an academic discipline. The events of the mid 1980s, most importantly the Supreme Court ruling on Shah Bano case, Roop Kanwar's sati-suicide and the subsequent issues related to cultural and religious upsurge under the garb of Ramjanmabhumi have set the agenda for the women's liberation movements and paved the ways for a disciplinary approach in academic parlance. Until that point women's roles were seen as home-makers and as agency of religio-social liaisons. At a later period with the rise of English educated upper caste and middleclass women, women moved along with their male counterpart to participate in Nation Building. In real sense their participation in freedom struggle, freedom movements and engagement in 'Nation Building' cannot be considered as women's liberation movement. Women's participation was more a solidarity with men in achieving freedom for the nation. Their participation manifested India's *narisakti. Sakti* being a Hindu abstract symbol for goddesses it created space for woman's power within the framework of Brahminical patriarchy. Hence Sarojini Naidu, Rani Jhansi Bai and others were depicted as Hindu warrior goddesses who zealously protected *stridharma. Narisakti* is power of woman, in that it is an abstract and outside power that neither be claimed nor owned as women's power. Therefore, it cannot be empowering to women.

It is imitative power, hence it can be taken away through the process of domestication and spousification when *narisakti* becomes 'out-of-control'. In essence marriage spousifies and domesticates women. Power is removed and transferred in marriage, thus making women powerless.

However, in the 1980s with the rise of women's movements, *narimukti* was emphasised as an alternative to *narisakti*. Since there is no *mukti* for women in religious parlance of India, *narimukti,* liberation of women was proposed by identifying it with the 'body metaphor' as opposed to the 'spirit metaphor' of *narisakti*. Hence, *narimukit* is secular, inclusive and pluralistic. *Narimukti* moved beyond familial role, role socialisation, cultural ethos and religious norms of *dharma*. This also helped in getting rid of religious, communal and cultural identities and brought women together as community of sisters to struggle for justice and celebration of liberation in anticipation.

The revolution of information certainly helped women to come together. There was a greater interaction with the Western counterpart which led to the recognition of the presence of the women in history and position in society. Since *narimukit* challenged the exclusive religious foundations of *narisakti,* soon women's movements were branded in India as Western, elitist, upper class and 'white.'

Such allegations are not unfounded; however, *naimukti* provided a new agenda for women's liberation. In the 1990s the discourse have been very different—women's reservation in parliament, discussions on reproductive and sexual rights including alternate sexualities and an increasing attempts at using culture as the grounds for policing women's sexuality.

The question one needs to ask is how does one evaluate academic curricula for the Women's Studies in the light of the recent developments? The concept of *narimukti* must replace and engage in every Indian feminist discourse. Even in the Christian circles we have articulated women's freedom in line with *narisakti*. *Narisakti* subscribes to church hierarchy and patriarchal structure. There is a need of paradigm shift in our understanding of women's freedom. *Narisakti* does not empower women; rather it only validates the power of woman as the imitative power rooted in patriarchy. 'Power of woman' in reality is not empowering; rather powered to strike a compromise with the hierarchy of power.

If women have to be liberated, women should move from the manifestations of *narisakti* to the liberation in *narimukti*. Cultural and religious symbols are in themselves oppressive in India, and Christian symbols are no better. A re-reading of one or two women characters of the Bible in our preaching, symbolic ordination without an assigned responsibility of an ordained minister and token positions in church leadership will not help promote wholistic women's liberation. How often we hear church leaders admonishing us to go slow, be sensitive to culture, so on and so forth, when it comes to giving women the rightful positions in the church. Contrary to this phenomenon, how often we have decried injustice to women in Indian society and demanded 2/3 reservation for women in Indian parliament and at times joined Protest March to rally around liberation for women in society. Yet we have refused to transfer or share power with women in our churches. Can we commit ourselves to equal representation of women in church leadership by alternately appointing women Bishops, Presidents and Executive Secretaries? The time has come that Women's studies must simultaneously become a movement in the seminaries demanding justice, equality and rightful share of power.

i) Patriarchy remains at the root of oppression, injustice and inequality. This has been well identified since the time immemorial. Therefore, Feminism cannot construct methodology without patriarchy, as is the case for Dalit studies with caste analysis. Power is a means of social, economic and political control. Patriarchy is institutionalised and it is possessed by men. Power therefore is a male power. The attempt is not to kill the men but the male domination and unless Patriarchy is broken down, power will manifest always as gendered male. Mere generalisation of Patriarchy and male power does not bring liberation to women.[11]

Feminism as liberation struggle, resists all forms of domination, subordination and subjugation of women by patriarchy. Ideological patriarchy, though oppresses women based on gender discrimination; its agenda also promotes race, caste, creedal differences. But, one needs to distinguish feminism from other forms of liberation or else the concern with sexism may be diluted.

> Unlike many feminist comrades, I believe women and men must share a common understanding—a basic knowledge of what feminism is—if it is ever to be a powerful mass-based political movement. In Feminist Theory: From Margin to Center, I suggest that defining feminism broadly as "a movement to end sexism and sexist oppression" would enable us to have a common political goal … Sharing a common goal does not imply that women and men will not have radically divergent perspectives on how that goal might be reached.[12]

Feminisms objectives is to end sexism but sexism cannot be separated in its relations to other forms of oppressions. If feminist themselves are racists and Dalit, Tribal and Adivasi women's cause is not taken as multifaceted

---

11 Krishnaraj, "Methodological Concerns," in *Economic and Political Weekly*: 47.

12 Bell Hooks, *Feminist Theory: From Margin to Center* (Cambridge, MA: South End Press, 1989), 23.

oppressions rooted in sexism, the institutions of equality cannot be realised by all women. Patriarchy remains centre of all oppressions.

ii) Brahminism as a methodological tool is well established in the ancient classical philosophical traditions of India. It is founded on the structures of Caste. Brahminism as a dominant methodology has replaced colonial substructure in social sciences and humanities. Is Brahminism different from colonial methodology? Brahminism rather comes to us as a home-grown colonial structure, which is very difficult to get rid off unlike the Colonial power. Since Brahminism occupied significant position in Indian freedom struggle, it replaced by assuming power, thus an era of neo-colonialism began with the Brahminical-majority rule. Hindutva of today is natural outcome of decades of neo-colonial rule. Today Brahminic theorisation has affected all disciplines of the Social Sciences and Humanities. So, much so Brahminism as a mindset has invaded Indian Christian Theology and Indian Christian traditions. It also influences the Subaltern religions by reinterpreting Brahminic festivals as secular, therefore national. Brahminism today as a contemporary methodological tool promotes the same old oppressive ideals, such as, i) Vedic, more particularly the Upanisadic-Philosophical authorities. ii) Experiences as abstract, supreme and superior that takes place in the negation of the body. iii) The neo-classification of Caste hierarchy under M. N. Srinivasa's *Sanskritisation.* All these are antithetical to the liberation of women.

Brahminism as a methodology is more dangerous to Women, Adivasis and Dalits than any other methodological categories. Let us not be deluded by thinking it as an Indian hermeneutics. We must be careful in interpreting symbols and mythologies that are not liberating. In our zeal to be Indian in theology we have uncritically accepted Brahminical structures. Christian tradition must defeat the evils of caste by squarely rejecting both Brahminism.

Methodological Challenges for Indian Feminism

Patriarchy remains the common enemy of all women, irrespective of women's religion, sexuality and race. The distinctiveness of Indian Patriarchy is that it is also Brahminical. It not only challenges the status of women as inferior to male gender, it also makes women at the bottom of the caste hierarchy. Their bodily pollution cannot alleviate their position. Hence, feminist methodology and methodological tools of analyses must critically reject both Patriarchy and Brahminism.

I would like to point out few tools of analysis which may help construct an adequate methodology for Indian Feminist Theology.

i) **Critical Shift is needed from *Narisakti* to *Narimukti***: Much has been said about it in the previous section hence I am not going to elaborate any further. It is not eulogization of the power of woman that is important but the liberating power that make women celebrate 'here and now'

ii) **Emphasis on *Prakrti* Over and Above *Purusa***: The metaphor of body must be in the centre of the feminist discourse. Body experiences oppression, body is abused, body is made inferior, body is sexual-therefore body should be liberated.

iii) **Little Story and Oral History Constitute Herstory**: Women's Studies in social science use theories not so much to develop hypotheses but to develop wider understanding of women's issues. This is possible when theorisation becomes descriptive. Women's history is mostly found in oral and little traditions, sometimes hidden in the texts. Therefore it is essential to listen and understand women's experiences in their own stories and narratives. Written records are not necessarily more authentic by virtue of being found written.

iv) **Critiquing Tradition as an A Priori Engagement**: Feminist theology must engage in critiquing tradition at first place. While we have achieved in rereading and reconstructing the text by recovering the little traditions of the women, it is tradition that has been playing truant in liberating women. Tradition has become more sacrosanct than text for Indian church. Indian feminism must critique tradition because it is tradition that provides religious and cultural norms. Most often such norms do not have scriptural sanctions.

v) **Analysing Power**: It implies that someone 'powerful' delegates powers. Who are we to empower women? For example we hear very often so and so has ordained women, so and so has allowed women to be ministers. The giver of power is powerful in the hierarchy of patriarchy and bestowing power is the prerogative of the one who is at the top of the hierarchy of power. This structure defeats the notion of equality and creates power centres. For example, if an ordained woman is asked how she is liberated after getting Ordination, the answer would be that she is more respected, her status as woman is elevated compared to other women. It is construed as proof that she is empowered, never mind if she is still discriminated against because of her sex.

vi) **Experience**: The universality of women's experience of sexual violence, suggesting it is possible that in different cultural contexts the recognition of 'sexuality and sexual violence' may not be the same. However oppression is experienced by all women, no matter what is their social position. Therefore, experience must constitute as one of the important methodological category to recover the little and descriptive traditions.

vii) **Accompanying in the Struggles with the Dalits and Adivasis**: Women cannot achieve liberation by themselves. There is a need to align with others who are seeking liberation and at the same time allow men to convert so that all can engage in the struggles. Men are equally important in liberating women. For liberation in the final analysis is needed for both, men and women, oppressor and oppressed.

'Indian Feminism': An Alternative to Feminist Theology

What is Indian in Feminist Theology? Some may answer uncritically that the very preoccupation of Feminist Theology in India makes it Indian. But, the question is if Feminist Theology is rooted in the socio-cultural religious context of India. Feminist Theology has remained purely Christian and has not created a space for women of other religious traditions. Feminist Theologians in India have critiqued enough of the scriptures, including Hindu scriptures, like their western counterpart. It has not helped much, because in India critiquing scripture is seen much less as detached and distant experience that happens outside of women's body. The text does not appeal as much to the sentiment of women as the traditions, since scriptures have already have distanced from women as polluted beings. Rather the immediate locations of women's experiences are in the tradition – culture, liturgy, church traditions. Therefore, the first and foremost task is to critique tradition if liberation is to be realised in India.

Feminism must evolve tools to critique traditions, hierarchy and overarching patriarchal structure? No matter how we critique the text, unless we critique tradition as a priority we cannot eradicate discrimination against women and caste impediment from our churches.

Feminist Theology in India must make a paradigm shift, probably a total shift from their Western counterpart, in critiquing church traditions, church hierarchy and consciously challenging patriarchal leadership by starting movements as well as raising such issues in different academic forums. Not much has happened in shaking the church's patriarchal structure in last few decades by critiquing the text. Patriarchy is happy as long as domain of feminist critique remains within the bound of scripture. We have received enough hermeneutical tools to critique the texts from the West, but unfortunately there are few or no tools of analysis to critique traditions.

Secondly the Feminist Theology must articulate in multireligious context. Feminist theology has not addressed the issues and concerns of Indian women. 98 percent Indian women are not Christian, how do you approach Feminist Theology which is out and out Christian. If one has to foreground Feminist Theology, then consciously we must avoid using the nomenclature given by the West. In many ways Feminist Theology is hindrance to Indian women because of its deep roots in Western culture and Christian religion. There is a need to provide an appropriate nomenclature to 'Indian Feminist Theology'. While attempting to find an appropriate nomenclature one must realise there cannot be a feminist theology but feminist theologies for India. Further I doubt whether we can use the nomenclature feminist theologies in multireligious context like India where the word theology has become imperialistic and pejorative. There is a possibility to name the Study as Religious Feminisms under which we can study Dalit Feminism, Adivasi Feminism, Hindu Feminism, and Christian Feminism. In fact Feminism addresses the issues of tradition directly, while the Feminist Theology is text oriented.

4

Journey of Truth for the People of God towards Interfaith Harmony and Peace

Jetti A. Oliver

Study of religions is of paramount importance. Dialogue is essential to discover together the spiritual riches the religion offers for one's own inner wellbeing while on Earth and to enable the reward of Heaven when one ceases from the Earth.

This write up is to be part of a festschrift being brought out in honour of Rev. Dr. T. Swami Raju, Professor of Religions and a well-known author. His recent rich edition is a one volume Telugu Bible commentary titled 'Telugulo Bible Bhashyam'. An unassuming scholar, Dr. Swami Raju, is a great thinker, writer, preacher, teacher and a researcher par excellence. Committed to the cause of the Ministry of the Church. He brings to his teaching profession a very rich pastoral experience of rural and urban congregations of Andhra Pradesh. His student-centric life style is greatly admired and his writings are well sought after. He made us proud with scholarly papers presented at the national and international forums.

Turning 60 is a wonderful feat with so many achievements to his credit. We congratulate him for this his vibrant life and pray to God that he continues to enjoy the health and happiness, as the best is yet to come. We also congratulate the students, both the present and the past, the colleagues and the family members for being part of the task of honouring this spirit filled, mission oriented, highly dependable co-worker and a friend—Dr. Swami Raju.

God in His Grace wanted humankind the crown of creation to live for ever in the Garden of Eden. It was indeed a life of unmatchable blessings. True to the resultant nature, the vulnerable humankind could be convinced by the Satan to eat the forbidden fruit. It was a defiance of God's commandment resulting in the eviction from the Garden of Eden. Consequently, death dawn upon humankind and the rest of the creation. But, the God of love and compassion, post eviction, also blessed Adam and Eve to be fruitful, to multiply, to replenish and subdue the Earth. In this scenario, within the limitations, humankind continued to prosper a great deal even though death became inevitable.

To the misfortune of generations to come, the crime of Cain brought into the world the curse with its related hatred; enmity; violent approaches to issues; unjust way of living and a total rival culture to that of the originally intended culture of love and tolerance. Generations grew under the direct command of God the Almighty. Then, the intermediaries like leaders of deliverance, the judges, the prophets, the kings and such other stood in between God and Humankind punishing the wicked and upholding the righteous.

Thus, humanity grew, firstly, as the Blessed and the Cursed. Then, they grew as the Chosen and the Others; the Circumcised and the Uncircumcised; as the People of God and the Heathen; and then as the Jews and the Gentiles. Jews were supposed to be the oldest known faith group of people with blessings passed on from Abraham to Isaac and on to Jacob. This clan came out of one of the twelve Tribes risen from Jacob, the second and the son of Isaac whom God has blessed to become nations of the world and gave him the name 'Israel'. Judah, Jacob's fourth son was the source for the kingdom of Judea and the people—the Jews. As history reveals, we need to take note of the generations of the people born to the cursed Cain, and the blessed third son of Adam—Seth. In this manner, generations were born to the blessed Jacob, the second son of Isaac and the one left with minor blessings, Esau. Generations of people were also born in the family tree of Ishmael that Abraham had through Hagar who became the nation of Egypt with its neighbourhoods. As per the promise God made to Abraham, the population was exploding like countless stars of heaven and the sand on the sea shore with settlements in the known lands, the new found lands and in that order. People were opting for different forms of worship and different deities of worship.

As per the historical research, Pyramid texts of ancient Egypt and the Dead Sea Scrolls are some of the oldest available religious texts. When the art of writing was invented, philosophical theories started emerging resulting in innumerable forms of beliefs. People developed their own deities having suffered the tragic disconnect from God the Creator. These philosophical theories laid the spiritual foundations for humanity. Over a period of time, these were institutionalised and resulted in organized religions; served as a means of security and economic stability. It also justified a central authority. Thus, kings and emperors were playing the twin roles of political and spiritual leaders gaining justification of political authority by the Divine sanction. Organized religion also emerged as a means of maintaining peace between unrelated individuals and groups of people. It also served as a bonding factor for people of varying cultures and languages. Philosophical traditions such as Monotheism in Persia and Canaan (Middle East); Platonism in Greece; Sanathana Dharma, Buddhism, Jainism in India; and Confucianism and Taoism in China are few of the spiritual foundations for humanity.

Life after 'Garden of Eden' grew to a very complex and complicated societies and communities each shaping itself a unique form of culture, the language, the nations, the vocations, the royals and the less mortals and so on. The interventions of God, to reform the humanity did bear fruit though not fully, and the disconnect that exists between Man and God kept the faith perceptions far apart. While the day of judgement is to sort out the matters, the life until then has to be 'just', 'peaceful' with opportunities for people to live life to the fullest measure. This remains a great challenge to all Truth seekers to move beyond the discovery of truth for one's own benefit but also as a common endeavour to discover the Truth.

In our own context, we are of the land of Buddha, the land of Mahatma Gandhi, the land on which the Gospel of Jesus Christ was preached for over 2000 years. It continues to have many cultures, many languages and many people and yet one nation. Ours is a land of religions with three Crore deities. Sanathana Dharma together with the dharmas and the cultures that existed on this side of the Indus valley are Hindu by culture though different in Faith. Fortunately, a great many scholars from every religion admit the fact that God is One and the only One who is the Creator, the Sustainer, the Rock and the Refuge. There are many who would like to see an image of God of their imagination. Naturally, comprehension vary from person to person. In Telugu, it is popularly known as 'kodi kalu kinda koti nelalu untaye'. That is the kind of complexity and the diversity. Therefore, we need to look for unity not uniformity, unity in diversity and unity of purpose.

Religion and spiritually, are two different things. Religion promotes spirituality while religiosity may undermine the significance of spirituality with potential danger to create disunity leading to destruction. This will be a negation to the spiritual well-being of humanity. It warrants personal perusal of spiritual growth for one's own enlightenment and also to promote live and let live approach of humanity for a life of abundance on the earth and moksha in heaven. It is therefore necessary and essential to inculcate in the study of religions, dialogue with living faiths; understanding of religions and practising the gift of love; the gift of forgiveness and the gift of peace in the day to day lives of the people we live with. What we disagree should not be the basis but what we agree upon can be the basis to build human relations to promote peace and prosperity for all, After all, when we come to know the Truth, the Truth will set us free.

5

Re-visioning Methods and Approaches in the Study of Religions

Arun Gopal

In world history, religion has made immense contribution to the betterment of both societal, as well as individual lives. Several service organizations and voluntary agencies associated or inspired by one religion or the other, either in terms of social concerns or moral values have sprung to action, to rescue the victims of natural calamities, wars, epidemics, and poverty. It is also true that every religion has its own myths, faith-formulations, scriptures and patterns of worship and also observances in the form of festivals and celebrations, made explicit through music, hymns and lyrics, dance, drama, art, architecture and paintings. This has informed a spectrum of religious philosophies and spiritualties, theologies and ethical principles that have nurtured human sensibilities, convictions, commitments and value orientations. The list is unending. Seen in that perspective, religious pluralism in a sense is a gift of God.

Religion also has had its darker side that has been tarnishing the image and putting blocks, so that it would not play its legitimate role to enhance the humanity of the inhabitants of this planet earth. There have been moments of violence and blood-shed, causing large scale un-warranted migration and uprooting of communities from their native soil, resulting in hunger, ill-health, homelessness and mass-poverty, in thc name of religion. The recent history of India presents a dismal account of the vision of the architects of the constitution—'Unity in Diversity'. This has resulted in rise of hatred, suspicion accompanied by desecration of religious monuments, icons and worship centers of minority communities, through what may be termed as State sponsored violence, becoming the order of the day.

In such a context, the initiative to explore at deeper depth on the topic—"Re-visioning Methods and Approaches in the Study of Religion"—certainly holds a great promise. Although there have been several approaches, the author has selected to examine just four namely, the Triumphalistic Approach, the Dialogue Approach, the Pluriform Approach and the Dalit Hermeneutical Approach. It is obvious that the first three approaches are inter-related. The Dalit Hermeneutical Approach is included in this article in view of its uniqueness and significance. For, it reflects the perceptions of the sizable number of Indian masses and majority of Christians who originally were outside the purview of organized religion.

Triumphalistic Approach

Triumphalism, it is widely agreed has characterized what is described as the early missionary enterprise. In simple terms it is asserting the superiority of Christianity, over against other religions. The basic conviction of the missionaries as well as the early converts was that Christianity possessed the truth about God that is necessary for human salvation. This being the so called uniqueness of the Church's teaching and her evangelistic activities. The silent and yet powerful message conveyed to the people of other faiths was that the services rendered by Christian institutions and the style of functioning in Church organizations and administrative structures were of a higher quality. Hence, people of the different religions were invited to relate to the Christian missionaries with an attitude of 'co-existence, collaboration and solidarity.'[1] It was obvious that the ultimate objective of the foreign mission boards, who had sponsored and supported their representatives in India, as well as the indigenous evangelists who had worked hand in hand with them, was to establish Christianity as the world religion. The discussion below elaborates the thinking of the mission agencies with particular reference to Non-Catholic International Missionary Conferences.

The first International Missionary Conference held at Edinburg in 1910 was very supportive of J.N. Farquhar's 'Theory of Fulfilment', as far as Indian religions, especially Hinduism was concerned.[2] The author summarizes here the stand taken by Farquhar on Inter-Faith relations, as there will be references

---

1 V. M. Jose, "Religious Harmony in a Multi-Religious India," *Jnanadeepa - Pune Journal of Religious Studies* 1&2 (January-December, 2012), 29.

2 James Massey, ed., *Indigenous People: Dalits – Dalit Issues in Today's Theological Debate* (Delhi: ISPCK CTE-5, 1994), 215.

to that in the following pages. In an article published in 1910, Farquhar had expounded Matthew 5:17 to present his idea of 'fulfilment'. A more developed version of is found in his classical work *Crown of Hinduism*[3] published in 1913. His fundamental affirmation is:

> Christ's own declaration, 'I came not to destroy but to fulfil' has cleared up for us completely all our difficulties with regard to the Old Testament... Can it be that Christ Himself was thinking of pagan faiths as well as Judaism? If Christ is able to satisfy all religious needs of the human heart, then all the elements of pagan religions, since they spring up from these needs, will be found reproduced in perfect form, completely fulfilled, and consummated in Christ.[4]

It may be noticed that in the thought of Farquhar there was an evolutionary connection between Hinduism and Christianity, as of lower to higher. So, he hoped that days were not far when Christianity would replace Hinduism, rather than reforming it.

The Second International Missionary Conference held at Jerusalem in 1928, inspired by Natural Theology and the concept of Cosmic Christ affirmed that the "... rays of light that shone in Jesus Christ were to be found where He was unknown or even rejected."[5] Pointing out that "... the Father has nowhere left Himself without witness", the Jerusalem Conference presented a different version of the 'Fulfilment Theory.' To substantiate what is stated above the Conference report referred to the "... sense of the majesty of God and the consequent reverence in worship in Islam, the deep sympathy for world's suffering and search for a way of escape found in Buddhism, the desire for union with the ultimate reality in Hinduism and insistence on moral conduct in Confucianism,"[6] as pointers to further openings in future.

It may be seen that the International Missionary Conferences of 1910 and 1928 initiated a process whereby those areas in other religions, and especially Hinduism, could be identified and used as a fertile ground to sow the seed namely, the Gospel, that would eventually replace those religions. But, the International Missionary Conference held at Tambaram in 1938 caused much tension and led to disagreements, among the participants on some crucial issues. While responding to the W.E. Hocking's "Report of the Commission of Appraisal of the Layman's Foreign Missionary Enquiry", the Dutch theologian

---

3 R. S. H. Boyd, *Introduction to Indian Christian Theology* (Madras: Christian Literature Service, 1975), 89.

4 Boyd, *Introduction to Indian Christian Theology*, 89.

5 A. Haque, *Mission and Dialogue in the New Millennium* (Delhi: ISPCK, 1999), 6.

6 Haque, *Mission and Dialogue in the New Millennium*, 6.

Hendrick Kraemer through his treatise entitled, "Christian Message to Non-Christian World", asserted drawing input from Barthian Theology and Biblical Realism, that there is discontinuity between Christianity and other religions.[7] The three point program outlined by Kraemer was first to convince the world that other religions were purely human attempts to reach God and devoid of revelation. Second, the mission of the Church was to evangelize and call people to respond to the Gospel. And, third to present the challenge of the Gospel should continue as the majority priority of the missionary movement.[8]

Of course, such a posture was not relished by the 'Re-thinking Christianity Group' in India too. The participants at the conference resolved: "We see and readily recognize that in them (other faiths) are to be found values of deep religious experiences and great moral achievement."[9] They called for positive and constructive relations with the followers of other religions and encouraged the churches to cooperate with them in community movements for social transformation. The Re-thinking group on the other hand laid down that the Hindu culture, heritage and traditions were common to all Indians. Further, the work of the Holy Spirit who transcends the boundaries of religions cannot be controlled by the Church.[10] With the outbreak of World War II discussions on the Christian attitude towards followers of other religions was not pursued seriously with a view to break a new ground, either at the International Missionary Conference held in Whitby in 1947, the First Assembly of the World Council of Churches convened in 1948 at Amsterdam or the International Missionary Conference Session in 1952 at Willingen. However, the Christian Institute for the study of Religion and Society, Bangalore, established after the New Delhi session of the World Council of Churches in 1961, to conduct studies on the theme, "Word of God and Living Faiths", under the leadership of its first Director, P.D. Devanandan, a young Professor of Religions began to work on a balanced Christian Approach in Inter-Faith relations.

Today "Triumphalism" on the part of the Christian denominations planted by the missionaries has ceased with the declaration of the "Moratorium on Missions", and the Emergence of the Indian Church, with its own ecclesiology and Theology of Missions. However, another form of "Triumphalism" is raising its head with the slogan 'One Religion, One Nation and One Language' under the present Bharatiya Janata Party rule, committed to 'Hindutva' ideology and saffronization. In the current situation there is an urgent need for the Christian churches to help identify the meeting

7 Haque, *Mission and Dialogue in the New Millennium*, 7.

8 Vincent Rajkumar, "Inter-Faith Conversations in Asia: New Challenges," *Religion & Society* 3&4 (September – December, 2016), 132.

9 Haque, *Mission and Dialogue in the New Millennium*, 7.

10 Rajkumar, "Inter-Faith Conversations in Asia: New Challenges," 132.

points between several Indian religions and promote common brotherhood/ sisterhood.

Dialogue Approach

In the present shrinking world, religious pluralism is becoming a global phenomenon. To the well-meaning people such a plurality through inter-faith conversations and other partnership programs could contribute to enriching one another's faith perspectives, besides fostering communal harmony necessary for peace and justice. In a multi-religious context as obtained in India today, it is all the more imperative on the part of the Church to make every effort to identify the extent of collaboration between the followers of different religions, so that those who pursue a policy of what S.J. Samartha terms as "... Politicization of religion and communalization of politics"[11] may not use religion to serve the vested interests. Reading the signs of the times at the beginning of this century, both at the national and international levels theologians had initiated a process of inter-faith dialogue that had gained popularity as the Dialogue approach.

In inter-religious dialogue forums, the participants meet with 'an informed understanding' of one's own faith. Further, they come as pilgrims walking hand in hand, and moving towards a common goal which is to perceive truth in all its manifold facets. In this journey, each one has to shed his or her prejudices and recognize some indication of God's revelation in other's religion, and also what is that one could draw from other religious traditions to broaden one's faith perspectives. Vincent Rajkumar provides clarity on what dialogue involves saying:

> The goal of inter-faith conversation is not to achieve agreement on matters of doctrine. It is not about finding the lowest common doctrinal denominator, to which all can give assent, nor is it about striving to find correspondence between our faith traditions, though it may be that resonances might emerge. But, it demands us to collaborate in the interests of common people for common justice and political stability to build a healthy and sustainable human community.[12]

With this mature understanding of dialogue, the author proceeds to outline the parameters of dialogue from four perspectives viz. Biblical, Theological, Missiological and Ecumenical.

---

11 Israel Selvanayagam, "Commitment and Openness in a Multi-Faith Context," *Religion & Society* 4 (December 2012), 63.

12 Rajkumar, "Inter-Faith Conversations in Asia: New Challenges," 137.

Viewing Dialogue from a Biblical perspective, Jose Kuttianimattathil begins with the pre-existent 'Word-Logos' that became incarnate in Jesus, the Christ[13] (John 1:1-18). This divine Logos who had brought everything visible and invisible into being (John 1:3) had entered history in human form and revealed Himself. This word has been communicating powerful messages through the creation, historical events and also human conscience. Kuttianimattathil, in his penetrative analysis categorically states that the 'Word-Logos' without partiality has been active both among the Jews and non-Jews. According to him one has to affirm in Faith that:

> What was shown partially and in an obscure way to all peoples has been revealed totally in the incarnation. Jesus Christ is the incarnate manifestation of the Divine Logos, which has been active always and everywhere in the world. Therefore, there is continuity between 'not-yet' incarnate Logos and the Logos made flesh.[14]

Pointing out the essential unity between the Logos and the Holy Spirit Kuttianimattathil claims that although the Son and the Holy Spirit are distinct, in their mission they are inseparable. Pointing out John 16:13 he says that Jesus Christ is the truth. And, the Spirit guides "… into all truth." Thus, it is his conviction that the same Spirit, who has been leading all religions in the direction of truth, has been active in the incarnation of Logos. So, it is dialogue that opens the eyes of Christians to those elements of revelation present in other religions, but not made fully explicit in the teachings of Jesus.

To examine dialogue from the perspective of Christian theology, the author has drawn from the ideas of Raymond Panikar. Panikar feels that the truth is always relational and so it is absurd to talk about absolute truth. Therefore, whatever may be the claims of world's great religions to possess the full truth, their affirmations need to be understood only in a limited and in a tentative context. In this connection, Panikar refers to the question posed to Jesus by Pilot at the time of Jesus' crucifixion—"What is truth?" He interprets the silence of Jesus as conveying that there is nothing like absolute or objective truth. Further, truth cannot be fully conceptualized. He exegetes the statement of Jesus "I am the truth" to extend an invitation to join the way that leads to truth. Panikar articulates his theological position metaphorically as follows:

> I am convinced that each of us participates in the truth. Inevitably my truth is that I perceive from my window. And, the value of dialogue between various religions is precisely to help me perceive

13 Jose Kuttianimattathil, "The Basis of Creating A Culture of Encounter to Travel Together with All People in Understanding and Solidarity," *Vidhyajyothi Journal of Theological Reflection* 6 (June 2018), 415.

14 Kuttianimattathil, "The Basis of Creating A Culture of Encounter," 16.

> that there are other windows, other perspectives. Therefore I need the other in order to know and verify my own perspective of truth. Truth is a genuine and authentic participation in the dynamism of reality.[15]

Thus, in the thought of Panikar dialogue is a necessity in the process of search and discovery of truth that dispels the darkness of ignorance.

The Missiological perspective on dialogue is contained in the writings of P.D. Devanandan. He starts from the 'Fulfilment Theory' of J.N. Farquhar. In his thinking neither Christians nor Hindus need to build on the past believing that there is a process of evolution. His thesis is that the future has already broken in on the present, the future which is Christ, the hope of glory, the new creation. The same Christ who is at work within the Church, through the Spirit is also at work outside it. As far as Hinduism is concerned Christ is at work in all the reform movements, which indicate that religious Hinduism is being replaced by renascent Hinduism, providing a new understanding of God and the world. Devanandan conveys his radical ideas in the form of a question stating:

> If all 'new creation' can only be of God, where else could these 'new aspects of other beliefs in the thinking and living of people have sprung from? If the whole creation being directed by the redemptive power of God in Christ Jesus, towards the final 'hope of glory', a total transformation of the present existence is the *fulfilment* in the end the result of the present, being fulfilled in the future or does it consist in the ultimate future being *realized* (and so fulfilled) in the temporal present? If the true reading of salvation history (Heilsgeschichte) is in terms of eternity flowing into time, the 'coming' of the eternal kingdom in the temporal order of man, how doing we restate the distinctiveness of the Gospel, in the context of religions of the world?[16]

Devanandan sees in this 'newness' the hand of God, and hears in it the call to Dialogue with those who belong to other faiths, so that Christians as well as those who are outside might meet each other in the area of God's new creation.

It may be seen that Devanandan does not subscribe to Farquhar's 'Crown of Hinduism' theory, wherein 'fulfilment' is understood as the culmination of a historical process with the establishment of Christianity. On the other hand, it is the breaking in of the 'end' here and now, in history where both sacred

---

15 Kuruvilla Pandikattu, "Identity, Memory and Healing: In Search of Dialogical Wisdom," 80.

16 Boyd, *Introduction to Indian Christian Theology*, 195.

and secular converge in Christ. To Devanandan, what is important is the living interpretation of Christian faith, which through the dialogue with the followers of Hindu faith would satisfy their spiritual longings while remaining true to the faith 'once delivered to the Saints.'

Finally, the Ecumenical perspective emerges from the World Council of Churches, affirming that proclamation and dialogue are not the same, and yet each compliments the other in the witness of the Church. The Uppsala Assembly of the World Council of Churches held in 1968, stated that the foundation for *Christian Dialogue with men of other Faiths*, is the common humanity or one stock to which all people of all races, languages, religions and cultures belong. The report affirms:

> The meeting with men of other faiths or no faith must lead to dialogue. A Christian's dialogue with another implies neither a denial of the uniqueness of Christ, nor any loss of his own commitment to Christ, but rather that a genuinely Christian approach to others must be human, personal, relevant and humble. In dialogue we share our common humanity … Christ speaks in this dialogue.[17]

The common humanity refers to the common experiences of woundedness caused by sin. In order to come out of it people of different faiths need each other. The answer of God to the innermost longings of human hearts and the soul penetrating questions comes through His revelation in and through Christ, who through the Holy Spirit reaches people of religions other than Christianity, through things that are noble having salvific significance.

It may not be an exaggeration to say that dialogue in the present Indian context is most preferable because it happens in an environment of collaboration, rather than discord and antagonism. For, the Gospel to penetrate and generate a favorable response people need to develop a 'listening ear.' When the people of other faiths find Christians as co-pilgrims moving towards a common goal namely, to comprehend the full truth, it would foster partnership and brotherhood/sisterhood where the light of Christ would enlighten all people. In a sense, dialogue has to replace the Triumphalistic attitude whoever might nurture it. For, the objective of dialogue is not religious propaganda but comprehension of truth sharing each other's experiences and perceptions. However, it needs to be stated that the dialogue approach should not be confined mainly to theological consultations or Ecumenical forums, it should come down to the level of local congregations which are the witnessing units of the Church.

---

17 A. Haque, *Mission and Dialogue in the New Millennium* (Delhi: ISPCK, 1995), 12.

Pluriform Approach

The Pluriform approach to the study of religions or what might better be termed as the pattern of relationship between religions, in the contemporary world in general, and the Indian society in particular is presented by Samuel Rayan, within the framework of his "Theology of the Other."[18] His "Theology of the Other" is undergirded by four fundamental affirmations that are summarized below. Before leading the reader to consider the affirmations the author points out the foundation of Rayan's thesis. In order to give content to his "Theology of the Other" Rayan exegetes the 'Great Commandment' of Jesus and the Pauline exhortation on humility that characterizes Christian spirituality. He holds that:

> His (Jesus') great command to love our neighbor as we love ourselves, I suggest that the commandment covers not only individual persons, but cultures as well as religions and spiritual traditions. It includes the other's right and need for a world of justice and a community of equality and creative freedom.[19]

Samuel Rayan further adds:

> Paul's recommendation to consider the other superior must be valid for religions and cultures and political formations and ethnic groups, as they are for individual persons. The grace of the Gospel of God keeps us from developing boastfulness and superiority complexes.[20]

The four affirmations are as follows. First, Rayan firmly believes that there is no religion, Church doctrine or cultural tradition, or even a spiritual experience that adequately, exhaustively and comprehensively grasps or communicates divine revelation. According to him, the divine reality is revealed, experienced and articulated in manifold ways. Rayan who has mature and seasoned faith perspectives lays down that there are three principles underlying religious pluralism namely, 'the utterly free and personal nature of divine self-revelation, the unfolding historical character of human perceptions and human bondedness.'[21] So, he submits that each tradition has something that is meant to be shared as a gift from God. The gracefulness of the Christians lies in shedding self-complacency and readiness to learn from others. Samuel Rayan appeals to Christian sisters and brothers to identify those areas in their

---

18 Kurian Kunnapuram, ed., *Selected Writings of Samuel Rayan Vol. III The Mission of the Church* (Mumbai: St. Paul's Press, 2013), 348.

19 Kunnapuram, *Selected Writings of Samuel Rayan*, 340.

20 Kunnapuram, *Selected Writings of Samuel Rayan*, 340.

21 Kunnapuram, *Selected Writings of Samuel Rayan*, 344.

doctrines, liturgies, faith-formulations and religious observances, where sister traditions could make their rich contribution for further growth and fresh insights.

Second, in as much as the searching faith opens itself to God, it should simultaneously be open to discerning God's revelatory activities in the events and religious histories of the non-Christian neighbors, in whose midst Christians live. Hence, its natural corollary is that any attempt to ignore, caricature or destroy other religions, would amount to being blind to God's presence, unique gifts and deeper truths embedded in other religions. Above all it is tarnishing the image of one's own faith-tradition and undercutting its credibility.

Third, Rayan does not approve any implicit or explicit move towards the fusion or assimilation of all religions, ending in syncretism. Claiming that all particularities and specificities in different religions are God's gifts he calls the adherents of all religions to strive towards evolving what Samuel Rayan envisions as:

> A family of religions, each with its own race and voice and heart loyalties, yet all living together for the construction of a new human world, living and working from each other for each other, especially from the promise and the reality of the coming reign of God and for it.[22]

He elaborates it using the imagery of a garden, where the common ground or the field is the earth. But, out of that which is common grows the rose plant, coconut and palm trees and then lotus in the pond. The profound insight of Rayan is that the common is there to produce the particular and the special. He sees this phenomenon in every culture and history of religions. He states that as the 'Common Whole' advances, the achievements of the 'Specific' add colour and flavor.

Finally, as a true disciple of Jesus Christ, Samuel Rayan takes a firm stand saying that Christ is the only authentic self-disclosure of God. According to him, Jesus is the personification of the 'tenderness, goodness, and philanthropy' of God. In the same breath he also without mincing words declares that all spiritual traditions claims of theophanies are the variations of that 'One-Word' that was speaking throughout human history and finally made flesh in Jesus of Nazareth.

Hence, the Church has to work towards this wider ecumenism, for a family of religions, each echoing and reflecting in its rituals, rights, teachings and doctrines, that ever present eternal voice of God's redeeming love. The final exhortation of Samuel Rayan is:

---

22 Kunnapuram, *Selected Writings of Samuel Rayan*, 346.

> Religious thinkers and witnesses thus stand summoned and challenged to serve the people, by working out from within the people's own experience, a theology of the other and a spirituality of mutualness. They are all called upon to enable their communities and all who come to be open and respectful to the other and thereby to the ultimate "other" who is also the 'self' of our deepest 'self' who is other and not other *paraparah*.[23]

It may be noticed that Samuel Rayan a distinguished Jesuit theologian has in his 'Pluriform approach', based on the "Theology of the Other" expresses his theological convictions, that Christ is the singular disclosure of God and all other religions are the variations of that revelation. The mission of the Church is to recognize the common soil that is God from whom grow the particular manifestations, as individual trees and plants and not destroy or annihilate other religions with a triumphalistic attitude, but to resist the triumphalism of every other religion. He appeals to Christian seekers to join hands with the followers of different religions, for promoting mutual faith enrichment, but not syncretism.

In a sense the 'Pluriform Approach' or 'Spirituality of Mutualness' of Samuel Rayan may be interpreted as the dialogue approach in a different form but it may be appropriate to say it is a further development of the concerns that figure in dialogical approach. In fact, Rayan is not interested in projecting Christianity as the hope of the world. For, even as other religious faiths reflect the light of Christ, Christianity also does it in its own way. But, Christ who cannot be imprisoned in any religious doctrine or dogma is the ultimate self-revelation of God and all claims of revelations made by all religions including Christianity, have to be subordinated to this 'Finality of Christ', standing in need of their own their perfection.

Dalit Hermeneutical Approach

Hitherto the discussion has been on the insights gained through biblical and theological research, critical and penetrative analysis of the past and present methods and approaches, not only to the study of religion in general, but inter-faith relations involving a closer look at the Indian religious and cultural realities. The author feels that a responsible and serious discussion of the subject at hand will not be complete without taking into account an altogether non-elitist, 'experience' based perceptions of those who have been trampled-down and victimized by the caste-class power structure that is being nurtured and sustained by the middle-class ethos of India for centuries. They are those who are labelled as 'Panchamas', outside the caste-ladder, blessed by the dominant religious culture namely, Hinduism. They had no access to

23 Kunnapuram, *Selected Writings of Samuel Rayan*, 348.

temple worship or written religious Scriptures. Their approach to the Study of Religions emerges from what Masilamani Azariah terms as the "Wounded psyche."[24] Their understanding of religion is based on their physical pain and psychological trauma. When A. P. Nirmal[25] opines that Dalits "Know God in and through their suffering ... It is in and through pain ... pathos that sufferers know God", he is pointing towards the "Bottom-up" approach rather than "Top-down" approach to religion. Since, pathos is also the starting point for Dalit hermeneutics that serves as a window to grasp the impact of the factors that underlie Dalit religious affections and perceptions, the graphic picture painted by Evangeline Anderson Rajkumar is worth considering. In despair she remarks:

> The skin, body and blood thus stand at the center of Dalit Hermeneutics. While the violence is meted out against the bodies, the skins bear the painful scars, testifying to the struggles of life. The blood of the Dalits is shed every single day in this country, and it cries out to God for justice.[26]

While the voice of the shed blood and painful scars provide the framework to evolve an authentic Dalit Hermeneutic, the ultimate objective to envision what it really needs to achieve is outlined by Vincent Rajkumar. He says, "Dalit approach ... is around their own liberation and humanization as advocated by Dr. B. R. Ambedkar who set the direction for Dalit liberation."[27]

Hence, it may be inferred that the goal towards which Dalit hermeneutics leads one, particularly the Indian Dalits is liberation from the subtle psychological mechanisms that are driven into the consciousness of the Dalits under the auspices of religious Hinduism. The reader would notice that the basic premise of the Dalit hermeneutical approach is that religion has to be the 'hand-maiden' of individuals and groups fostering justice and peace that contribute to genuine humanization, rather than being a 'task-master' or a whip employed by the vested interests, promoting self-perpetuation, with the connivance of State authorities, as may be observed in contemporary Indian context.

Having this mind, the author discusses below the implications of the Dalit hermeneutical approach, for the Dalits in general and also the Christians of Dalit origin in particular. At this juncture it needs to be highlighted that

24 John. C. B. Webster, "Exploring 'Pastoral Theology' Dimension of Dalit Liberation," *Religion and Society* 2 & 3 (June & September, 2004), 50.

25 Franklyn J. Balasundaram, "The Contribution of A. P. Nirmal to Theology and Especially Dalit Theology, *Religion and Society* 2&3 (June & September, 2004), 90.

26 Rajkumar, "Skin, Body and Blood: Exploration of Dalit Hermeneutics," 115.

27 Rajkumar, "Inter-Faith Conversations in Asia: New Challenges," 135.

'protest' or countering the world views, beliefs, values and patterns of behavior imposed by hierarchical caste ideologies comes as a natural corollary, while exploring the methodology for Dalit hermeneutics. Evangeline A. Rajkumar who has thoroughly investigated the area of Dalit pathos had proposed a five point program that is summarized below. To all those who are genuinely interested in working out a credible Dalit Hermeneutical Approach to Study of Religion, the author believes that these proposals would indicate the areas, where serious re-thinking and concentration are needed, if a non-casteist, non-elitist and indigenous Hermeneutics from 'below' should replace the conventional-status quo oriented Hermeneutics.

According to Evangeline A. Rajkumar[28] there needs to be a psychological revolution among the Dalits themselves. It is necessary so as to develop a strong conviction that it is certainly possible to demolish the mental images of a person of Dalit origin, whose personality and human existence is defined by caste structures. Every attempt should be made to restore in her or him the image of God as a human being.

Secondly, the Dalits have to remove from their psyche the implanted 'human-made' constructs ascribed to their identities bearing the seal of religion, that they are the polluted—untouchables, precisely, the apartheid of India. Thirdly, the Dalits have to acquire an alternative mindset that would no longer own the impure, inferior and hazardous tasks assigned only to them, amidst rites and rituals such as those in crematoriums. They are also employed in manual scavenging and exploited in the organ transplant markets, on account of their poverty, in spite of the life-threatening consequences.

Fourthly, through a process of de-mystification, the Dalits themselves have to sharpen their sensibilities and critical faculties to discard those age-old stories and narratives authenticated by Brahminic-Hinduism, that unlike other castes they do not belong to the body of Brahman their 'Casteist-God'. Hence, whatever status is prescribed to them has divine sanction. Finally, the Dalits have to expose to the public the conniving attitude of politicians and the government officials, who either support or are silent about the atrocities committed on Dalits, in the name of casteism and patriarchy. It is gratifying to note that in Tamil Nadu way back in early sixties, E.V. Ramaswamy Periyar, through his anti-Brahmin 'Dravida Kazhagam' movement adopted the principles similar to those outlined by Evangeline A. Rajkumar, in his hermeneutics rooted in atheism.

As one whose heart bleeds at the plight of the Christians of Dalit origin, the author wishes to complete this section, with a brief discussion on Christian Dalit hermeneutical approach. Needless to say that the history of the Church in India is tainted by the frustrations, disappointments and a sense

---

28 Rajkumar, "Skin, Body and Blood: Exploration of Dalit Hermeneutics," 116-120.

of defeatism experienced by the Christians of Dalit origin, who feel in the words of Kottapalli Wilson that they are "twice alienated." A vast number of Dalits embraced Christianity during the early missionary era, unable to bear the brunt of Hinduism, manifested in innumerable ways discussed above. They embraced Christianity with the hope of experiencing equality, sisterhood/brotherhood and commonality. Irrespective of being treated as "Second-class citizens" or "Back benchers" in some denomination—with separate places inside the Church and also in burial grounds—a majority of them have not left to return to the Hindu fold or join some other faith, although the present State policies encourage that. By the efforts of the Dalit theologians like A.P. Nirmal, James Massey, Kottapalli Wilson, Fr. Arockiadoss, Fr. T.K. John, Mrs. Mary Celia, Sr. Shalini, V. Devasahayam and Sathianathan Clarke, Christians of Dalit origin in India are breaking their "Culture of Silence." They are taking responsibility for their own liberation, and authentic Christian discipleship, through a new hermeneutic. T.K. John describes this fresh initiative as follows:

> The Christians of 'Dalit Origin' now turn to the traditional interpreters and do tell them: please allow us to read the Bible ourselves, introduce our perspectives and receive the liberating message unblocked in order to bring about change in our iniquitous system. For, our world is seen or experienced only by those who are in it, or come to it. The word of God was read to us, interpreted to us, for over thousand years but not much happened… We resolve to have direct dialogue with the God that understands us from within.[29]

To empower the Christians of Dalit origin, John. C.B. Webster opposes what he calls as the "trickle-down theory of spiritual aid."[30] He feels that hitherto the Indian Church's hermeneutical and homiletical practices were the extension of the practices in the Western churches. Now the Dalit hermeneutics centering on freedom and humanization has to emerge from their suffering. According to Webster, V. Devasahayam elaborated it saying that Pastor and Preachers normally begin their sermon preparation processes by exegeting a series of Bible passages. In reality what is needed is to exegete their congregations, especially the inner world of Dalit pain and suffering, the 'Dalit Reality' and 'Dalit pathos.' Hence, Devasahayam pleaded for a paradigmatic shift from a "Sociological bias" that took into account the external pressures and strictures imposed by structures, customs and practices on the Dalits, to a "psychological bias" that would provide an understanding of the 'in-depth experience' of the

29 Leonardo Fernando, et al. *Dalit World and Biblical World: An Encounter* (New Delhi: Centre for Dalit/Subaltern Studies, 2007), 190.

30 Webster, "Exploring 'Pastoral Theology' Dimension of Dalit Liberation," 55.

worshipping Dalit Christians.[31] The suggestions of John C. B. Webster and V. Devasahayam to percolate to the level of local congregations starts with seminary training, so that the clergy may in turn equip the lay preachers by instilling the basic components of Dalit hermeneutical approach in their minds.

While concluding this section on 'Dalit Hermeneutical Approach', it may be underlined that the approach of the Dalits in India and that of the Christians of Dalit origin towards the study of religion, cannot be a reflection on the religious concepts or faith-formulations, but the day-to-day experiences and particularly the pain inflicted on their bodies and minds. Seen in that perspective, it is a hermeneutics of departure from inherited patterns. Dalit hermeneutical approach focuses on an 'inductive-method' starting with Dalit reality which is 'Pathos.' Further, their philosophical speculations and theological perceptions generate not from intellectual mode of consciousness but intuitive mode of consciousness. Their method of articulating their perceptions is dialogue and group interaction. The symbol of Dalit solidarity and expressions is the Drum.

In this article, the author has attempted to present an in-depth analysis of the selected approaches adopted at different stages of the systematic study of religion, with particular reference to Inter-faith relations. Of course, at each stage the particular emphasis/interest was different. For, in a pluralistic society like India, religion cannot be subjected only to an intellectual analysis, neglecting the practical issues confronting the masses. A holistic treatment of the subject necessitates a closer look at Missionary Triumphalism and the concerns emerging from the current Inter-religious dialogue, which is further developed in the Pluriform Approach. The author has included the Dalit Hermeneutical Approach because it is altogether different from the approaches cited above. As indicated earlier as far as the Dalit are concerned, it is the reflection on their pain, rather than any doctrine or constructs based on any claim of revolution. It is their path way to gain understanding of religion. The discussion in this presentation is not exhaustive, but it highlights the important concerns underlying the whole envisioning process, in the study of the Methods and Approaches to acquire a global perspective of religion, that is increasingly becoming a divisive force in the present Indian context. The author sincerely hopes that this academic investigation would in some ways afford religion its rightful place, as a binding force fostering brotherhood/sisterhood in an otherwise disintegrating Indian society, at the hands of the communal-minded politicians.

31 Webster, "Exploring 'Pastoral Theology' Dimension of Dalit Liberation," 55.

6

Sri Sri Ravishankar's Interpretation of Jesus Christ: A Critical Appreciation

Rodinmawia Ralte

Introduction

Sri Sri Ravishankar may be considered as the greatest and most popular living Hindu guru in terms of his followings and worldwide recognition. He was born on 13th May, 1956 in Papanasam, a village in Tamil Nadu. He showed religious interest at a very early age and it is said that he learnt Sanskrit and could recite part of Bhagavad Gita at the age of four. When he reached the age of nine, he protested the practice of untouchability in her maternal grandmother's village.[1] According to her sister, Sri Sri was a very different person right from childhood; he was very brilliant, "when he was eighth standard, students from tenth standard would come to him for advice. In his company, everyone felt good... He was very artistic. He would write poem, write and direct play."[2] As a young boy he would often tell his friends, "People all over the world are waiting for me."[3] He studied science and graduated at a very early age from St. Stephen's College, Bangalore. They used to say, "By age seventeen, He had

---

1 Francois Gautier, *The Guru of Joy: Sri Sri Ravishankar & The Art of Living* (New Delhi: Hay House Publishers (India) Pvt. Ltd., 2011), 39.

2 *India Today*, November 12, 2001, 64.

3 In the Appendix of the book, Sri Sri Ravishankar, *Bang on the Door: A collection of Talks*, Second Revised Edition (Bangalore: Sri Sri Publication Trust, 2008).

completed his education in both Vedic literature and modern science."[4] After graduation he has a choice to make: a bank job or a job with God: he chose the latter.

He joined Maharishi Mahesh Yogi who is a famous guru of 'Transcendental Meditation' and worked with him for some time. Though very young, Maharishi recognized his ability and he was sent to various places in India and abroad to give talks on Vedas and science.[5] He had a successful time with Maharishi but in 1980 he parted company.[6] He explains, "There was no ill feeling. (But) I was not very comfortable with his claims of people flying... I was more interested in rural development. So, I went into villages and help people to integrate their lives and get stress out. I helped children study both ancient and modern science."[7]

It was in the year 1982, in Shimoga, where a course conducted by him was going on, something phenomenal happened in the life of Sri Sri Ravishankar. He decided to go silent for ten days. He says, "An instinct comes that you want silence and so you follow it... On the bank of the Tunga river in Bhadravati in Karnataka."[8] It was during this ten days silence the *Sudarshan Kriya*, a powerful breathing technique was revealed to him. "It came like a poem, an inspiration. I learn it and I started teaching it."[9] Soon after this, in the same year, Sri Sri Ravishankar founded the Art of Living Foundation which is "an international, non-profit, educational and humanitarian organization. It's educational and self-development programs offer powerful tools to eliminate stress and foster a sense of well-being."[10]

Sri Sri Ravishankar is undoubtedly the fastest growing guru in the world at present. According to the official website of Sri Sri Ravishankar, his Art of Living, though it is only some thirty years old, has expanded and covered 151 countries of the world.[11] Like many contemporary gurus, he is associated with miracles, though it is not the primary feature of his teaching or ministry. Miracles like changing stone into diamond or silver or gold, healing of sick from cancers, heart problems, mental illness, etc. are reported to have taken

---

4 Ravishankar, *Bang on the Door: A collection of Talks*.

5 Gautier, *The Guru of Joy*, 57.

6 Gautier, *The Guru of Joy*, 58.

7 *Reader Digest*, February 2007, 96.

8 *Reader Digest*, February 2007, 96.

9 *Reader Digest*, February 2007, 96.

10 In an official website of Sri Sri Ravishankar *http://srisriravishankar.org/biography* (27.07.2011).

11 In an official website of Sri Sri Ravishankar *http://srisriravishankar.org/biography* (27.07.2011).

place in his ministry.[12] But the greatest miracle of all associated with Sri Sri, according to Francois Gautier, is changing the lives and natures of his disciples which is a near-impossible.[13]

Philosophical and Religious Teachings of Sri Sri Ravishankar: An Overview

Michael Fischman, an American instructor of Art of Living (hereafter AOL) knowingly or unknowingly summarizes the main purpose of Sri Sri Ravishankar and his AOL when he says in the introductory speech of one of the LOL courses: "We all want happiness, love, and peace. We fail to realize this because we are stressed. The breathing techniques that we learn here will help to release stress."[14] This is in consonance with the vision of Sri Sri Ravishankar: 'Violence-free, stress-free world'.

Philosophically, Sri Sri follows Advaita Vedanta system which he praises as: "Einstein's theory of relativity correlates with the *Avdaita* (non-dual) philosophy."[15] God is not easy to explain in human terms and categories. God is beyond all concepts. It is an experience. "God is the eternal 'I don't know."[16] In the midst of the unknowable-*ness*, the good part according to Sri Sri is "You can be God. You can live in God." Though you cannot know God, but "You can experience God. Whether you know it or not, experience it or not, you are That."[17] No doubt that with these words Sri Sri reflects Upanisadic explication of Brahman as *neti neti* and *tat tvam asi*. He explains the indwelling God, the *tat tvam asi* God as follows:

> God is the junction of presence and present. Whenever every cell, every atom of the mind and body get totally immersed in the

12 For further study on this subject Ref. Francois Gautier, *The Guru of Joy*, where chapter ten of this book talks about miracles associated with Sri Sri Ravishankar. Cf. for miracles Sri Sri Ravishankar, *An Intimate Note to the Seeker Volume 4,* 80; Sri Sri Ravishankar, *An Intimate Note to the Sincere Seeker, Volume 5*, compiled by Anne Elixhauser & Bill Hayden, (Bangalore: Vyakti Vikas Kendra, 2002), 31, 68, 77, 84, 97. Cf. also Sri Sri Ravishankar, *An Intimate Note to the Seeker Volume 6*, compiled by Bill Hayden and Anne Elixhauser (Bangalore: Vyakti Vikas Kendra, 2002), 25, 27, 65; Sri Sri Ravishankar, *An Intimate Note to the Seeker Volume 1*, compiled by David L. Burge (Santa Barbara: Art of Living Foundation, 2002; first published in 1997), 61. Also Sri Sri Ravishankar, *An Intimate Note to the Seeker Volume 2*, compiled by David L. Burge (Santa Barbara: Art of Living Foundation, 2000), 66.

13 Gautier, *The Guru of Joy*, 159.

14 Gautier, *The Guru of Joy*, 21.

15 Sri Sri Ravishankar, *An Intimate Note to the Sincere Seeker, Vol. 7,* compiled by Bill Hayden & Anne Elixhauser, (Bangalore: Vyakti Vikas Kendra, 2003), 71.

16 Sri Sri Ravishankar, *God loves Fun* (Bangalore: Sri Sri Publications Trust, 2008), 41.

17 Ravishankar, *God loves Fun*, 41.

> presence and present, you experience something ecstatic, something beyond this world. An experience of eternity comes. This is "Me! Me! dissolves... There is something. And what is that something? You don't know? That is presence. A presence where only knower remains, is God.[18]

According to Sri Sri, God is Omnipresent which means He is everywhere, in the rich or in the wicket as much as He is in the wonderful. Every thought is in God. The thinker is God. We are not separate from God. It is wrong to say "God is speaking to me" or "I have a message from God", because, this is just our consciousness split into two where one part of our own consciousness becomes God, and another part becomes our mind. That is not God. God is the totality. Everything is in God. There is nothing that can be outside God. Whether good or evil, both exist in God.[19]

An interesting feature of Sri Sri Ravishankar's concept of God is that for him God and Love are synonymous, that is why he emphasized so much about love in all his lectures and discourses. Responding to a question: "Who is God", Sri Sri says, "You and me and all that is. The totality. Love is God and everything is love. The whole creation is filled with love." Moving away from the general conception of love as 'feeling or emotion' he says, "Love is what you are made up of. The consciousness in you is love. Love is not just emotion. It is the very state of your being. It is the pulse in you. You may call it God. You may call it pure consciousness. You may call it the supreme or unseen power... When you become love you dissolve, you go beyond."[20] The place he assigns to love is interesting:

> Love is present in the entire creation... Because of love the planets are moving in their orbits, the sun is shining, and the stars are there. There is love in every atom, and that is why the electron is moving around the charged particle. The charge of attraction, the charge in this entire creation is a power, is love.[21]

Sri Sri Ravishankar explains God in relation to human being beautifully as follows:

---

18 Ravishankar, *God loves Fun*, 53.

19 Ravishankar, *God loves Fun*, 41.

20 Sri Sri Ravishankar, *Bang on the Door: A collection of Talks*, Second Revised Edition (Bangalore: Sri Sri Publication Trust, 2008), 93-94, Cf. Sri Sri Ravishankar, *An Intimate Note to the Sincere Seeker, Vol. 3,* compiled by David L. Burge (Santa Barbara: Art of Living Foundation, 2000, first published in 1998), 43.

21 Ri Sri Ravishankar, *Wisdom for the New Millennium* (Mumbai: Jaico Publishing House, 2005), 74.

> God is never an object of isolation but the very core of your being. The difference between Self (human) and God is just like the wave and the ocean. Can there be a wave without the ocean?... So you are made up of God!... Do not think God is sitting somewhere in heaven. God is here and now!... When you want to see God as something, as an object, then it is not everywhere. Then you are not God. This wanting to see God as separate from you is also an illusion. God is not an object of senses, but the feeling of feelings, the presence of presence, the sound of silence, the light of life, the essence of the world and the taste of bliss... God is never an object of isolation. God is the sum totality. When you dissolve, God remains. When you are there, there is no God. Either you can be there, or God can be there, not both. So when you meditate, you become one with God. You are God. That is why it is said, *Tat tvam asi*, meaning, 'Thou art that.'[22]

As a non-dualist, Sri Sri has high regard for human being. He said that when a river meets the ocean, the river no longer maintains separate identity, it becomes the ocean. Likewise the moment a devotee meets God, he or she becomes God.[23] So, human being is potentially divine.

Sri Sri Ravishankar teaches several processes or practices by which one can elevate his/her spiritual life. *Firstly*, it is by *Seva* (service) which is strongly emphasized by him. He maintains, "Our first and foremost commitment in the world is to do *seva* or service." The realization that we are here in this world to do *seva* dissolves the "I" and when the "I dissolves, worries dissolves.[24] Nevertheless, the motive of service should be right. He says, "Most of the work in the society is done out of ego... Real service is when you feel that you have not done enough."[25] Again, "*Seva* is not something you do out of convenience or for pleasure. The ultimate purpose of life is to be of service... when you make service your sole purpose in life, it eliminates fear, brings focus in your mind and purposefulness,"[26] it will reward you immediately, the

---

22 In an official website of AOL: (4 July 2011).

23 Sri Sri Ravishankar, *An Intimate Note to the Seeker Volume 6,* 18.

24 Sri Sri Ravishankar, *Celebrating Silence*, Second Edition (Bangalore: Sri Sri Publication Trust, 2008), 108.

25 Gautier, *The Guru of Joy*, 214, 217.

26 Sri Sri Ravishankar, *An Intimate Note to the Seeker Volume 4: July 30, 1998 – July 28, 1999*, Compiled by Anne Elixhauser & Bill Hayden, (Bangalore: Vyakti Vikas Kendra, 1999), 37.

reward is for sure and is always more than your doing.[27] His emphasis on *seva* makes him and his AOL International run several social service centers.[28]

Secondly, having stressed the importance of joy because of which he earned the appellation 'Guru of Joy', Sri Sri also emphasizes the importance of singing, dance and laughter for the improvement of the quality of life and growing in spiritual life. He even exaggerates its essentiality by proclaiming thus— "There is nothing in life that is more worthy than your laughter," writes Sri Sri, "God will dance in our life when the day dawns in laughter and love. The true prayer is laughing in the morning. Don't just be laughing outside but from deep inside. Laughter comes from the center of our Being, from the core of our heart… True laughter is true prayer."[29] He advises his disciples to see life as a game to play joyfully. "You are God, you know it. I am God, I know it. So let us play." This will result in oneness. God is inviting us every day to sit with Him, "I am doing everything. You come and sit with me. Whatever needs to be done, I will get it done through you. You simply stop existing."[30] Here Sri Sri suggests that our ego, our pride, the 'Me-ness' should be put to death in order to have oneness with God.

Thirdly, the seeming opposite to what is suggested above as another important practice to be cultivated is *Silence* which is another watchword of Sri Sri. It is no wonder that he emphasized so much on silence because it is silence, we may say, that made Sri Sri Ravishankar as he is now – as pointed out earlier, it is during his ten days silence in 1982 that the *Sudarshan Kriya* was born. Sri Sri believes that communication is possible, sometime more effectively, in silence. He says, "You should have belongingness to silence. Silence is the mother of all creativity. Silence is the mother of invention. Silence is the basis of love."[31] For him silence is the key to reach God in

---

27 Sri Sri Ravishankar, *An Intimate Note to the Seeker Volume 2*, 84.

28 Along with AOL programme Sri Sri Ravishankar founded several organization for the service of human beings. Organizations such as International Association for Human Values, Ved Vignan Maha Vidhya Peeth, Vyakti Vikas Kendra and The Sri Sri Ravishankar Vidya Mandir Trust – all founded by him, carry on a wide variety of service projects including – (1) Education: Free schools, (2) The Prisoner Programme, (3) Trauma & Disaster Relief (4) Peace Initiatives, (5) Sustainable Rural Development that includes the 5H (Health, Hygiene, Homes for the homeless, Human values, Harmony in diversity programmes, The Youth leadership training programme, Organic farming, Women empowerment, Rehabilitation of Drug & Alcohol Addicts. The Art of Living service projects and educational programmes are carried out in over 146 countries. The organization works in special consultative status with the Economic and Social Council (ECOSOC) of the United Nations. Cf. Sri Sri Ravishankar, *Belongingness to Silence* (Bangalore: Vyakti Vikas Kendra, India Publications, 2006), 45-50.

29 Ravishankar, *God loves Fun*, 33.

30 Ravishankar, *God loves Fun*, 61.

31 Ravishankar, *Belongingness to Silence*, 1-2.

us: "The moment you relax, and go deep into silence, you perceive the Self, right there." So, he advices his listeners to observe silence at least once in a while—"Take some time off – three-four days, and go deep into silence. This is essential", because this will make you grow in your spirituality very fast.[32]

So, in deep silence there is the absence of feeling somebody, some things, some objects, only one feels God. Here, duality ends, oneness is attained. Celebration such as singing, dancing, which are integral to Sri Sri's programme and silence look contradictory, but, he says that they are not. "Spirituality is a harmonious blend of outer silence and inner celebration; and also inner silence and outer celebration!"[33]

Fourthly, Sri Sri suggests four techniques for spiritual life such as *Sama, Dana, Bheda* and *Danda*. *Sama* refers to maintaining of equanimity in pleasant and un-pleasant moments; meditation, yoga are all pertaining to *Sama*. However, this is not easy for many people. So, there is *Dana* which means giving up that which disturbs you, that which cannot put you in the royal seat of equanimity. The third one, *Bheda* is separating the permanence and the impermanence; body is impermanence soul is permanence. One should be able to separate them. This separation can be helped by the last one, i.e. *Danda* which means support. Determination and commitment are the *Danda*. Listening to spiritual discourses, *satsang*, Guru's presence are all the support, the *Danda*.[34]

Sri Sri Ravishankar's philosophy is never deviated from Advaita Vedanta, his concept of God as the indwelling God; human being in his/her true nature as God—all reflect Sankara's Advaita Vedanta. However, he seems to be more concerned for the life here and now—a stress free, violence-free, productive and happy life. His *Sudarshan Kriya* is also primarily sailing towards this. This emphasis brings the importance of celebration, singing, dancing and laughter which all have their place in Sri Sri Ravishankar's teaching. Otherworldly motif is not fundamental and primary in his thought, though it is not altogether missing. He talks less about '*moksha*' and cessation of cycle of birth and rebirth, but more on happiness in life. His lectures and discourses are more of 'wisdom sayings' that deals with day to day life of a human, but less a scriptural discourse. He is a model of religious tolerance; he does not shy away from using Bible alongside Buddhist teachings to elaborate his philosophical proposition. He teaches us that we should own religious resources of others as others own ours. His positive attitude towards human as 'potentially Divine' encourages Sri Sri to take up tremendous social services for those who are in need, because, according to him, we are one, we belong together.

---

32 Ravishankar, *Belongingness to Silence*, 28-29, 40.

33 Sri Sri Ravishankar, *An Intimate Note to the Sincere Seeker, Volume 5*, 20.

34 Ravishankar, *God loves Fun*, 23-32.

Sri Sri Ravishankar's Interpretation of Jesus Christ: *Jesus, the Embodiment of Love*

Sri Sri Ravishankar does not produce huge literatures on Jesus Christ and this leaves us with a limited source to construct his Christology. One of the most important sources is his lecture on 'Jesus the Embodiment of Love' which is available in the form of Audio CD[35] and also part of which forms a Chapter of his book *Wisdom for the New Millennium.*[36] A part from this, another book—*Living the Mystery of Life*[37] contains a chapter on 'Jesus and Christianity', which also helps us in our investigation. Few other books also contain his references to Jesus.[38] The author of this essay met Sri Sri at his Bangalore *āśram* on the 27th October, 2012 and had personal interview with him. By using these sources we venture to advance Ravishankar's interpretation of Jesus Christ.

The Background of his Interpretation

As underlined before, Sri Sri Ravishankar has three basic commitments in relation to religion and spirituality—commitment to Advaita Vedānta school of thought, commitment to traditional Hinduism and commitment to the validity of all religions as the expression of One and the same God. It is natural that Sri Sri would have been influenced by these factors in his interpretations of Jesus Christ as no interpreter is free from subjectivity.

Sri Sri states that the true knowledge of Jesus is gained only with the heart by people who have the Spirit, the Life Force (*prāṇa*). You cannot understand what Jesus said if you are not living with the Life Force; concepts will be there at the head, but heart can be understood by the heart only. Mind cannot understand Jesus, only heart can feel the presence of Jesus. The Jews who crucified him were not bad people, they were ignorant. As they were not born out of the spirit though they have read all the scriptures and books, they could not understand Jesus. To know Jesus one has to be born twice, born of the Spirit, *Prāṇa*, the Life Force.[39] Sri Sri asserts that vision of Jesus is possible, "When you go deep in meditation, there are other realities. There is the world of light… When you go deep in meditation mind is still, there are no thoughts, there is no eye, then the knowledge become very spontaneous… In that level in meditation, you are in touch with the world of light. Jesus is

35 Ravishankar, "Jesus Embodiment of Love."

36 Ref. Ravishankar, *Wisdom for the New Millennium.*

37 Sri Sri Ravishankar, *Living the Mystery of Life* (Bangalore: Sri Sri Publication Trust, 2012).

38 Sri Sri Ravishankar, *Hinduism and Christianity* Second Edition (Bangalore: Vyakti Vikas Kendra India, 1999, and Gautier, *The Guru of Joy.*

39 Ravishankar, "Jesus Embodiment of Love."

definitely part of that light."[40] So, he acknowledges intuitive, mystical and experiential knowledge of Jesus as more authentic than the knowledge gained from the reading of scriptures and theological books.

Jesus as One of the Prophets

Ravishankar is reluctant to give any special status to Jesus Christ; his philosophy of religion allows him not to do so. As all are conceived as one, higher and lower concepts have no room in him. So, Jesus is also understood as one of the prophets. He is unique in his own way but not in comparison with others. Sri Sri puts Jesus in the same category with Lord Kṛṣṇa and Lord Rāmā and declines to comments who is higher and who is lower just as it is not possible to say which is higher between banana and apple.[41] Jesus is the son of God just as we all are. He is also God in so far as he is Love,[42] the embodiment of love. For that matter we are also God because all is God. Hinduism testifies that father, mother, guru, guest—all are God. In this sense, Jesus is also God.[43] The uniqueness of Jesus lies, according to Sri Sri, not on his body but on he being the manifestation of love. "That is the uniqueness of Jesus, not as a body but as love, as consciousness, he is in your heart, in everywhere. In that sense he all permeates."[44] Ravishankar, therefore, is not interested in interpreting Jesus as the Son of God, a member of the Trinity, an incarnate God or God himself as most Christians believe him to be. Those are not the categories in which he sees Jesus.

Jesus the Embodiment of Love

Ravishankar exalted Jesus as the embodiment of love. "Jesus and love are synonymous. If you say love, you need not say Jesus."[45] Love makes people courageous. That is why Jesus was courageous. He completely overthrows the common concepts of people such as the strong shall inherit the earth; for Jesus it is the meek that will inherit the earth, for love makes people meek. "Love is the strongest force in this universe and yet, it makes you meek, it makes you weak."[46] When Jesus says, "It was better Judas had not been born at all", he did not say those words out of anger but of love. He could feel the pain and

---

40 This is the answer he gave when the present researcher asked him, "Have you ever have vision of or communion with Jesus", indicating faintly that he knew Jesus not only from the scripture but by experiencing personally in mystical union. Personal interview with him at his *āśram*, Bangalore on 27.10.2012.

41 Personal interview with him at his *āśram*, Bangalore on 27.10.2012.

42 Personal interview with him at his *āśram*, Bangalore on 27.10.2012.

43 Personal interview with him at his *āśram*, Bangalore on 27.10.2012.

44 Personal interview with him at his *āśram*, Bangalore on 27.10.2012.

45 Ravishankar, *Wisdom for the New Millennium*, 113.

46 Ravishankar, *Wisdom for the New Millennium*, 113.

suffering Judas would go through. "His love for him was so great that saying, 'I wish he was not born' shows the height of love he had for him."[47] Jesus' love for the people is seen in his identification with his disciple as 'friend'. He says, "See, I call you friend, I treat you like my friend, not as servant." It is the best way to share love. Because of love Jesus identified himself as 'friend' and not as king or lord or one who is in authority. He is opening his arm and says, "Come, you are my friend... Give me a seat in your heart. See me in everyone you see around you. Love everyone as much as I love you, or as much as you love me. Share that with everyone around."[48]

Sri Sri emphasizes the importance of loving Jesus who is living today. He says, "When you are truly in love with Jesus, you will see Jesus in every name, in every form, in every nook and corner of the planet and beyond."[49] He cautions people not to limit Jesus to a certain time in history and place. He advices his audience to go to the values that Jesus truly represents so that they will know that Jesus "is not the past, he is here now. And he will be in future, also forever and ever and ever."[50]

The Kingdom of God is within You

The disciples fought for a place in the right and left hands of Jesus because they did not know that in the Kingdom of God there is not right or left. "Once you go within, there is not right or left! There is no front or back."[51] Jesus did all he could to make the disciples get into the soul, the spirit, the source of life, the Self. In order to do this we need to break through the limited concepts of relating ourselves with something or somebody or identities and recognize the Divinity within us. That is to realize that we are much more than just a human. "You are part of the Divine and you will inherit the kingdom, which is right here, right within you."[52] Jesus may have lived two thousand years ago, but Christ consciousness being eternal was in existence even before, because, the Divine consciousness is beyond time and space.[53] This is suggestive of the possibility and importance of realizing the living Jesus, or what we may call 'Christ consciousness'.

47 Ravishankar, *Wisdom for the New Millennium*, 115.

48 Ravishankar, *Wisdom for the New Millennium*, 118.

49 Ravishankar, *Wisdom for the New Millennium*, 122.

50 Ravishankar, *Wisdom for the New Millennium*, 123.

51 Ravishankar, *Wisdom for the New Millennium*, 114.

52 Ravishankar, *Wisdom for the New Millennium*, 115.

53 Ravishankar, *Hinduism and Christianity*, 18.

Jesus is *Not* the Only Way!

Hindu spiritual leaders who try to interpret Jesus positively have always struggled with the exclusive claim of Jesus: "the only begotten Son of God" and "I am the only way. No one come to the Father except through me." Ravishankar is no exception. He explains - When Jesus said that he is the only Son of our Father, he meant 'our Father', the Father of everybody. Jesus' intention was to say "I am the son of the only Father." He explicates this problem as follows

> This has been wrongly understood. If Jesus is the only son of the Father, who are the others then? Is the whole mankind the sons of Satan? Then you would call him Jesus' Father, not 'Our' Father. From the original Hebrew when the words were translated, a lot was lost on the way. Often Jesus has said, 'Let us pray to Our Father in heaven'. Again he says 'Our Father', and he means the Father of all the living beings in the world.[54]

It is clear from this quotation that Sri Sri is not well-versed in Christian scripture, but what he wanted to convey is clear, that Jesus is not the 'only' Son of God. However, Sri Sri gives compensation to Jesus when he says, "Of course, he is worthy calling 'the only son' because he embodies what the Father is, totally. Though everyone is still the son of the same Father, or daughter of the same Father, it is, in a way, justified to call Jesus the only son."[55]

Ravishankar, while defending the validity of 'other saviours' in accordance with his theology of religion and at the same time trying to be true to Jesus, fosters an interesting interpretation of Jesus' words "All those who came before me are robbers and thieves." He says that Jesus meant to indicate that those who came before him—possibly other saviours like Kṛṣṇa or Rāmā, etc.

> are robbing your mind of the present moment... You are dreaming of somebody in the future or glorifying someone in the past! The Divine is in the present... Your mind has been stolen by the past or the future. I am here to bring it to now, the present moment. I am the only way. If you cannot see the Divinity in me when I am right in front of you, do you think you are going to see the Divinity in the

54 Ravishankar, *Hinduism and Christianity*, 18. Cf. Sri Ravishankar, *Living the Mystery of Life*, 131.

55 Ravishankar, *Wisdom for the New Millennium*, 118.

> future or in the past? Forget about it. I am the gate. Look at me, see what I manifest and that is what you are…[56]

When Jesus says, "I am the only way," he does not mean that you cannot attain the Kingdom of God unless you believe in Jesus. Kṛṣṇa and Buddha also made the same exclusive statement. God is one eternal and omnipotent; we cannot limit the scope and mercy of God that he makes only one way. "I am the only way" means that the abstract cannot be approached directly, but only through persons like the teachers, the enlightened ones. Another reason for saying this is to draw the attention of the people. Still another meaning of this statement is that the teacher comes to be a bridge so that you can move from what is known to what is unknown.[57] It was his way of saying, "I am the only goal for you. What are you looking for here and there? Come to me… When I am here in front of you, you are thinking about Moses and Isaac…No, drop all this, surrender to me. When you surrender here, right now, that is how you reach my father."[58] So, Jesus' words should not be taken literally because there could be contradictions and problems. For instance, Jesus is described as the only begotten Son of God, at the same time he instructs us to pray, "Our heavenly Father." Is there one son or many sons? These things need to be pondered upon.[59]

Therefore, Jesus is the 'only way' for those who are listening to him. If one is not able to see Divinity through Jesus, there is less hope for him/her to see through 'other saviours' also, because "Jesus leads you to your own Being, your own Self, your own Divinity, that is deep within you."[60] So, the validity of 'other saviours' is not rule out, oneness—*advaita* is held high to show the fact of the existence of such saviours other than Jesus in this world. Sri Sri treads this path because his Hindu commitment *does not* allow having only one unique Saviour for the whole humanity, and his *advaitic* experience *does allow* him to hold all the divergent spiritual experiences as the expression of the One Ultimate Reality.

---

56 Ravishankar, *Wisdom for the New Millennium*, 119. Elsewhere Sri Sri also says - Jesus said 'they are robbers' because they have stolen your mind. You are always thinking about the past, longing for some great person in the past. So he said, "NOW! NOW! You see greatness right NOW, in front of you. See it and surrender," in Ravishankar, *Living the Mystery of Life*, 128.

57 Gautier, *The Guru of Joy*, 201-203. Cf. Ravishankar, *Living the Mystery of Life*, 128.

58 Ravishankar, *Living the Mystery of Life*, 127-128.

59 Gautier, *The Guru of Joy,* 203.

60 Ravishankar, *Wisdom for the New Millennium*, 120.

The Cross of Jesus

Jesus Christ is acknowledged by Christians as one who suffered and died on the cross for the sin of humankind. But Sri Sri does not endorse this view, because according to him, Jesus never said - "I am suffering for your sin." This statement is "just a way people used to awaken other people," a tactic to wake the sleeping people, another way of saying "Look, doomsday is coming, come on, wake up. Hell is going to open." In those days, this type of waking up call is needed because of the context. But today, we do not need to induce fear; we can use the tactic of love.[61] For Sri Sri, whether Jesus died on the cross or not is not important. "It does not matter to me whether he died on the cross or he did not die or he went to Kashmir (after crucifixion)… It does not matter. What is most important is the teaching, the message of love and universal brotherhood (*sic*)."[62] So, the significance of Jesus Christ is not what 'he did' on the cross – his death and resurrection, but his message of love. It was Jesus, who brought the idea of piety and love among the Jews who "only perceived God as one who is punishing, an angry God, a chief dictator,"[63] and the message of love that Jesus introduced to the Jewish thought is innovative and it is that which is the most significant.

Transcending Mind

Jesus said, "I have come to put man against man, father against son, daughter against mother." Quoting this verse, Ravishankar says that very few people have really understood what it means. According to him, this particular verse indicates that some people whom we consider as friends are making us to have faith in the material things thereby weakening our faith in the spiritual thing. So, they are not our friend! When Jesus said, "I have come to put fire, not peace," it shows that he knew the depth of slumber. When we talk something nice, peaceful, everybody will go to sleep and when there is something sensational, people wake up and listen. These rather harsh words of Jesus should not be taken to indicate that Jesus did not show love, but it is his method to wake you up. This is how human mind operates. Ravishankar, thus, concludes saying, Jesus made all efforts so that people may cross the mind and get into the soul, the spirit, the source of life, the Self. Jesus wanted us to recognize that we are not limited human being, small and helpless. Divinity is within you.[64]

---

61 Ravishankar, *Wisdom for the New Millennium*, 124-125.

62 Personal interview with him at his *āśram*, Bangalore on 27.10.2012.

63 Personal interview with him at his *āśram*, Bangalore on 27.10.2012.

64 Ravishankar, *Wisdom for the New Millennium*, 115.

Jesus at the Doorsteps

Jesus said, "I am not yet one with my Father", but at the same time he also said, "I and my Father are one". There is no contradiction here. In reality Jesus was already at home, if he is not, nobody will follow him. But, when he said that he is not yet one with his Father, he meant to say that he is at the doorstep, waiting for the others to come, waiting in the rain, in the snow, in the storm, in the sun—a perfect demonstration of perfect love.[65]

Jesus Lived in India

Ravishankar appears to believe in the popular notion that Jesus at the age of around fourteen came to India and lived here till he reached the age of thirty when he returned to Palestine to finish his mission. During his stay, he visited many places, preaching and teaching to the Indian people side by side learning from them. "Christianity has so many similarities to Indian traditions that is a good indication that Jesus spent a lot of time in India."[66] He maintains, "If you look at many of the teachings of Jesus you find that all are from the Upaniṣadic lore."[67] Sri Sri observes that by a direct knowledge from the consciousness, through deep meditation, which is a more reliable knowledge than any other, we can see that Jesus lived in India and went back to Palestine wearing an orange robe—the typical attire for a spiritual leader in India.[68] However, as this is a contentious issue, Sri Sri, in attempting to evade controversy, softens his stand on this issue by saying that the authenticity of Jesus lived in India is not yet proven, though "there is a lot of thing to believe that Jesus spent twelve years in India," so, he leaves this controversy to scholars and historians.[69]

Our study reveals few innovative ideas in his interpretations, such as:

- Jesus as the manifestation and embodiment of Love where Love is understood by him as another name of God. By saying that Jesus and Love are synonymous, Sri Sri, consciously or unconsciously admits Jesus as God.
- The possibility and importance of realizing the living Jesus, the Christ Consciousness is implicit in his teaching.
- Contact with Christ, an ecstatic union with him, communion with the living Jesus is possible when one is deep in meditation, deep down at the level when the mind is still without any thought. The authentic and direct knowledge of Jesus Christ is possible at this

65 Ravishankar, *Wisdom for the New Millennium*, 116.

66 Ravishankar, *Wisdom for the New Millennium*, 127.

67 Ravishankar, *Hinduism and Christianity*, 18.

68 Ravishankar, *Hinduism and Christianity*, 2-3.

69 Personal interview with him at his *āśram*, Bangalore on 27.10.2012.

stage as the knowledge gained through deep meditation is more reliable than knowledge acquired through logical understanding.

Critical Appreciation

Sri Sri Ravishankar neither uses the Bible as his main source nor is faithful and serious to its passages, though he quotes verses from the Bible loosely from time to time. Again, he is not systematic in his interpretation of Christ but simply quotes him here and there to support his teaching. He is committed to the theology of religious pluralism that all religions are essentially the same and from this perspective he interprets Jesus' life and message with a view to bring harmony between religions. As the exclusive statements of Jesus such as 'No one comes to the father except through me' and 'the only begotten Son' become a hurdle on the way of achieving the dream of religious harmony, he leaves no stone unturned to show that Jesus did not mean to say that he is the only way for all people and for all time.

Sri Sri Ravishankar does not explicitly mention in his writings that Jesus is an *Avatara*, but he appears to have believed in the incarnation of God in and through Jesus Christ. This is evident in his interpretation of Jesus Christ when he compares Jesus with Krishna and Buddha and also says that Christ consciousness being eternal was in existence even before, because, the Divine consciousness is beyond time and space.[70]

Like many Indian interpreters of Jesus Christ, Sri Sri Ravishankar looks at Jesus from the perspective of Advaita Vedānta. There is no wrong in trying to understanding Jesus in relation to Advaita Vedānta; as this system is the most popular system of thought in India, it is likely that such an attempt will be most welcomed in India. But, he is selective, selecting what he feels suiting to his own line of thought, an advaitic stream of thought, instead of taking the teachings of Jesus comprehensively. Sri Sri Ravishankar shows no acquaintance with the Bible or extra biblical materials that talk about Jesus.

The greatest Christological contribution of Sri Sri Ravishankar is his understanding of Jesus as the embodiment of love. Others Indian interpreters call Jesus as an *avatara*; for Sri Ramakrishna, Swami Vivekananda and Swami Akhilananda Jesus is the great advaitin, for Gandhiji he is the Ideal Satyagrahi, for Swami Akhilananda Jesus is a Yogi of the highest type,[71] but for Sri Sri Ravishankar, Jesus is the embodiment of love. He does not talk about Jesus as an *avatara*. But, for him Jesus and love are synonymous. If you say Jesus,

70 Sri Sri Ravishankar, *Hinduism and Christianity* (Bangalore: Vyakti Vikas Kendra, India, 1999), 18.

71 Cf. S.J. Samartha, *The Hindu Response to the Unbound Christ* (Madras: CLS, 1974) also K. P. Aleaz, *Jesus in Neo-Vedanta*, 95.

you do not need to say love.[72] Sri Sri even says, "When you are truly in love with Jesus, you will see Jesus in every name, in every form, in every nook and corner of the planet and beyond"[73] Following his own maxim "Love is God, God is love", we can deduce another maxim from this: "Jesus is also God". So, the Jesus he presents is definitely not less a God as God is God. His emphasis on love, thus, becomes the foundation for the tremendous social works his organization—Art of Living—is carrying on.

Indian interpreters of Jesus univocally pressed their assumption that there is no essential difference between a pure religion of Jesus and the Indian religions especially that of Vedanta, the seeming differences is only in the outward expression of religion. For example Swami Vivekananda takes few verses like "the kingdom of God is within you" and "I and my Father are one" as the evidence for the similarity between Jesus' teaching and Advaita Vedanta philosophy.[74] Sri Sri Ravishankar also approves the essential similarity between Jesus' message and Advaita Vedanta. He lists a numbers of practices that are similar between Hinduism and Christianity. The saddest part according to him is we focus on the skin of banana, the outer visible aspect of religion and throw away the banana, the inner spiritual reality of each religion.[75] Having the true spirit of Hinduism with its pluralistic vision, his main intention is bringing all religions together that will end so much of hatred between people of different faiths.

In his attempt to interpret Jesus Christ, Sri Sri sets his vision clear, the vision for harmonious living, owning each other in the true spirit of oneness taught by Advaita Vedanta, which is also the core message of Jesus. Considering others as belonging to us, and us belong to others. This mutual belongingness will enhance mutual spiritual growth where a new understanding of Jesus plays a pivotal role. Attempting to arrive at the harmony of religion in order to achieve mutual sharing, mutual enrichment and mutual owning is an welcome gesture, but harmony in Advaitic perspective alone may not produce the needed result. It is presumptuous to consider 'mis-interpretation' of what the Church through the ages had faithfully propagated. Mutuality and harmony can only be reached when the two parties respect each others' view point and try to agree in disagreement.

One of the most important contributions towards the understanding of Jesus may be his suggestion to have intuitive experiential knowledge of

---

72 Sri Sri Ravishankar, *Wisdom for the New Millennium* (Mumbai: Jaico Publishing House, 2005), 113.

73 Ravishankar, *Wisdom for the New Millennium*, 113.

74 *The Complete Works of Swami Vivekananda (CWV) Vol. I, Thirteenth Edition* (Calcutta: Advaita Ashrama, 1994), 46-48.

75 Sri Sri Ravishankar, *Bang on the Door* (Bangalore: Sri Sri Publication Trust, 2008), 10.

Jesus. As Jesus is a living reality, living even today, there must be possibility to commune with him and experience him in an ecstatic spirituality. So, for Sri Sri Ravishankar a direct knowledge from the consciousness, through deep meditation, which is a more reliable knowledge than any other, is the best way of knowing Jesus Christ. The emphasis on direct-intuitive knowledge of Christ appears to be a valid proposition, but the practicality is in question. This may be possibly achieved only by those who have extra-spiritual and ecstatic gift, endowed with supernatural spiritual strength. Can this be applied to the common people? Again, a total denial of the importance and role of the written scripture is dangerous and it is not even in line with the method of Sankara whose Advaita Vedanta philosophy, which is firmly rooted in scriptures, is followed by Sri Sri himself. So, we cannot go together with their suggestion to discard Scripture in our interpretation of Christ. We rather follow the synthesis of these two – a written scripture and an intuitive-ecstatic communion with Christ in our attempt to interpret Jesus and his message.

Sri Sri Ravishankar, though not systematic in his interpretation of Jesus, definitely shows some attachment and appreciation to Jesus Christ. His all time emphasis is 'love' where he even goes to the extent of pronouncing that Love is God[76] and at the same time declares that Jesus and love and synonymous. So, his attachment to Jesus is fairly evident. Again, Sri Sri Ravishankar, though less attached to Jesus, still willing to quote with approval Jesus as saying: "I am the only way. If you cannot see the Divinity in me when I am right in front of you, do you think you are going to see the Divinity in the future or in the past?"[77] It only shows how Sri Sri has a deep and unshakable faith in Jesus as the way for those who cling to him and follow him.

Conclusion

Ravishankar did not give serious effort to look at the Bible or the context and interpret it systematically but he rather picked verses of his choice randomly and gave his own meanings. He shunned away from some of the crucial Christological issues such as incarnation, death and resurrection as significant for salvation. There is always a danger of making hermeneutical mistake in picking verses from the Bible selectively out of the context without taking the whole message into consideration. That is where Sri Sri is found to be wanting. It is apparent that his knowledge of Christian history and theology is also very limited. He reads Bible and speaks of Jesus mainly for the purpose of inter-faith meetings and relations. His interpretation of Jesus is not enough to bring to light a comprehensive understanding of Jesus and his mission.

76 Sri Sri Ravishankar, *Bang on the Door: A collection of Talks*, Second Revised Edition, (Bangalore: Sri Sri Publication Trust, 2008), 93.

77 Ravishankar, *Wisdom for the New Millennium*, 119.

However, in spite of several flaws in his treatment of Jesus and his message, Sri Sri's understanding of Jesus as the embodiment of love, the one whose essential identity is love, is definitely innovative and encouraging. His assertion that a living Jesus can be known with more accuracy by means of personal experience in a mystical communion at the deeper level of meditation than from the written scripture appears to be in line with the other select gurus' argument. This is significant in the context of Christian churches' emphasis on the written Word of God as the sole or primary authority for the knowledge of Jesus and his message.

7

Messianic Love: Personal Reflection from Inter-Faith Perspective

V. Kanagu Nelson

The Socio-Religious-Cultural Setting in India

India where we live, is the land of many religions and many faiths. They are pre-historical Primal religion, Tribal religion, Dalit and Dravidian religions, Hinduism, Jainism, Buddhism, Zoroastrianism, Judaism, Christianity, Islam, Sikhism, Bahaism and so on which is the combination of forest, mountain/hill born religions, river born religions and desert born religions. These religions have been shaping, equipping, molding and transforming the various inter-faith communities/societies with a composite culture and complex cultures. The people of different religions and cultures have their own religious and cultural values and secular visions. Thus, we may say that there is no religion and culture without human history.

Apart from these religious faiths, there are many other faiths such as Marxism, Leninism, Gandhism, Ambedkarism, Periyarism, etc., which have been raising their liberative voices for the emancipation of marginalized people in various sectors of the inter-faith societies. The people of those faiths are working differently at various levels against the pernicious ideologies of Hindutva and the divisive forces like Sanskritization, Saffronization, Brahmanization and privatization, ignoring the presence of neighboring religious people who are showing love and concern in day today life. At the same time, they are also vigilant to condemn the polemic attitude of Christians and Muslims towards Hindus. Thus, conservative and narrow minded people of every religion disturb Indian sovereignty of secularism, socialism, democracy and republic. Rather, one may search God genuinely, practicing the love of God/Messiah in their life.

In this connection, Messianic love commands being religious as being inter-religious in a religiously plural India. All scriptures of every religion comprise of different religious, cultural and national aspects. As far as our country is concerned, these natural characteristics are of intra-religious and inter-religious; intra-cultural and inter-cultural; intra-faith and inter-faith; intra-scriptural and inter-scriptural; intra-Truth and inter-Truth, etc. These realities of a multi-faith context of India live side-by-side since many centuries. The scripture or scriptures portray monotheism and polytheism. According to India's plurality, there are two concepts about God: one God and many deities. Whatever it may be, in God's creation we see that everything is pluralistic. God created male and female in His image and likeness. In God's creation, sustenance and liberation is the grace of God in which we see God's love for all kinds of people. However, personal experience is needed to understand God's/Messianic love.

Personal Journey of Faith

I was born and brought up in village/popular Hindu religious traditions. According to popular Hinduism, there are polytheistic, pantheistic, and henotheistic concepts about God and gods and goddesses, including personal and family deities and nature worship. I was a staunch Hindu, observing all rituals and ceremonies including fasting. Since popular Hinduism is flexible, I was also free in worshipping gods and goddesses. My favorite deities were Ayyanar, Mariamman, Karumalaiyan and Murugan. Till twenty five years, I was living as a village Hindu and experienced those deities' love and blessings. My family members had been maintaining loving friendship and relationship with neighbors and extending hospitality. As a young boy, I liked this attitude of openness and friendship extended to my native people irrespective of religion and caste for which I think even now my Hindu family has been rooted in God's love.

As I grew up in my Hindu family, I did not understand religious matters that were observed by family members and my fellow Hindus. I was not aware of the differences between Hinduism and Christianity. I even did not know why we were Hindus and they were Catholic Christians in my village. Yet, I remember my Hindu family as a devout family and their God fearing and prayerful life is profoundly and genuinely meaningful. Due to this, I was impressed, and I could boldly say that my Hindu family has been a religiously and ethically conscious family. Not only that, during my middle school studies, tracts were distributed to the inter-faith students like me to know about Christianity and Jesus Christ. Before and after my teenage, I did not know Christianity even at a minimum level.

After leaving from middle school, I studied in a Hindu school for higher secondary studies. When I was growing in my village, I remembered always my teachers Regina Mary and Kanagavalli for their genuine love and concern towards my personal development and character building. Thus, my Christian teachers were more compassionate with love and concern during my Primary and Middle school studies. Personally, I experienced and enjoyed God's love from my teachers' life and deeds. From this perception, I understand that God intervened into human history and God's love is inclusive and open for all, irrespective of religion, caste, colour, race, gender and language. This is my personal experience and understanding even before my conversion to Christianity.

After I became a CSI Christian and studied major and minor Religions at some depth—as a theologian and dialogian—I deeply respected Popular Hinduism as a religion and admire several aspects of it. At the same time, I have serious engagement in inter-faith dialogue movement with Christian faith and hope; I experience the Messianic love in Jesus Christ without any dilution.

At this juncture, we need to be careful to exhort the following passages: like preaching the gospel and planting the church extensively even today is dictum of Mission mandatory for many denominational churches and sectarians (Matt. 28:19); that "there is salvation in no one else, for there is no other name under heaven given among mortals by which we must be saved" (Act 4:12). This kind of determination may come from the idea of covenant, election or chosen, people of God, revelation, no other name and so on. Then how do we understand that Messianic love is inclusive and accommodative in a religiously plural society? Can we take salvation for granted?

In relation to the matter of mission mandate, for Christians, preaching the gospel values is our bounden duty to fulfill the requirement of mission of Jesus which is the traditional understanding of the church. At this point, what is the vision and mission of Jesus? If we are not able to internalize and exercise the gospel values in our life and ministry then what is the use of preaching? This is the question of Hindu and Muslim and secular thinkers. It is the prerogative of theologians and ministers of the churches to know and understand the requirement of the present and the need of the suppressed and poor people.

Generally, Messianic love may be perceived from personal and people's experiential perspective. From time to time, individual to individual, the nature and character of God's love may be understood differently. But, the love of Messiah or God is for the universe, without any limitations and boundaries. The God of creation and redemption who manifested in Jesus Christ is in different ways. For which we may mention the Biblical reference "now there are varieties of gifts, but the same Spirit; and there are varieties of services, but the same Lord: and there are varieties of activities, but it is the same God who activates all of them in everyone. To each is given the manifestation of the Spirit for the common good" (1 Cor. 12:4-7). Therefore, we need proper understanding of God and His activities.

How do we exercise and express Jesus' demand: 'love your neighbors as you love yourself? Jesus as Messiah revealed God's love through the Cross for all. Mark 10:45 reads that the Son of Man came not to be served but to serve, and to give his life as a ransom for many. 1 John 3:16 also reads that we know what love is by Jesus' act of laying his life for everyone; it is a call to do likewise. From these we understand that the Messianic love is attached with grace, compassion and commitment to peace, justice, equality and liberty. Therefore a mere confession of faith and hope in Jesus Christ ignores and fails to experience messianic love.

This reflection invites and raises several questions about our own faith and hope in Jesus. In the contexts of discussions on inter-faith dialogue forums, wider ecumenical fellowships and peace movements, what does mission mean in a religiously plural and diverse and multiple society? How do we understand the sacrifice and significance of Christ Jesus? Should this be understood exclusively for Christians or for all people? As a matter of fact, what do we believe in God who has done in Christ within this wider ecumenical relationship, crossing over all the boundaries? How do we mobilize religious resources to know and discern the Messianic love through theological education?

Towards Theological Education on Religious Pluralism

We live in a world full of greed, envy, religious fundamentalism, communalism and other divisive and evil forces which has resulted in heartless and merciless generation from which emanate violence, wars and killings. Most of our educated congregations appear to be both sensitive and insensitive towards deprived and marginalized sections of our Indian plural society. At a global level, some educated people have also created destructive armaments; and divided multi-faith society. The challenges we are facing is whether theological education can be a platform that upholds peace, integrity and accountability.

All religions express God's intervention in human history from their religious point of view. From this interaction of God with the people, we learn that the Messianic love is not a word or a concept but experiences and events at personal, family, regional, national and inter-national level. All religions speak of God's love in general terms. Likewise, Christianity speaks of unconditional and sacrificial love of Jesus Christ. In this context, the life sustaining theological education needs to be imparted oriented in peace, justice and humanization. At present, most of the Seminaries and Colleges have their own theological education according to their ethos, thrust, vision and missions. The concern however is the integration, coordination with the ground realities and expectations of congregations. It is the need of the hour to formulate concrete workable and practical programmes with a good vision for the development of congregations and betterment of inter-faith society.

8

The Study of Religion: Islamic Perspective

S. S. Waheedulla Hussaini Quadri Multani

It is an honour and privilege for me to contribute an article to the Festschrift in honour of Prof. T. Swami Raju on the occasion of his 60th birthday. He is a celebrated religious scholar, most esteemed scholastic theologian and renowned educator endowed with special leadership abilities and charismatic personality. His contributions on spirituality, peace, and interfaith dialogue are immense. In his academic scholarship over these decades, he has authored number of books and research articles on varied subjects. His life and contributions in the academic circle have been inspirational for all.

This paper attempts to understand the study of religion from Islamic perspective. All religions are foundations for morality and belief, which should be internalized within our family and with the outside world. Religion, with its objective beliefs, is a significant part of our lives, representing a force in the public realms of society. Humankind has been familiar with religion for such a long time that it covers the entire recorded history of human society.[1] Different activities of people and their spheres of social life are still influenced by religious rites and ceremonies. It is apt to say that human nobility is the result of spiritual education of religion as it promotes acts of selflessness, humanity, charity, and responsibility on one hand, and provides natural boundaries for communities to develop, on the other. Therefore, many people turn to religion

---

1 For further detail see The Qur'ān 30:30.

for encouragement in a time of trouble and they concluded that religion assists them to deal with the most stressful moments of their lives; that it gives them hope to move on. Due to these reasons, we cannot ignore the role of religion if any serious attempt to consider the future of our society has to be made, because, religion builds societies and binds them together.

The laws God has communicated to human beings over the ages have been revealed on the level of intuitive knowledge—that is, in language that is accessible to people of all levels of intelligence.[2] For this reason, all people of mature mind are equally accountable for their response to the basic requirements of their religion.[3] Each religion is perfect in its own way and teaches the same basic values and principles. Religion unites us, but in bits and pieces. Therefore, Judaism, Christianity, Islam and other major religions of the world legislate themselves in distinction to other religious practices and beliefs—a trend that continues throughout history. Though Islam has different methodologies and forms of religious practices, it shares three fundamental concepts, i.e., Unity of God, Prophethood and Life hereafter, with Judaisim and Christianity.[4] The religion sanctioned in the Qur'ān is the same as the religion entitled in the Old and New testaments.[5] Islam is not a new religion, in the sense that most of its teachings are those that were also given to earlier peoples like the Jews and the Christians. Islam, however, does bring together in one place the best of all earlier teachings and presents them in a perspective completely unknown before.[6] According to Muslim traditions, all prophets are brother or a spiritual heir of ancient prophets, therefore, any individual cannot enter Islam until s/he believes in the truth of the Holy Books given to all nations of the world and in all the prophets commissioned to these nations.[7] Numerous Qur'ānic verses also express the idea that humanity had been united in faith during the primeval stages of its existence.[8]

2 For further detail see The Qur'ān, 14:4.

3 For further detail see Balil Abd Al-Karim, *Qur'anic Terminology: A Linguistic and Semantic Analysis*, 151.

4 For further detail see The Qur'ān, 4:125; 42:13.

5 In some religions all following common factors are found; in others some of them. Like belief in supernatural creatures like God, angels, jinn, and spiritual creatures; separation of the sacred and mundane worship, rituals and ceremonies; sacred book and moral code of laws; connection to the superhuman by means like revelation, prophets, prayer, supplication and inspiration.

6 For further detail see The Qur'ān, 2:41, 91, 97, 101; 3:3, 50, 81; 4:47; 5:46, 48; 6: 92; 35:31; 46:30; 61:6.

7 For further detail see The Qur'ān, 40:79.

8 For further detail see The Qur'ān, 2:213; 10:19. See also Yohanan Friedmann, *Tolerance and Coercion in Islam: Interfaith Relations in the Muslim Tradition*, 13-53.

The definition of religion has occupied the minds of scholars for a long time, but scholars have failed to agree on a definition of religion as different intellectuals highlight either of the aspects but none can give us a comprehensive understanding of it. The description of religion is even, to some extent, negotiated in the streets of present-day multicultural communities all over the world. Some scholars are of the view that religion means divine things that are set apart from society as exceptional, inspiring awe, and deserving of respect. According to others, religion means a social system that comprises a consolidated way of beliefs and practices that identifies the holy. Within the structure of a secular academic approach, 'religion' has been to a considerable extent defined in terms of beliefs, internal conditions, and systems of symbols. However, more recently, actions and behavior have been added to the definition. Anthropologist Talal Asad has argued that all attempts at a universal definition of religion are doomed to fail, because, religion as a concept is itself the product of a specifically Western modern discourse.[9] The most central question of Western modernity has been concerning the notion of 'religion,' be they questions of metaphysics, epistemologies, morals, aesthetics, or anthropology. The responsiveness to this issue is heightened by the recent flood of publications on the genesis of the notion of religion. Likewise, an attempt has been made in this paper to discuss the definition of religion from Islamic perspective.

Islam is a religion, but not in the western meaning of religion. One of the connotations of the term 'religion' is one that relates between the believer and God. Thus, everyone is totally free concerning his/her metaphysical beliefs, rituals for worship, and social customs; the state won't interfere in any of these. At the same time, religion must not intrude or intervene in the running of the state either. Therefore, the modern Western norm of the separation of religion from power came into existence.[10] This is the first time in the history of humankind that human being has taken out God from their collective lives. Due to which, in all existing systems of the world, divine guidance has been dismissed as irrelevant to collective lives. It creates many problems like injustice, inequity, haves and have nots, immorality, and all sorts of corruption,

---

9 Talal Asad, *Genealogies of Religion: Discipline and Reasons of Power in Christianity and Islam*, 40-43.

10 The phrase "separation of church and state" can be traced back to a letter written by Thomas Jefferson in 1802 to Baptists from Danbury, Connecticut, referencing the First Amendment to the United States Constitution. The letter says: "Believing with you that religion is a matter which lies solely between Man & his God, that he owes account to none other for his faith or his worship, that the legitimate powers of government reach actions only, & not opinions, I contemplate with sovereign reverence that act of the whole American people which declared that their legislature should 'make no law respecting an establishment of religion, or prohibiting the free exercise thereof', thus building a wall of separation between Church & State. http://www.loc.gov/loc/lcib/9806/danpre.html, Retrieved 15th August, 2019.

unwed mothers, unisex marriages, single parents, and high rate of divorces in the society. These issues would not have happened along religious guidance in which each community of faith has full right to abide, be it personal laws and laws of land. It is to be noted that the law of the land may be applied to any religion, however, without contradicting the divine laws.

We all have bitter experience of the function of various forms of government that prevailed in different parts of the world. For instance, democracy, in which number plays a vital role legitimizes the worth of three rotten tomatoes to one diamond—it is a game of majority! In republic form of government, personal priority take precedence over collective well-being. This discourages democratic participation but encourages deception. In absolute monarchical form of government, citizens receive fewer privileges, which may lead to societal rebellion. This form of government is usually built at the expense of the working class. Consequently, it leads to abuse of power, which in turn leads to war.

Therefore, the implementation of human-made laws in the society is termed as the way of devil in the Qur'ān,[11] as it is diametrically against the fundamental teachings of Islam. According to Islamic teaching, the idea of organized religion must not only be to establish or define the interaction between human and god. It must also be to expedite human interaction and cooperation, so that one soul may inspire and ennoble others. Islam is a religion of complete and comprehensive set of religious laws which is meant to dominate all domains of life and all human-made systems and ideologies. It covers all the practices of human being from the moment of birth till death. This distinguishing element of Islam (from other religions) was confessed by Michael Hart when he remarked,

> My choice of Mohammad to lead the list of the world's most influential persons may surprise some readers and may be questioned by others, but he was the only man in history who was supremely successful on both the religious and secular level.[12]

The Qur'ānic term *dīn*, a word usually translated as religion,[13] is undoubtedly one of the most significant terms and appears in the Qur'ān ninety-eight times with different connotations. It provides sanctions for the principles

11 For further detail see The Qur'ān, 4:60.

12 Michael Hart, *the 100: a ranking of the most influential persons in the history*, p. 33.

13 It is a Qur'ānic word commonly translated by modern interpreters as religion. The root of the Arabic word *din* is *dyn* which has Semitic cognates, including Hebrew, Aramaic, Amharic, and Ugaritic. This root has four primary meanings: mutual obligation, submission or acknowledgment, judicial authority, and natural inclination or tendency. When one considers the four primary meanings of the root *dyn*, one realizes that in Islam, religion (*din*) is natural to the human condition. Religion conveys the idea of obligation

of morality like justice, honesty, rectitude, righteousness, brotherhood, equality, virtuousness, tolerance, sacrifice, help to the needy and other kindred virtues. The Qur'ānic term *dīn* refers to eternal part of divine guidance which has been given equally to all the prophets which consists of beliefs, dogmas, traditions, practices, and rituals. The term *dīn* has two different meanings in regard to the Creator and created. When this word is associated with the creator, it gives the meaning of being in control, making obedient, taking to account, and giving punishment-reward. If this word is related to the created, it means bowing down, understanding one's helplessness, surrendering, and worshipping. In other words, the literal meaning of religion in Islam is obedience—following the path and the commands of God. In technical term, it is the collection of divine laws that enables people with intelligence to attain goodness and happiness both in this world and the next.

While describing the Arabic term *dīn*, Islamic scholars have taken into consideration the way concept of religion was taken up in the Qur'ān and Islamic beliefs. The word *dīn* is more holistic and encompasses the entire depth, breadth, and richness of the three general aspects of Islam—both exoteric as well as esoteric—namely, the guardian of faith, the process of spiritual transformation, and the realization of truth. In other words, *dīn* is the quest for the Master's assent in both outwardly inwards[14] and inwardly outwards,[15] until the inwards and outwards have lost distinction.[16] The word *dīn* gives expression to a methodology for engaging the purpose of life—the Divine purpose, not human purposes—which elevates human nature to its highest potential; advocates moderation and balance; presents a lasting upright value system based on mutual consultation; prescribes good manners and fair dealings; and ultimately permits one to realize primordial spiritual potential.[17]

Apart from the English word religion, the comprehensive term *dīn* carries other various dictionary meanings. Firstly, it means a state of abasement and submissiveness.[18] Secondly, it is used to denote a particular

---

or indebtedness, the acknowledgment of indebtedness, and the requirement to repay one's debts. For further detail see The Qur'ān, 7:172; 9:111; 10:62; 2:245; 92:5-10.

14 It means those endeavors that bring us closer to God by our interaction with fellow creatures.

15 It means those percepts of faith that we cultivate and which then become the underlying motive of our actions.

16 For further detail see, Saeed Malik, *A Perspective on the Signs of Al-Qur'ān: Through the Prism of the Heart*, 23-48.

17 For further detail see, Anab Whitehouse, *Spiritual Abuse, A Sufi's Perspective*, 109-122. See also Darla K. Deardorff, ed., *The SAGE Handbook of Intercultural Competence*, 179-195.

18 For further detail see The Qur'ān, 2:193; 39:3; 7:29; 39:2; 40:14, 65.

law, statute or ordinance or dominion or government.[19] Thirdly, it is also used to refer reward and punishment.[20] Fourthly, the word *dīn* neither consists merely a collection of some rituals, nor a theoretical ideology, rather it refers to complete code of life or system of governance.[21] The composite factors of religion includes sovereignty and supreme authority; obedience and submission to such authority; the system of thought and action established through the exercise of that authority and retribution meted out by the authority.[22] It is seen that this word is used in the Qur'ān mainly with these meanings: rule, ruled, obedience, law, worship, uniting with Allāh, Islam, laws, regulations, limits put by Allāh, tradition, punishment, accounting, and group of people with the same belief etc.

Ḥazrat Abul 'Ārif Shāh Syed Shafīullāh Ḥusaynī al-Qadrī ul-Multānī[23] (*Sajjādahnashīn*) of the shrine of *Pīr Quṭb al-Mashā'ikh*,[24] is of the view that in the usage of *dīn*, it is incorrect to call Islam as mere religion in its restricted and narrow sense, because, religion deals with private affairs of life, set of dogmas, some rituals, and other social customs, whereas, the Qur'ānic term *dīn* applied to religion,[25] in the widest sense of this term is both practical and doctrinal. It includes all religio-socio-politico-economic aspects of human life and detailed regulations of Islam. It regulates both the individual as well as collective life on one hand, and touches upon the spiritual dimensions of human existence on the other.[26]

---

19 For further detail see The Qur'ān, 12:77; 24:2.

20 For further detail see The Qur'ān, 1:4; 37:20, 53.

21 For further detail see The Qur'ān, 109:6; 3:19.

22 For further detail see Syed Abul Ala Maududi, Eng. tr. by Abu Asad, *Four Basic Qur'ānic Terms*, 76-77.

23 He is the son of Ḥazrat Abul Qāsim Shāh Syed 'Abdul Wahāb Husaynī al-Qadrī ul-Multānī (May Allāh sanctify his secret) (1326-1415/1908-1995) bin Ḥazrat Abul 'Irfān Shāh Syed Aḥmad 'Ārif Husaynī al-Qadrī ul-Multānī (May Allāh shower His mercy on him) (1300-1330/1882-1912).

24 This *dargāh* named after Ḥazrat Shāh Syed Pīr Husaynī al-Qādrī ul-Multānī al-Muhaqqiq (May Allāh perfume his resting place) (1293-1305/1823-1887), who is one of the greatest Sufi Saint of the Deccan, Founder of Multānī Order (a sub-branch of Quadri Order) in Hyderabad and Spiritual Mentor of Ḥazrat Syed Shāh Muḥammad Husaynī al-Qadrī ul-Multānī (May Allāh sanctify his soul) (1279-1342/1862-1923), founder Islāmia College Warangal. The first president of this prestigious educational institute was Nawāb Jivan Yār Jung Bahādur, B.A. (Cantab), Barrister at Law of the Lincoln's Inn, London, Judge of the High Court, Hyderabad, Deccan, India. Nawāb Jivan Yār Jung Bahadur belongs to a famous Mughal family of Chogathā'ī clan which was related by marriage and blood with the historical imperial family.

25 For further detail see The Qur'ān, 9:29; 2:257; 3:20.

26 For further detail see The Qur'ān, 5:30.

Therefore, there is no dualism of religious and secular affairs in Islam, rather, it implies the establishment of the sovereignty of Allāh in the religious and secular domain. The Divine guidance needs prevalence in complete way of life.[27] It was vehemently argued that God is the only legitimate legislator, and, by extension, of all matters pertaining to human existence. The Qur'ān clearly says that the upright way of life or system of governance is the one in which the Ultimate Authority belongs to Allāh alone.[28] Hence, *dīn* is an all-round movement in the light of faith in Allāh; a system of life in which human beings consciously surrender themselves to the sovereignty of a higher authority; life of total obedience under the system of that higher authority; a sense of responsibility for the formation of thought and belief; and for the promotion of higher principles of human morality for the establishment of good relations among members of the society and the elimination of every sort of undue discrimination in order to gain rewards from it and to save themselves from its punishment.[29]

The basis of all Islamic teaching is non-coercion.[30] Islam calls for genuine piety not hypocrisy—something the Qur'ān considers to be worse than disbelief. Compulsion in religion does not lead to a life of sincerity and genuine religiosity. Therefore, the concept of religion in Islam has been laid on the solid bed-rock of freedom of will and on the fact that everybody is accountable for his own deeds. The Qur'ān says,

Each one is a hostage to one's deeds[31]

In the light of the above quoted Qur'ānic verse, everyone is absolutely free to choose their way of life. This fundamental rule of the Qur'ān guarantees full freedom on anyone to practice religion of their choice in their personal lives. It also provides security and protection for places of worship.[32]

Islam preaches commitment to peace and love. An escalation of violence in recent years and its attribution to Islam in the name of *jihād*[33] has drawn attention of scholars all over the world. It is a historical fact that there is no role of Muslim community in the First World War (1914-1918), Second World

27 For further detail see The Qur'ān, 48:28.

28 For further detail see The Qur'ān, 3:83; 5:44, 45, 47; 12:40; 16:53; 39:2-3, 11, 14, 17; 64:65; 98:5. See also.

29 For further detail see The Qur'ān, 49:13. See also Zamir Akhtar Khan, "Islam: A Deen Not Mere Religion", *The Dialogue*, iv, no. 1, 97-108.

30 For further detail see The Qur'ān, 2:256; 10:99; 11:118.

31 The Qur'ān, 74:38. See also 2:256.

32 For further detail see The Qur'ān, 6:159; 42:13.

33 It is noteworthy to mention here neither *jihād* included in *arkān al-Islam* (Pillars of Islam) nor a part of *arkān al-īmān* (Articles of Faith).

War (1939-1945), The Holocaust (1941-1945) nuclear attack on Japanese city Nagasaki (1945), Vietnam War (1968), Cambodian Civil War (1967-1975), Bosnian War (1992-1995), and in other state sponsored persecutions in which millions of people were mercilessly killed, imprisoned, annihilated and handicapped. It is also a fact that nuclear weapon and explosive devices are not manufactured by any Muslim countries. But some biased scholars and critics try to blame Islam for promoting terrorism and malign Islam as a tyrant religion by quoting the Qur'ānic verses out of context. Contrary to it, a large number of prophetic traditions deal with kindness, even compassion to animals. How would Islam allow killing a human being who is the precious, most perfect and greatest creature of Allāh?[34] Because Allāh has certainly blessed human beings with some of the abilities that only human possess, for instance, they have been given a choice to choose from right or wrong.

No one has the right to label any religion as terrorist based, because we all agree in principle that no religion advocates violence or terrorism. Therefore, the best way to understand any religion in general, and Islam in particular, is a thorough study of Holy scriptures and sources rather than the practice of a few whose heinous crimes violate the tolerant teachings of religions and a pure betrayal of it. Islam has awakened in people capacities to love, to forgive, to create, to dare greatly, and to sacrifice for the common good. The model of Islamic reality as preached in Qur'ān and Ḥadīth is completely different from those perceived by some. As a matter of fact, the basis of Islamic teachings is peace which is evident from the fact that the Qur'ān is replete with exhortations for peace and prefer to peace and forgiveness over war and hatred respectively.[35] It is also evident from the word of Islam—itself derived from the root word س ل م —which connotes to making peace, being in a mutually peaceful environment, greetings, rescue, safety, being secure, finding peace, reaching salvation and well-being or being far from danger, attaining goodness, comfort and favor, keeping away from troubles and disasters, submitting the self and obeying, respect, and being far from wrong. Islam enjoins peace even in war when the enemy is inclined to peace.[36]

The Islamic concept of peace encompasses whole range of human sphere be it political, social, family or personal life. Muslim scholars remarked that any act which leads to violence and destroy peace does not come under the purview of Islamic teaching. Amitabh Pal rightly pointed out that the Arabs never had a military class, unlike the Prussians in Germany, the Samurais in Japan, or the Rajputs in India. Instead, the elite were of a merchant nature. And

---

34 For further detail see The Qur'ān, 2:30; 15:29; 17:70; 23:14; 31:20; 33:72; 49:13; 95:4; 98:7.

35 For further detail see The Qur'ān, 2:224; 5:32; 10:25; 7:50, 56; 42:13.

36 For further detail see The Qur'ān, 8:61.

even the behavior of the Arabs after their conquest was not that of a militaristic people. Instead, Baghdad became known as a center of learning and the finer arts.[37]

In Islam, submission to God does not imply the abandonment of reason, or the determination of reclusion. Contrary to popular belief, reason does not stand in the way of God. The essence of religion will always be sacred, though the interpretation by fallible human beings may not be not sacred, and therefore, can be criticized, modified, refined, and redefined. So there's no single, inflexible, or absolute interpretation of Islam for all time because the diversity of interpretations is the very source of the richness and beauty of the belief, as the purity of a Divine verse is not served by its narrow interpretation. This is the reason why there are numbers of school of Islamic law in Islam. But at the same time it is our basic responsibility, not to indulge in self-serving interpretation of textual material, or taking teachings out of their appropriate context, distorting and skewing meanings thereby. For instance, the primary notion of *jihād* focuses on an individual's conflict with one's own lower nature which is the best and most superior form of *jihād* according to the prophetic tradition, and not on armed conflict with an external opponent who were threatening to exterminate Islam. The latter is called as lesser *jihād* by the noble prophet.[38] Yet, the propaganda continues that *jihād* is only about using arms in order to convert others to the fold of Islam, which is totally baseless. Because, Muslims are spiritually prohibited from oppressing the adherents of other faith groups.

It is necessary, therefore, that while evaluating a religion, the idea and life style recommended to the people addressed should be taken into consideration; it should be suitable to human nature in regard to both sustainability and morality. A religion that claims universality should be able to address every human being, take into consideration the needs of people at every level. It is the need of the hour for Muslim scholars in spite of engaging in response to those questions raised by biased scholars, to have a strong focus on re-engaging with the classic texts with rationality and employing *maqāṣid al-sharī'ah* (objectives of *sharī'ah*)[39] to advance new, modern interpretations which are necessary for strengthens civilian rights, scientific and technological advancement. The process of *ijtihād*[40] allowed Muslims and Muslim societies

37 Amitabh Pal, *"Islam" Means Peace: Understanding the Muslim Principle of Nonviolence Today*, 6.

38 For further detail see, *Spiritual Abuse, A Sufi's Perspective*, 109-122.

39 Protection of Religion, Life, Intellect, Progeny, and Wealth.

40 The Arabic word, اجتهاد *Ijtihād* (Lit. Exertion) is extracted from a three-letter Arabic root, جهد *juhd*. Linguistically it means conscientiousness, hard striving, strenuousness, exert one's power of efforts and ability. *Ijtihād* (independent thinking) as a technical term in Islamic law, means technical estimate, discretion of the expert in order to reach some

to continually adapt in the face of changing societal conditions and new advances in knowledge. It constitutes a bridge between eternally valid divine injunctions and time specific requirement of every age. It is the key to provide an Islamic interpretation of modern developments and circumstances. The radical transformative effects of realizing Islam in society and the state provided the Muslim community with the opportunity to enact renewal of itself at a time of decline. It is the right way to leave no room for critics to equate Islam with violence or terrorism. Islamic civilization was equipped with a dynamic legal tradition that had a set of intellectual mechanisms which allowed it to shape and construct an Islamic way of life. The great poet of his time, Sir 'Allāmah Iqbāl called for a re-examination of the intellectual foundations of Islamic philosophy which influences many contemporary Muslim reformers.

difficult matter" or "the exercise of Judgment in the light of Islamic law to meet new circumstances.

9

A Critical Reading of 'Modernity and Religion' in the Sociology of Peter Berger

Satvasheela Pandhare

Introduction

The study of religion has contributed to the wider understanding of different religions and the contributions of different scholars have facilitated the students of religion with multi-dimensional viewpoint to the study. One such eminent sociologist, Peter Berger, has enriched the study of religion by his scholarly contributions.[1] This paper is focused on one of his famous concerns—Modernity and Religion. He believed that modernity is an avoidable phenomenon.[2]

Life and Contributions of Peter Berger

Peter Ludwig Berger was born in Vienna (Austria) in the year 1929. He received his doctorate in 1952 from the New School for Social Research in New York

---

1 Some of his contributions are: *Invitation to Sociology* (1963); *The Social Construction of Reality* (1966) with T. Lukman; *The Sacred Canopy* (1967); *The Homeless Mind* (1973) with B. Berger and P. Kellner; *Facing up to Modernity* (1977); *The War over the Family* (1983); *The Capitalist Revolution* (1986) and *Redeeming Laughter* (1997).

2 James Nuechterlein, "Remembering Peter Berger," in First Things, 276 (Oct 2017), 12. Available at http://web.a.ebscohost.com/ehost/resultsadvanced?vid=2&sid=04f33351-d742-4abc-9306-86865e5342f2%40sessionmgr4007&bquery=Remembering+Peter+Berger&bdata=JmRiPWxzZGFyJnR5cGU9MSZzZWFyY2hNb2RlPVN0YW5kYXJkJnNpdGU9ZWhvc3QtbGl2ZQ%3d%3d. (31/8/2019).

City. After teaching at several universities, including the New School and Rutgers University, in 1981 Berger took the post of Professor of Sociology and Theology at Boston University. It is here that he initiated the Institute of the Study of Economic Culture.[3] His principal interests were social theory and the sociology of religion. However, he has also written on Third World issues like the sociology of the family and political sociology.[4] Peter Berger died on 27 June, 2017 in Massachusetts (United States).

Peter Berger's Definition of Religion

Berger defines religion concisely as the human enterprise which establishes a sacred cosmos. Humankind creates a universe with sacred meaning through a process of sacralisation. However, the way in which religion is expressed, is culturally determined. The result is a religious pluralistic environment in which society consists of various religions stemming from different cultural backgrounds.[5]

Berger proposed definitions and descriptions of religion; and the purpose of his efforts is to place some boundaries around the area of scientific study of religion. He is much concerned with such classifications as the secular (the ordinary reality of everyday life) and the religious, i.e., 'otherness' of religious experience (the transcendental). Berger is concerned with the nature of the scientific study of religion that demands exhibition of a methodological skepticism which would surely lead to secularization. However, it must be noted that this dichotomy of Berger is not universal in character. Supportive examples could be taken from some of the religions. For instance, Judaism considers every act right from rising in the morning till sleeping at night as an act of worship. This is also true in some aspects of Islam and Hinduism. Nevertheless Berger feels uneasy about the dichotomies as "secular" and "religious." He opines that spiritual delights are experienced through socially acceptable and useful activity such as moral conduct.[6]

---

3 Richard K. Fenn (ed.), "Peter L. Berger," in *Key Thinkers in The Sociology of Religion* by Richard K. Fenn, (London, New York: Continuum International Publishing Group, 2009), 139.

4 Nicholas Abercrombie, Stephen Hill and Bryan S. Turner, "Peter L. Berger," in *The Penguin Dictionary of Sociology* (London: Penguin Books, 2010), 30.

5 Beyers, J., 2011, "Religion, civil society and conflict: What is it that religion does for and to society?," *HTS Teologiese Studies/Theological Studies* 67(3), Art. #949, 8 pages. doi: 10.4102/hts.v67i3.949. Available at *http://www.ajol.info/index.php/hts/article/viewFile/70933/59889* (14//8/2019).

6 Nathan Grossman J. D, "On Peter Berger's Definition of Religion," *Journal of Scientific Study of Religion* 14, no. 3 (September 1975), 289-292, available at *http://www.jstor.org/pss/1384911* (14/8/2019).

Berger interprets religion on the observation that very little in human life is determined by instinct and that the human are constantly forced to choose how to interact with the society and with the world at large. He explains that one must choose how to relate to and shape the environment around us. He terms this as "externalization." As a response to the process to externalizing, the environment changes and creates a new set of choices. The sociological view demands a stable order as society's main project is to create a sense of stability although it has been a false illusion since the world and the self is not stable. Society does this by teaching the individual to make the same choices over and over again as one externalizes, which is called "obejectivating". The role of the society here is to make the individual believe that those choices are necessary and inevitable. The process of learning these roles is called "socialization."[7]

Along with Luckmann, Berger acknowledges the presence of religion in identifiable religious institutions such as churches, synagogues and temples. However, both of them do not wish to restrict the social reality of religion to these institutional forms. For them, sociology of religion that deals only with institutions concentrates upon motionless forms of religion. Religion, in larger sense, legitimates the fundamental values of a society by constructing symbolic universes of meaning. Berger, in particular, thinks that religion legitimates social institutions firstly by bestowing upon an ultimately valid ontological status that is by locating them within a sacred and cosmic frame of reference; and secondly by maintaining the reality of that socially constructed world within which human exist in her/his everyday life.[8]

Modern Society and the Rediscovery of the Supernatural

Berger defines modernity as people's behavior and action that intends to take charge of the world and their own life. According to him *fate* in previous days is replaced by *arena of choices*. He also describes modernity as completely unimaginable growth of human life, which is open to choices.[9] Berger puts in simple words that modernity is not characterized by the absence of God, but by the presence of many gods.[10] Marion Levy defines the measure of

---

7 Ira Chernus, "Summary of Peter Berger, The Sacred Canopy," http://www.colorado.edu/ReligiousStudies/chernus/2400/Readings/SumariesOfTheSacredCanopy.htm. (21st August, 2019).

8 Walter H. Capps, "Society and Religion," in *The Encyclopedia of Religion* Vol. 13, edited by Mircea Eliade (New York: Macmillan Publishing Company, 1987), 383.

9 Peter L. Berger, *Pyramids of Sacrifice* (New York: Anchor Books, 1976), 20.

10 Peter L. Berger, "Secularization Falsified," in *First Things: A Monthly Journal of Religion and Public Life;* New York Iss. 180 (Feb 2008), 24. Available at https://search.proquest.com/openview/2ad8a999002fde985d4f71f32fe418e2/1?pq-origsite=gscholar&cbl=45949 (2/9/2019).

modernization as "the ratio of inanimate to animate sources of power."[11] This definition points out that modernity does not take place equally but it takes form in different degrees. Another important point underlined through this definition is that the essential factor in the process of modernization and core of modernity (*ipso facto*) is technological.[12] According to Berger, technological revolution is the result of a convergence of manifold causes. Therefore modernity, as we understand today, was also caused by other forces like capitalist market economy, the bureaucratic nation-state, the pluralistic city and the intricate ideological trend introduced by the movements like Renaissance and the Reformation. However, it is evident that among all these transforming forces, only technology is continuing till today.[13]

Impacts of Modernity and Religion

It is often discussed as to whether religion, at least in its traditional forms, will survive the ongoing cultural changes of modern times. Over the period, undoubtedly many traditional and current formulations and perhaps entire traditions will go through a thorough change or even disappear. However, another rises to take its place immediately after one form of religion disappears. Human situation surrounded by enormous mysteries and uncertainties of the world and human's enquiring and evaluating self-conscious nature makes it inevitable for a human to be a religious being.[14]

The age of modernity has witnessed a thick layer of dissatisfaction that has affected human life. Some of the discontents are specially derived from the pluralization of social life-worlds; which, according to Berger, can be counted under the heading of 'homelessness'. Due to the pluralistic structure of modernity, people have to be migrated and always be mobile. In the process of migration, people get detached from their original social setting and the succeeding milieu does not truly make them own it. This pushes them into a continuous fear of isolation and meaninglessness that causes due to the loss of collective and individual security.[15]

This 'homelessness' of the modern individual's social life has affected religion very badly. The pluralization of everyday life and biography in modern society cause cognitive and normative uncertainty, which further

11 Marion Levy, *Modernization: Latecomers and Survivors* (New York: Basic Books, 1972), 3. cited in *The Heretical Imperative: Contemporary Possibilities of Religious Affirmation* by Peter L. Berger (London: William Collins Sons and Co. Ltd, 1980), 3.

12 Peter L. Berger, *The Heretical Imperative. Contemporary Possibilities of Religious Affirmation* (London: William Collins Sons & Co. Ltd., 1979), 4.

13 Berger, *The Heretical Imperative*, 5.

14 Winston L. King, "Religion," in *Encyclopedia of Religion* Vol. 12, Edited by Mircea Eliade (New York: Macmillan Publishing Company, 1987), 292.

15 Berger, *Pyramids of Sacrifice*, 23.

generates crisis about the credibility of religion. It could be seen in the shaken nature of function of religion, that assures ultimate certainty in midst of the demands of human condition. The religious crisis contributes in making the social 'homelessness' the cosmic 'homelessness.'[16]

As an impact of modernity, religion loses its hold on the level of institutions and human consciousness too. A religious worldview needs to be supported by society. In the pre-modern society there were conditions created in the life of an individual, under which religion has certainty. However, in the modern society, religion has acquired 'taken-for-granted' status.[17]

Necessity of Rediscovering the 'Supernatural'

Considering the contemporary situation of religion, it could be said that the supernatural has departed from the modern world. In Thomas Altizer's own words, "We must realize that the death of God is an historical event that God has died in our cosmos, in our history in our *Exixstenz.*[18]

Berger informs that different scholars have criticized the term 'supernatural' for various reasons. According to the historians of religion and cultural anthropologists the term 'supernatural' suggests that there is a division of reality into a system of rationally comprehensible phenomenon and an inexplicable world which is beyond it. Biblical scholars provide their criticism on the basis of the failure to express the concreteness of the religious experience of the Israelite. Christian theologians argued that the term offends the implications of the doctrine of incarnation, which are universally acknowledged. The term suggests that there is some 'other reality' than the empirical reality which unfolds everyday human experiences. Rudolff Otto, a historian of religion, emphasizes the 'supernatural' as something completely different than that of the human phenomena. In this 'otherness' the sacred is understood as strange fascinating power.[19] However, social philosopher Alfred Schutz argues that in the empirical reality wherein human carry on her/his normal activities in association with others, she/he experiences the natural attitude as a reality.[20] This reality becomes the taken-for-granted natural experience of her/him. It is before such a natural reality, religion puts-forth

16 Peter L. Berger, Brigitte Berger and Hansfried Kellner, *The Homeless Mind* (England: Penguin Books, 1973), 165-166.

17 Berger, *The Heretical Imperative*, 26.

18 Thomas J. J. Altizer and William Hamilton, *Radical Theology and the Death of God* (Pelican, 1968), 26, cited in *A Rumour of Angels. Modern Society and the Rediscovery of the Supernatural,* by Peter L. Berger (England: Penguine Books, 1969), 13.

19 Rudolf Otto, *The Idea of the Holy: An Enquiry into the Non-Rational Factor in the Idea of the Divine and its Relation to the Rational* (Oxford University Press: London, 1936), xix.

20 Alfred Schutz, *Collected Papers,* Vol. I (The Hague, Nijhoff, 1962), 208, cited in Berger, *A Rumour of Angels,* 15.

the reality of 'Supernatural.'[21] The empirical experiences of a human are full of crisis of suffering and death. In this context Marx Weber opines that there is a social need for *theodicy.* Theodicy refers to theories that justify suffering. These theories are explanations about the ways God, who is all-powerful and ever good, can permit suffering in the world.[22] Religion has offered meaning to the most painful experiences of human life. Modern society has been successful in creating threats to the validity of religious theodicies but it has not been successful to remove the invoking experiences of these theodicies. Modernity has weakened the definitions of reality which helped human to bear the challenges of life.[23]

With the beginning of secularization the fully accepted divine fullness started declining and the god-talk became fairy tales. In such situation, Berger thinks that the transcendence has been reduced to rumour. For him the secularized consciousness is not the absolute as it seems. So, it is better that the rumours are explored and traced till the end. This would facilitate a rediscovery of the supernatural and better perception of reality in our times.

Contemporary Possibilities of Religious Affirmations

In the context of modernity Berger suggests the following possibilities for religious affirmations.

Deductive Possibility: Reaffirming Tradition[24]

Religious tradition helps individuals to ascertain the religious claims again and again. Berger elaborates this with the help of the illustration of religious life of Muslim communities. The call to prayer that sounded from minarets serves as a continuous proclamation of the background of the human lives. This call to prayer creates an internal as well as external antiphony that affirms the religious conviction of the Muslims. However, modernization creates disorder in this antiphony and the external affirmation continues while the internal response faints.[25] Still, many people in modernized situations, when confront with the memory of the traditions, experience the coherence between the internal and external antiphony. Such kind of memory allows oneself to return to her/his biographical roots. Thus the antiphony gets restored to the previous intact. A mass movement of powerful Islamic renaissance is the best example that Berger gives. This can happen even on intellectual level. In this case the

21 Berger, *A Rumour of Angels,* 14-15.

22 Berger, *Rumour of Angels*, 40.

23 Peter L. Berger, Brigitte Berger and Hansfried Kellner *The Homeless Mind. Modernization and Consciousness* (England: Penguin Books Ltd., 1973), 166.

24 Berger, *The Heretical Imperative*, 66.

25 Berger, *The Heretical Imperative,* 66.

term "neo-orthodoxy" is used. However, the prefix "neo" creates problems as it suggests that the tradition is affirmed anew and there was an interval before it.[26] Nevertheless, a postmodern outlook suggests that neo-orthodoxy has valued unity instead of plurality. An authentic postmodern religion should not draw people to one tradition rather than being centrifugal. It should foster freelance approach.[27]

Reductive Possibility: Modernizing Tradition[28]

In human history, gods were experienced very closely as that of the presence of fellow humans. However, in the present situation gods' presence is not felt so close and sometimes they seem as if they are vanished. The situation, where human feels gods' presence or not, both the situations could be the starting point for human experience and reflection. Western countries live in modern situation, which is characterized by a high degree of secularization. Modern consciousness does not promote close contact with the gods. It is difficult for the orthodox minds to perceive the character of modern situation. On the other hand, the neo-orthodox minds resist it. Berger suggests that the example of this is found in the "death of God movement" which took place in 1960 in America. The death of God was perceived as a starting point for an enterprise of Christian Theology. From this it could be said that modern situation has changed the religious experience and religious thought.[29]

Inductive Possibility: From Tradition to Experience[30]

The term "induction" is used in its most common sense that suggests argument from empirical evidence. The term suggests two things:

i. Taking human experience as the starting point of religious reflection, and,
ii. Using the methods of the historian to reveal religious traditions.

It poses the questions like what kind of experience would be counted as evidence for starting point of religious reflection? In what way? To these questions, Gregory Baum responds that biblical religious experiences reflect God's majesty and as Otto suggests they are inextricably linked to the sense of God's justice and holiness. Thus, the sacred becomes the bearer of a judgment

26 Berger, *The Heretical Imperative*, 67-68.

27 Don Cupitt, *Radicals and the Future of the Church* (London: SCM Press, 1989), 77.

28 Berger, *The Heretical Imperative,* 95.

29 Berger, *The Heretical Imperative,* 95-98.

30 Berger, *The Heretical Imperative,* 125.

on human life and society and an assured corrector of the present ills. Thus, religious experience had to do with human transformation.[31]

Nevertheless, Liberal Protestant theology stands unique in following these two methodological principles. Hence, it creates interest for those Protestant theologians, who are disturbed with the substantive issues (they argued that in the Holy Communion, the bread and wine actually turns into Jesus' body and blood). The inductive approach demonstrated by Protestant liberalism is helpful as a possible model for thinking not just about Christianity but religion on the whole.[32]

Friedrich Schleiermacher is considered as a pragmatic figure of Protestant Liberalism. He proposes a method of inquiry through which every religion is traced back to its experiential source. Here he included even those religions that have reduced to mere rituals and theoretical assumptions. This method is historical as well as phenomenological at the same time. It allows the discovery that "all the dead embers were once glowing effusions of inner fire."[33] The expression "inner fire" makes it possible to evaluate the specific forms of religion whether they are intimate or distant from the core experience of God.[34]

However, this model is being criticized on the ground that by its very nature, this model occupies a position of compromise, which is a vulnerable position. Therefore, possibly, theologians, who begins with an inductive approach ends up with formulations that seems like reductionism.[35]

Critical observations

Peter Berger's thoughts about sociology, modernity and religion are assessed as follows:

i. Berger's analysis of pluralism's extend and consequences has invited debate. Some scholars questioned whether pluralism was particularly a new phenomenon in human history. Berger himself has no problem with as far as the existence of pluralism in early eras was concerned. His argument has been that the scope and intensity

31 Gregory Baum, "The Sociology of Roman Catholic Theology," in *Sociology and Theology: Alliance and Conflict,* edited by D. Martin, J. O. Mills, O. P. and U.S.F. Pickering (Brighton: The Harvester Press Ltd., 2004), 135. E-book available at https://epdf.pub/queue/sociology-and-theology.html (2/9/2019).

32 Berger, *The Heretical Imperative,* 127.

33 Über die Religion: Reden an die gebildeten unter ihren Verächtern, in Sämtliche Werke, I (Berlin: Reimer, 1843), 249, translated by Peter Berger, cited in Berger, *The Heretical Imperative,* 131.

34 Berger, *The Heretical Imperative.*

35 Berger, *The Heretical Imperative,* 140.

of modern pluralism are historically exceptional. Like any other social construction, however, pluralism (and modernity itself) is inevitable. While ascribing metaphor of the *Homeless Mind* to the modern individuals, Berger has consistently pointed out the impact of modernity on an individual's life and the need for a critique of modernity. However, it should be understood that Berger importantly aims at the sociologists and theologians to make them understand the characteristic of modern pluralism and its limitations as well as its probable impacts on religion.[36]

ii. Berger looks at the rediscovery of supernatural as a possibility for theological thought in contemporary situation. So, there is possibility that this endeavor remains the property of the isolated academic minority.[37] In such situation the idea of rediscovery of supernatural has less to do with the life of the majority people, who are not highly learned.

iii. Socialization and individualization are inter-related; so also modernity and individualism. Individual respond to the structure of modern social life by a stronger sense of personal identity.[38] Religion is increasingly experienced more as personal experience than collective and communal obligation. Religion is personalized and viewed more intimately. Having this perspective on mind, the decline of religion in modern society as Burger suggests, does not seem realistic.[39]

iv. Berger's emphasis on affirming religious tradition as a possibility of religious affirmation is appreciable given its nature of keeping people together and making them affirm their identities. However, it is also to be seriously noted that the tradition tend to reduce religion to historic events and does not offer further space to freely exercise it.

Conclusion

Peter Berger's overall impact on sociological and theological thinking is remarkable. In early works, like many others, Berger maintained that the two

---

36 Bruce Karlenzig, "Berger Peter L," *Encyclopedia of Religion* edited by William H. Swatos and Peter Kivisto. 53. Available at http://books.google.co.in/books (1 September, 2019).

37 Berger, *A Rumour of Angels*, 120-121.

38 Charles Taylor, *Sources of the Self: The Making of the Modern Identity* (Cambridge: Cambridge University Press, 1989) cited in Michael S. Northcott, "Sociological Approaches," in *Approaches to the Study of Religion,* edited by Peter Connolly (London and New York: Cassell, 1999), 216.

39 Michael S. Northcott, "Sociological Approaches," 216.

ideas, pluralism and secularization, were mutually strengthening. Increased religious choices underlined the necessity of religion.

His special mention of modernity, its impacts on religion and human life is the most attractive feature of his writings. When other scholars seem to be ignoring the phenomena of modernity, Berger has not only criticized modernity but pointed that even in such circumstances there is so much significance for religious possibilities. In terms of sociology Berger tends to follow a humanistic approach.

Berger has a unique way of analyzing contemporary situation by using the intellectual tools of the sociology of knowledge. 'A rediscovery of supernatural' is a catchy theme in Peter Berger's writings. While he discusses the changes in modernity in a general way, he also shows concern for religion and its changes. Further he relates those responses to social change and sees religion as contributing to social change.

10

A Study of Religion from Postmodern Perspective

Pranay Bin

Like any other disciplines of the academy, the study of religion owes much of its orientation to the intellectual interests of the European Enlightenment and to the dominance of a particular kind of rationality and subjectivity, which in recent year have undergone a radical critique by postmodernist. There are numerous approaches in the study of religion. Defining religion is a perilous task in the study of religion, so no approach is absolute in the study of religion. Postmodern approach to a certain degree nullifies any claim and proffers the importance of all or helps to deconstruct and reconstruct. This disquisition is one such attempt.

The Term Postmodern

Postmodernism is an exasperating term, and so are postmodern, postmodernist, postmodernity, and whatever one might come across in the way of derivation. American literary critics brought the term postmodernism into circulation in the 1960s and early 1970s. Postmodernism is a move away from presented narrative. It is a turn towards self-reflexivness.[1] The prefix 'post' suggests that any postmodernism is inextricably bound up with modernism, either as a replacement of modernism or as chronologically after modernism.

1 Hans Bertens, *The Idea of the Postmodern A History* (New York and London: Routledge, 1995), 4. ProQuest Ebook Central.

Indeed, with *postmodernism*, *postfeminism* and *postindustrialism*, the 'post' can be seen to suggest a critical engagement with modernism, rather than claiming the end of modernism, or it can seem that modernism has been overturned, superseded or replaced.[2] The relationship is something more akin to a continuous engagement, which implies that postmodernism to survive, so that they exist in something more like a host-parasite relationship. Therefore, it is quite crucial to realize that any definition of *postmodernism* will depend upon ones' prior definition of *modernism*. Modernism was generally the name given to the earth-quake in European culture in the first half of the twentieth century, which undermined many aesthetic tenets and principles throughout the arts.[3] Despite the prefix 'post' suggesting postmodernism as a chronologically later period in social and cultural history, there are many theorists who argue that postmodernism is not a chronological period, but more of a way of thinking and doing. Perhaps the term postmodernism is a term which denotes the continuation of the modern by affirming its worth and its Achilles heel and goes further in adding and analysing as well as accounting all the existing facts. Therefore, it is a recurrent historical phase within modernism.

Postmodernity: A Historical Backdrop

The European society lives in a postmodern world. While the idea is very familiar by now, it has not yet been described exactly. The emergence of postmodernity is accounted for several reasons in the west. It is alleged that in its history that is during the era of modernity[4] human kind was oppressed. It is

---

2 The *post*modern age rest partially covered by the late modern. The *post*-prefix of postmodernism has several possible connotations. First, *postmodernism* is after modernism; second, *postmodernism* is against modernism; third, *postmodernism* is a continuation of (high) modernism. The difficulty with defining the *post*-prefix comes from its positioning within the temporal order. The *post* suggests something somewhere in history. Postmodernism often is placed under the umbrella of postmodernity. This, however, is not sufficient in so far as postmodernity marks an historical era, and is most widely used as a sociological term to the social order under late capitalism. Postmodernism is more than annoying symptom of post-industrial-late-capital social organization. In fact, postmodernism is more than temporality, and more than history and the process of history. In fact its postmodernism developed in continuation with the modernism. Taylor, Victor E. *Para/Inquiry: Postmodern Religion and Culture*, Rutledge, 2008. ProQuest Ebook Central, https://ebookcentral-proquest-com.library.

3 Tim Woods, *Beginning Postmodernism* (New Delhi: Viva Books, 2010), 6.

4 The word modern was almost always used in the field of art and literature. It is said that the world first experienced renaissance, and then, enlightenment and thereafter modernity and postmodernity. Modernity, is regarded as the norm of human society toward which all history has been aiming and into which all societies should be ushered-forcibly if necessary-is increasingly seen as an aberration. A new respect for the wisdom of traditional societies is growing as we realize that they have endured for thousands of years and that, by contrast, the existence of modern society for even another century seems doubtful.

because of it that postmodernism is critical of universalizing theories, that is grand narratives or meta narratives[5] as they have been dubbed by Jean-Francois Lyotard. These theories are authoritarian in their outlook. It was assumed that the fundamentalism we discover in the West generated horrible religious clashes. The grand narratives are now recognized throughout the globe as a threat to individuals. India too has its share of grand narratives in the context of its great tradition and small historical ups and downs, its victories and defeats, its absorption of invaders and its inability to cope up with fanatical, bigoted, bigoted violent hordes. From the Epics, Brahmanas and scriptures, these traditions draw their power. Based on these mythological text, those who advocate cultural nationalism promote religious fundamentalism. All these narratives are reconstructed by postmodernity.

The history of the word 'postmodernity' goes back to 1870s, and although proceeds to crop up periodically over the next few decades, sometimes with positive, sometimes with negative connotations, it is only in the latter half of the 20th century that it comes to take on the precise meaning against modernism

Likewise, modernism as a worldview is less and less seen as The Final Truth. However, in a broader way to state modernity is associated with industrialization and urbanization, development, democracy, superiority of power, free market, the serach for absolute knowledge in science, technology, society and politics, the idea that gaining knowledge of the true self was the only foundation for all other knowledge and rationality. David Ray Griffin, "Constructive Postmodern Thought," Introduction to SUNY Series in *Primordial truh and Postmodern Theology* edited by David Ray Griffin and Huston Smith, xi-xiv (New York: State University of New York Press, 1989), 1.

5 By narratives means, grand narratives. The grand narratives are also called meta narratives or mega narratives by Lyotard. The things which is told or narrated or described in detail, is a narrative. The assumption of meta narratives is not acceptable to Lyotard. The society and their kit of knowledge are in a damaging state of affairs. They have become irreparable and degenerated. On the other hand, the met narratives and theories propounded by their authors have failed to do justice to the mankind. These theories, their impact and their application are, in fact, responsible for the degeneration of the society. They cannot be allowed to continue as such any more. Therefore, it an emergency to generate new knowledge for the health of this society. He also further divides the Metanarraives into two: emancipatory and scientific. Emancipatory meta narratives are associated with the notion of reason, experience, scepticism of religion and traditional authority. With regard to scientific meta narrative Lyotard says that there is no truth in scientific knowledge. Science has no direct access to truth. Both these narratives are considered as form of knowledge. S. L. Doshi, *Postmodern Perspectives on Indian Society* (New Delhi: Rawat Publications, 2008), 39-41.

and modernity.[6] Historically, postmodern subsumes poststructuralism.[7] In its

---

6 "Earlier, the meaning of postmodernity was related to art and painting. The English painter John Watkins Chapman suggested that any art that went beyond impressionism, the revolutionary new art style of period, would be definable as 'postmodern painting'. By 1917, the concept was used in terms of militaristic and anti-humanistic culture which was prevalent in Europe during the war. During 1020s and 1030s, the concept in America was used for religious matters. Arnold Toynbee, the British Historian, in his celebrated work, *A Study of History*, mentioned that the period from 1835 onwards was the "postmodern age of western history". During this period, there was cultural decline-it was the period of 2nd world war. It is clear that postmodernity had its affiliations to fine arts and fashion. Moreover Stuart Sim mentions the history of the development of postmodernity. Postmodernity has proved to be in the field of architecture as a conceptual term. The architectural theorist, Charls Jenckens, has done more than anyone to popularize postmodernism as a theoretical concept. Jenckens is highly critical of modern architecture, which he thought had lost touch with the general public. Jencks illustrated the revolt against modern architecture by bulldozing of the award winning Pruitt-Igor housing complex in St. Luis, Missouri in 1972. It showed the public mood for rejecting modernity or modern architecture was found to have alienated people from the community. Jencks favoured architecture which freely mixed the old and new styles. Thus, postmodernity had its first revolt against modern architecture sometime in the middle of the 20th century CE. In the later part of this century, it appeared in ecology movement, which found technology and factory harmful, environmentally. 'Green' political parties were formed in many western European countries to criticize the evil environmental effects of technology and industry. Many creative artists reverted to older style that audiences felt more comfortable with, rather as Charles Jencks was calling on architects to do in their field. Philosophers and cultural theorists reacted against theories such as structuralism, which reduced the dynamic or deep structure. The working of the entire world could be mapped out in terms of these deep structures, which dictated how all system operated. To explain the importance of postmodernity during this period of intellectual despair, this has been rightly said by Stuart Sim. Structuralism in dominance in mid-century intellectual enquiry (particularly in France) which led to a reaction, collectively called poststructuralism, which increasingly came to challenge the assumption on which structuralist analysis rested. Whereas structuralists emphasized difference and open-endedness. Structuralism was a universalizing theory, post structuralists spent their time demonstrating how such theories must always fall: the battle lines were drawn." Doshi, *Postmodern Perspectives on Indian Society*, 19-22.

7 "The origin of the term structure one finds that the term initially had an architectural meaning. In the 17th and 18th century, the use of the term broadened and came to describe the ways in which the parts of a concrete being are structure into a whole. This concept could apply to a variety of structures, including anatomical, geological, and mathematical. The application of the notion of structure to language and the social sciences in general came from development in the field of linguistics through the seminal course in general linguistics of Ferdinand de Saussure (1983), the founder of structural linguistics. His linguistics proposition is, a language is a system in which all the elements fit together, and in which the value of any one element depends on the simultaneous coexistence of all the others. But poststructuralism continues the central projects of structuralism-the inquiry into the organizing principles of language system. While structuralism posits that the language system can be described in an objective and scientific manner, poststructuralism suggests that such descriptions are themselves always highly contextual. Structuralism was confident that the principles by which language is organized can be fully determined

initial stages of development, it came as a part of art of painting when the art in its impressionist form was not acceptable to people, a new art form was invented. During the world war period, postmodernity took to militaristic form of expression. Culture declined during this period. And, then, it again appeared, in the form of modern architecture. The idea of deep structure and its analysis appeared in France as a theory of structuralism. This was rejected by postmodernity. Historically, postmodernity is rebellious. It rejects all the overarching theories of the totality of society, for example, Durkheim's theory of social fact, religion (sacred and profane), and solidarity of society. It also denies Karl Marx and argues Marx's attempt to find general pattern of history was inevitably doomed to failure. Postmodernist out rightly give up all such theories, which sought to develop over all interpretations of social change. Postmodernity, in short, has a history of reaction, rejection and rebellion.

Understanding Postmodernism

Defining postmodernism is a perilous and risky. Callum G. Brown says that it is not limited to one creed or people, position or standpoint. It is so big, it claims to be successor to the enlightenment which is a very large claim.[8] Postmodernism, then, means and has meant different things to different people at different conceptual levels, rising from humble literary critical origins in the 1950s to a level of global conceptualization in the 1980s. The word is highly used today, it is equally misused. Its critics defines it as a word of rejection. There is a saying: if you want to kill a dog, call it mad. In the similar strain, if you disagree with anything, want to reject anything, call it postmodern.

Postmodern thus is a cliché which is often used for rejecting anything. Since the postmodernism was made popular in English-speaking world by the English publication of Jean-Francois Lyotard (1984) *The Postmodern Condition* and its Appendix, "Answering the question: What is Postmodernity?" the debate has centred on question of knowledge. Lyotard's pivotal book is subtitled *A Report on Knowledge* and he makes clear in his first sentence that he uses the word postmodern to describe the state of knowledge in developed societies today.[9] Since Lyotard, postmodern thinkers have continued to pose epistemological questions-question about scientific methodology, the possibility of foundations for what is proposed as truth or knowledge, the relationship between this

---

and described, poststructuralism calls into question all such conclusions are always fragile and open to subversion." Gary P. Radford and Marie L. Radford, "Structuralism, post-structuralism, and the library: de Saussure and Foucault," Journal of Documentation 61, no. 1 (2005), 60-61. ProQuest Central. 60-78.

8 Callum G. Brown, *Postmodernism for Historians* (London and New York: Routledge Taylor and Francis Group, 2005), 9. Ebook Central ProQuest Ebrary.

9 Rekha Mirchandani, "Postmodernism and Sociology: From the Epistemological to Empirical," *Sociological Theory* 23, no. 1 (March 2005), 87.

knowledge and power, the role of the subject in knowledge, imperfections of representing knowledge through language, and the possibility of universal knowledge.[10] The postmodern debates over these questions extend through social theory, philosophy, religious and cultural studies as well as other disciplines. Further, it can be noted that the understanding of postmodernity will be determined by one's perspective, and that no one definition or system of it can be formulated. Accordingly, disagreement over what "postmodernity" is unavoidable.

In postmodernity, reason's capacity to critique and dismantle, and its inability to construct, perhaps find most extreme expression.[11] Lyotard writes, "I define postmodernism as incredulity towards metanarratives."[12] Richard Bernstein calls postmodernism as, "a rage against humanism and Enlightenment legacy."[13] Tyron Inbody compares it to "intellectual Velcro dragged across culture" which "can be used to characterize almost anything one approves or disapproves."[14] Postmodernity goes against the certainty, objectivity and progress orientation of modernity.[15] Because postmodernity often refers to the idea of a society characterized by widely dispersed cultural orientations that doubt the possibilities and blessings of this rationalizing project.

Zygmunt Bauman, one of the foremost social theorists, regards postmodernity as 'modernity conscious of its true nature,[16] in other words, it is a social and intellectual self-reflexive mood within modernity. In a moment of parodic insight, Tod Gitlin acutely lampoons the relationship by stating that 'modernism tore up unity and postmodernism has been enjoying the shreds'. Postmodernism is a knowing modernism, a self-reflexive modernism, a modernism that does not agonise about itself. Postmodernism does what modernism do, only in a celebratory rather than repentant way. Thus, instead lamenting the loss of the past, the fragmentation of existence and the collapse of selfhood, postmodernism embraces these characteristics as a new form of social existence and behaviour.[17] The difference between modernism and postmodernism is therefore, best seen as a difference in mood or attitude, rather than a chronological difference, or a difference set of aesthetic practices.

10 Rekha Mirchandani, "Postmodernism and Sociology: From the Epistemological to the Empirical," 88.

11 Thomas Finger, "Modernity, Postmodernity-What in the World are they?" *Transformation* 10, no. 4 (October 1993), 24.

12 Woods, Beginning Postmodernism, 6.

13 Richard Bernstein, ed., *Hebermas and Modernity* (Cambridge: Polity Press, 1985), 1.

14 Inbody Tyron, "Pstmodernism: Intellectua Velcro Dragged Across Culture?," Theology Today 51, no. 4 (January 1995), 524.

15 Alvesson, Postmodernism, 6.

16 Woods, Beginning Postmodernism, 6.

17 Woods, Beginning Postmodernism, 8-9.

Postmodernism pits *reason* in the plural-fragmented and incommensurable-against the universality of modernism and the longstanding conception of the human self as a subject with a single, unified reason. The subject is the space demarcated by the 'I', understood as a sense of identity, a selfhood which is coherent, stable, rational and unified.[18] Based upon this sense of individuality, it is believed that people possess agency and can use their capacities to alter, shape and change the world in which they live. Postmodern theory is suspicious of the notion of humans possessing an undivided and coherent self which acts as the standard of rationality, and guarantees all knowledge claims irrespective of time and place.[19] It is no longer believes that reasoning subjects act as vehicle for historically progressive change.

Postmodernism can be called constructive or revolutionary. It seeks to overcome the modern worldview not by eliminating the possibility of worldviews as such, but by constructing a postmodern worldview through a revision of modern premises and traditional concepts.[20] This constructive or revisionary postmodernism involves a new unity of scientific, ethical, aesthetic, and religious intuitions. It rejects not science as such but only that scientism in which the data of the modern natural science are alone allowed to contribute to the construction of our worldview.

Constructive postmodern thought provides support for the ecology, peace, feminist, and other emancipatory movements of our time, while stressing that the inclusive emancipation must be from modernity itself.[21] The term postmodern however, by contrast with premodern, emphasizes that the modern world has produced unparalleled advances that must not be lost in a general revulsion against its negative features. In fact, it is undeniable to say that postmodernism also is considered by many as a philosophy.

Post Modernism: A Philosophy

Postmodernism that began in France, is considered to be a system of philosophy. The leading figure in this regard to be noted is Jean-Francois Lyotrard whose book, *The Postmodern Condition: A report of knowledge* (1970), is widely considered to be "the most powerful theoretical expression of postmodernism." Lyotard's appeal that we should reject the grand narratives (that is, universal theories) of western culture because they have now lost all their credibility, sums up the ethos of postmodernism, derision for authority in all its many guises. There is no longer any point in engaging with modernism, which may assist to reach or to know the truth or to have appropriate knowledge. Rather,

18 Woods, Beginning Postmodernism, 9.

19 Woods, Beginning Postmodernism, 9-10.

20 Griffin, "Introduction to SUNY Series in Constructive Postmodern Thought," xii.

21 Griffin, "Introduction to Suny Series in Constructive Postmodern Thought," xiii.

we should ignore it as of no relevance to our lives. Postmodern philosophy provides us with the arguments and techniques to make that gesture of dissent, as well as with means to make value judgement in the absence of overall authorities.

When we mention postmodernism as a philosophy, it takes skepticism as its central point of argument. It is said that whatever we have received as our inherited wisdom, tradition, culture, and political norms must be put to a sceptical inquiry. Stuart Sim puts postmodernism as philosophy. He writes,

> Scepticism is essentially a negative form of philosophy, which sets out to undermine other philosophical theories claiming to be in possession of ultimate truth, or of criteria for determining what count as a ultimate truth. The technical term to describe such style of philosophy is anti-foundational. Anti-foundationalits dispute the validity of the foundations of discourse, asking such questions as what guarantees the truth of your foundation (that is, starting point). Postmodernism has drawn heavily on the example set by anti-foundationalists philosophers.[22]

For some, postmodernism is only branch of philosophy and should be discussed as such only. But, some argue that postmodernism as a social science. And S. L. Doshi he regards Lyotard, Jean Baudrilard, David Harvey, Anthony Giddens, Michael Foucault, Jacques Derrida, Fredric Jameson etc., as a postmodern sociologists rather than philosopher. In fact, asserting them as sociologist seems to be bias. Postmodern approach do not deal with any single streams rather it has wider scope. Perhaps the basic feature of postmodernism may help us to explore more on it.

Basic Features of Postmodernism

It is a term used roughly since the 1960s about cultural forms that displays certain characteristics, among which are: the undercutting of an all-encompassing rationality; incredulity towards metanarratives and a challenge to totalising discourses, which is a suspicion of any discursive attempts to offer a global or Universalist account of existence; and a rejection modernism.[23] Postmodernism is more of a way of thinking and doing.[24] Postmodern theory is suspicious of the notion of humans possessing an undivided and coherent self which acts as the standard of rationality, and guarantees all knowledge claims

22 Stuart Sim, *Fundamentalist World, the New Dark age of Dogma* (Cambridge: Cambridge University Press, 2004), cited by S. L. Doshi, *Postmodern Perspectives on Indian Society* (Jaipur: Rawat Publications), 24-25.

23 Woods, *Beginning Postmodernism,* 10.

24 Woods, *Beginning of Postmodernism*, 8

irrespective of time and place. It no longer believes that reasoning subjects act as vehicles for historically progressive change.[25] Postmodernism is a knowing modernism, a self-reflexive modernism, a modernism that modernism does, only in a celebratory rather than repentant way. Postmodernism denies the idea of knowable origin.[26] Thus, instead of lamenting the loss of the past, the fragmentation of existence and the collapse of selfhood, postmodernism embraces these characteristics as a new form of social existence and behaviour. The difference between modernisms is therefore best seen as a difference in mood or attitude, rather than a chronological difference, or a difference set of practices. Postmodernism seeks local or provisional, rather than universal and absolute, forms of legitimation.

Task of Postmodernism

The task of the postmodernism is to discover the contradiction, contingency, and indeterminacy; it uses the techniques of metaphor, narrative, and storytelling for discovering surprising new insights; it embraces a new neo-pragmatic position, and it justifies the use of "situated" and "local" critiques as a means for decentring foundational theories.[27] The objective of postmodern criticism is not merely one of exposing contradiction or indeterminacy. The goal is to recover contradiction, paradox and so forth. What is appealing about postmodernism is the possibility of recovering aspects of intellectual life that are generally erased by Enlightenment perspectives and knowledge. Postmodern attempts to bring to life the forms of thought and practices unheard and unseen. Moreover, postmodernity focuses on rationality seen as a guiding principle, as well as attainable objective, for the modern project.[28]

Postmodernism or postmodern is not, strictly speaking, a school of thought. It is not a unified intellectual movement with a definite goal or perspective, and it does not have a single dominant theoretician or spokesperson. This is because ideas about postmodernism have been adopted by virtually every discipline, from philosophy to cultural studies. From geography to art history. Each area has produced books and periodicals with their own particular angles on the topic, each has defined postmodernism in their own terms. In short, postmodernism has proliferated.[29]What postmodernism might mean in one discipline is not necessarily compatible with what it might mean in another. Postmodernism has more than one application. It can be used, for example, as a vague term for any contemporary artefact that seems in some way ironic. Or

---

25 Woods, *Beginning of Postmodernism*, 10.

26 Woods, *Beginning Postmodernism*, 3.

27 Gary Minda, *Postmodern legal Movements* (New York: NYU Press, 1995), 248.

28 Mats Alvesson, *Postmodernism* (New Delhi: Critical Quest, 2006), 6.

29 Glenn Ward, *Postmodernism* (Illinois: Teach Yourself Books, 1997), 3.

it can be used, even more vaguely, as a general name for our particular moment in history. Add to this, the fact that its meaning has argued over in the areas in which it was born, and postmodernism seems ever more resistant to definition.

Postmodern Approach to Religion

The pre-modern period does not view that social or religious change is progressive. The critiquing ushers in modernity. S. L. Doshi writes,

> A belief in the progress of human conditions, rational planning to achieve objectives, a belief in superiority or rational thought as compared to emotion; faith in the ability of technology and science to solve human problems; a belief in the ability and rights of human beings to shape their own lives and a reliance upon manufacturing industry to improve living standards.[30]

It is believed that it was possible for universalistic theories to solve the problems and lead to progress. This was felt by many though it is no longer helpful in doing research to finding the fact. There is a shift towards critical engagement in the study of cultures, society and religion. Postmodern critique opens up new possibilities for a more holistic and organic understanding of human existence at both personal and social levels. Critiques allow for new interpretive approaches acknowledging the interdependent, communal, ecological, and spiritual dimensions of human beings, their rootedness in earth and cosmos, and their interdependence with the evolutionary stream of becoming, thus evoking a new reverence for nature and the recognition of the overall sacredness of life.

Postmodern approach to religion is the avowed opposite of the modern one. Theorizing is to be spurned. For, in seeking only similarities among religions, a theory denies differences, where the focus should lie. Theories are suspect. Not merely do they account for all religions uniformly, but their accounts reflect the backgrounds and interest of the theorists. The goal of religion study is the appreciation of the distinctiveness of each religion. The most suitable metaphor for the postmodern study of religion is that of conversation, which in days of yore was called dialogue. The believer is the equal of the scholar. The two are "conversation partners."

In his introduction to *Critical Terms for Religious Studies* (1988) Mark C. Taylor maintains that the postmodern approach to religion is superior to the modern one:

> For interpreters schooled in postmodernism and poststructuralism, the seemingly innocent question "what is ...?" is fraught with

30 Doshi, *Postmodern Perspectives on Indian Society*, 26.

> ontological and epistemological presuppositions that are deeply problematic. To ask, for example, "what is religion?" assumes that religion has something like a general or even universal essence that can be discovered through discipline investigation... but what if religion has no such essential identity? What if religion is not a universal phenomenon? What if religion has not always existed or has never existed? ... Investigator create-sometime unknowingly-the objects and truth they profess to discover. Some critic claims that an appearance to the country notwithstanding, religion is a modern western invention . . . the very concept of religion entails a level of self-consciousness that is distinctively modern.[31]

> To make peace between premodern typologies and postmodern difference, it is necessary to develop comparative analyses that do not presuppose universal principles or reinscribe ahistorical essences. Whether or not it is possible to realize such a comparatives program, many critics schooled in poststructuralism insists that the very effort to establish similarities where there appear to be differences is, in the final analysis, intellectually misleading and politically misguided. When reason is obsesses with unity, they argue, it tends to become as hegemonic as political and economic orders constructed to regulate whatever does not fit into or agree with governing structures.[32]

This statement captures in essence the issue with postmodernism, such as the confusion of universality with essence, the confusion of universality of definition, confusion with the theory and failed theory and the confusion of the quest for similarities with the identical of differences.[33]

To deduce the postmodern approach to the study of religion few things can be noted. One of them is decentring the foundational theories. Religion often reflects the dominant culture in which it is rooted the ultimate reality. Postmodern approach is more of liberation of the unseen, underestimated or ignored aspects of the others. By spurning, suspecting, denying the absolute knowledge of anything that have been existing within the context of a study of religion could be attempted in order to achieve the goal.

---

31 Mark C. Taylor, *Critical Term for Religious Studies* (Chicago: University of Chicago Press, 1988), 5-6.

32 Taylor, *Critical Term for Religious Studies*, 15.

33 Robert A. Segal, "All Generalization are Bad: Postmodernism on Theories," *Journal of the American Academy of Religion*, 74, no. 1 (March 2006), 159-160.

Strength of Postmodernity in the Study of Religion

One of the strength of postmodernism is its sense of fluidity and open-endedness. It resists being conveniently summarised in easy 'sound bites' and refuses to lend itself fully to any single cut and dried definition.[34] Postmodern approach attempts to bring to life the forms of thought and practices unheard and unseen. Postmodernism gives equal importance both written as well as oral information. Postmodernism moves from universalizing to the localizing. It considers every aspect of the human affairs either great or remote knowledge, with value. Postmodernism regards each minute and subtle aspect of the religious value and information as worth. As a result, postmodernism is something that allows to exist anything. By not being an ideology, postmodernism is a way of understanding knowledge. It is a way of understanding how humans gain knowledge from the world. Postmodernism as a knowledge theory is concerned with many things such as,

i. Order, configure, assemble and display knowledge (in verbal, written or image form);
ii. Knowledge as experienced by every individual as he or she constructs and develops his or her personal identity; and
iii. Individual reflecting his or her identity (based on that knowledge) back into society.

These three things describe the functions of postmodernism. It has other applications. One is a way of understanding previous knowledge in the past. Past and present knowledge can be very different. On account of the fact that postmodern approach to the study of religion is worth adding to the study of religion.

Concluding Remark

It is difficult to deduce postmodern approach to the study of religion with any concrete definition. Postmodernism is critical of modernism or modern approach by providing an alternative avenue to explore the religion, which includes deconstructing metanarratives. Postmodernism, therefore, focuses on the mechanics of knowledge and identity, how these are constructed and circulated, and how they differ from century to century and place to place. Postmodernism is therefore an intellectual foundation for understanding society, religion, culture and psychology. Postmodernism decentralises the foundational theories of religion and reconstruct by adding from the remote aspect of religious value. It tries to unearth the unheard and unseen and ignored part of the religious knowledge. Likewise, postmodern approach is significant in the study of religion.

34 Glenn Ward, Postmodernism (Illinois: Teach Yourself Books, 1997), v.

11

Understanding the Concept of Guru in Hinduism

Gifta Angeline Kumar

Introduction

The idea of a *Guru* appears in one form or another in almost all culture and religions. *Guru* occupy a prominent place in Hinduism. Almost all the prominent deities of Hinduism act as *gurus* to reveal divine knowledge or teach specific skills. The notion of *Guru* is one of the central themes in the contemporary religious discourses. The impact of the Gurus has been experienced in every spheres of life in contemporary society. In the light of this discussion, this article is an attempt to understand the notion of Guru from post-modern perspective.

Etymological Meaning of the Term *Guru*

The word *Guru* is derived from *Gur* meaning 'to raise, to lift up, to hurt, to kill, to make effort, to eat, to go.' It also means 'to sing, or to swallow.' A person is called *Guru* because he/she preaches *Dharma* to his/her disciples. The word *Guru* literally means preceptors—one who guides the religious and spiritual life to the disciples. The word *Guru* also takes two derivatives: '*gu*' means darkness and '*ru*' means dispeller. Therefore, one who dispels "the darkness of ignorance is a *guru*"—'the *enlighter.*'[1]

1 Jagdhari Masih, *The Understanding of Guruship in Neo-Guruism* (Delhi: ISPCK, 2004), 7.

The Importance of Guru in Ancient Hindu Texts

The importance of a *Guru* is extolled in the ancient texts of Hinduism. The *Svetasvatara Upaniṣad* (6:23) emphasizes the importance of reverence for a *Guru* stating that the teachings will illuminate those great souls who have reverence for God as well as for a *Guru*. In the *Taittiriya Upaniṣad* (1.11.2), students are urged to treat their teacher as God (*Ācārya devobhava*). The *Guru Gītā* from the *Skanda Purāṇa* equates a *Guru* to Śiva himself. In a conversation with Parvati, Śiva, who is the universal *Guru*, declares thus, "Apart from the *Guru*, there is no other *Brahman*. O beautiful One, what I say is true, it is the truth." In the same text he further states, "A *Guru* is Śiva himself, manifested as a human." A popular Hindu prayer declares, "The Guru is Brahmā, the Guru is Viṣṇu, the Guru is Śiva. Indeed, the Guru is the Supreme Absolute. To that *Guru* I offer my reverent salutations."[2]

The Origin of the Concept of Guru

The life of a Hindu is theoretically divided into four *āśramas*. During the first *āśramas* of life—*brahmacharya*—one is a student and lived under a teacher or *Guru*. Usually many students lived under one *acharya-guru*, who taught them the *Vedas* and related subject such as grammar, interpretation, pronunciation, performance of sacrifices, astronomy, and sometimes subjects like mathematic and literature.[3]

In the absence of printed books and other modern facilities, the student was wholly dependent on the teacher for knowledge. Being young, a student could neither critically evaluate a teacher's opinions, nor generally check the opinions of one teacher against the opinions of another as can be done in modern universities. This almost total dependence on the *Guru* was given scriptural sanction. In fact, the student was virtually a servant to the teacher.[4] A. L. Basham writes: "The student was … expected to treat his master with the utmost reverence. Ministering to all his needs and obeying all his commands implicitly.[5]

Chaubey writes that according to later scriptures,

> *Guru* is to be worshipped specially because he alone shows what is *Dharma* and what is *Adharma*. Even when god Śiva is wrath, the *Guru* is the saviour, but when the *Guru*… is angered there is none to save. Ruin follows from the anger of the *Guru*; bad death from the

2 https://www.hinduwebsite.com/hinduism/concepts/guru.asp (30th August 2019).

3 Vishal Mangalwadi, *The World of Gurus: A Critical Look at the Philosophies of India's Influential Gurus and Mystics*, Revised Edition (Chicago: Cornerstone Press, 1992), 16-17.

4 Mangalwadi, *The World of Gurus*, 17.

5 Mangalwadi, *The World of Gurus*, 17.

criticism of the *Guru*, disasters from the displeasure of the *Guru*. It may be possible for a man who has entered the fire to remain alive; possible also to be alive after drinking poison or even caught in the hands of death; but not if he has offended the *Guru*. One should not lend one's ear to any censure of the *Guru*; where such criticisms occur, one should close one's ears. One should not criticize his tradition, whether based on *Vedas* or scriptures or *Agamas*.[6]

Different Understanding of *Guru*

Although the term *Guru* is commonly used across the globe to denote 'teacher', the word *Guru* implies far more than this. In the spiritual context, a *Guru* is the dispeller of *avidya* (ignorance) and unveiler of *māyā* (perceived reality). *Avidya* suggests the lack of true knowledge or knowledge as it should be, not necessarily as is normal perceived. *Māyā* is the perception of a false and delusionary reality, since our biological senses limit our assessment of the absolute.[7] A *Guru* also concentrates on concepts like life, death, and the afterlife. He/she changes the conditioning of several lifetimes and helps exhaust our *samskras* (conditioning of previous lifetimes). He/she teaches the theory and practice of *karma*, and the concept of being *karma mukt* (free of all *karma*-good and bad).[8]

Although the tendency to deify the *Guru* only gradually gained a doctrinal position, the idea can already be seen in *Svetasvatara Upaniṣad*, which speaks of a man/woman who has the highest love and devotion for God and his/her *Guru* as for God. The knowledge that was gained from a teacher only was capable of successfully leading one's aim. From *Chandogya Upaniṣad* 6.4. 1ff., it appears that the *Guru* is also necessary in order to cut through and disperse mundane, empirical knowledge and to become conscious of true spiritual knowledge. The *Guru* in the *Ṛgveda* is referred to as the *rsi* (seen) or *muni* (a sage or silent one), and considered to be the author of the sacred hymns.[9]

According to Jogeswar Sarmah, the *Guru* is also called *Ācārya* because he/she shows them right path. The right path here refers to cultivating moral virtue. The word *Ācārya* comes from the root *car* (to behave) and means one who trains others to behave well. The teacher's duty is to lead the student from darkness to light. The teacher is called *Guru* because he/she performed the *Upanavana* or the initiatory ceremonies and taught the Vedas. The residence of the preceptor was the institution where the students after their *Upanayana*

---

6 Mangalwadi, *The World of Gurus*, 17.

7 Hingori, *Guru Sūtra,* First Edition (Pali Hills Tourist Hotel Pvt. Ltd, 2017), 5.

8 Hingori, *Guru Sūtra*, 5.

9 Masih, *The Understanding of Guruship in Neo-Guruism*, 9.

or initiation ceremony gathered together from different parts of the land to receive their education.[10]

The word *Guru* does not always convey the same meaning to all. According to one interpretation, he/she is 'the venerable'. According to another, it gives the idea of one who enlightens. To one person he/she is an ideal teacher, to another a self-realised soul and the goal of human experience.[11]

For a common Hindu, the idea of the *Guru* has great importance. During his *pratah-manana* or morning worship he/she repeats the following *sloka* in praise of the *Guru*.[12]

> Gurur Brahmā, Gurur Viṣṇu, Gurur devo Maheswara.
> Gurur saksat Parabrahma, Tasmai Śrī Guruve namah.

According to this *sloka*, God himself is the *Guru*. He is invoked for help to explain the scriptures. Therefore, the understanding of *Guruship* is not simple. There are three elements in the *Guru* idea which are stated bellow.[13]

Śikṣā Guru

The *Guru* who teaches the knowledge of worldly arts is the *Śikṣā Guru*. The place of *Guru* in Hinduism is primarily considered as a religious teacher. *Śikṣā Guru* is one who makes his/her livelihood by giving instruction from the Veda*s*.[14] He is known as *Upadhyaya* or sub-teacher. The *Upadhyaya* charged fees from the disciples and imparted instruction only in some particular subject. *Śikṣā Guru*, on the other hand, give instruction in certain arts like dancing.[15]

Dīkṣā Guru

The *Guru* who shows the path of realisation is *Dīkṣā Guru*. *Dīkṣā Guru* is one who imparts the transcendental truths (*para-vidya*) to his disciples. There are two schools of thought concerning the concept of *Dīkṣā Guru*.[16] One school of thought regards the *Dīkṣā Guru* to be God. The conviction of this school is, "that individual soul is identical in the essence with the absolute *Brahman*." The *Dīkṣā Guru*, it maintains, is a person who has realized this fact. Śrī Sankaracharya belongs to this school of thought.[17] The other school regards

10 Masih, *The Understanding of Guruship in Neo-Guruism*, 9.

11 Masih, *The Understanding of Guruship in Neo-Guruism*, 9-10.

12 Masih, *The Understanding of Guruship in Neo-Guruism*, 10.

13 Masih, *The Understanding of Guruship in Neo-Guruism*, 10.

14 Oṁ Swami, *The Ancient Science of Mantras: Wisdom of the Sages* (Mumbai: Jaico Publishing House, 2017), 30.

15 Masih, *The Understanding of Guruship in Neo-Guruism*, 10.

16 Swami, *The Ancient Science of Mantras*, 30.

17 Masih, *The Understanding of Guruship in Neo-Guruism*, 10.

the *Dīkṣā Guru* as a righteous person. The *Dīkṣā Guru*, it maintains, "is a person, who has realised through *Bhakti*, the Supreme Lordship of God over the universe as 'the other' and man as His creatures." Śrī Ramanujacharya belongs to this school of thought.[18]

Guru as God

The idea of *Guru* as God is the development of the *Upaniṣadic Brahman-Atman* identification. Another idea is that the *Guru* should be learned in the scriptures and should be established in *Brahman*.[19] Furthermore, a *Guru* is one who knows *Brahman* and becomes *Brahman*. Śrī Sankarcharya states: "I bow down to my teacher, a knower of *Brahman*, who has collected for us the nectar of knowledge from the *Vedāntas* like a bee collecting the best honey from the flowers."[20] One of the most important contributions of Sankarcharya is the identification he makes between *Guru* and scriptures. Whenever he refers to scriptures as a source of knowledge, he invariably includes the teacher. He says, "Those who follow both scripture and teacher transcend ignorance."[21] The *Guru* dwells in *Brahman* because he/she is versed in scripture and dwells in *Brahman*.[22]

The Understanding of *Guru* According to Hinduism

Early Vedic literature (the Holy writing of Hinduism) does not have the word *Guru*. Even the idea of *Guru* is absent because Vedic religion was chiefly sacrificial. The word was first used and the concept developed during the *Upaniṣadic* times when the emphasis shifted from sacrifice to *jñāna* (knowledge) as the means to liberation. Someone who knows is needed to impart *jñāna*.[23]

During the *Upaniṣadic* era the *ashram* style was also established. The *Ācārya* who taught the students in the first *ashram* of life was different from the *Ācāryas* of the other three *ashrams*. The first was called *Ācārya-Guru*. The word *Guru* was and is used for many different people, but most commonly and traditionally it has been applied to a teacher, particularly to the one who gives religious instruction.[24]

---

18 Masih, *The Understanding of Guruship in Neo-Guruism*, 10-11.

19 Cf. Abid Mushtaq Wani, *Hinduism, Islam and Sikhism: A Comparative Study* (New Delhi: Educreation Publishing, 2018), 223.

20 Masih, *The Understanding of Guruship in Neo-Guruism*, 11.

21 Masih, *The Understanding of Guruship in Neo-Guruism*, 11.

22 William Cenkner, "The Pandit: The Embodiment of Oral Tradition," *Journal of Dharma* V, no.1 (1980), 24.

23 Masih, *The Understanding of Guruship in Neo-Guruism*, 6.

24 Masih, *The Understanding of Guruship in Neo-Guruism*, 7.

The advent of *Pauranika* and *Tantrika* religions (CE 300) added new connotations to the word *Guru*. A *Guru* was no longer only a teacher. The founder or inventor of a sect or creed also began to be called *Guru*. The followers who preached and propagated the master's doctrines were also referred to as *Gurus*. Thus, in the time of the *Puraṇas* the fundamental essence of guruship was preaching rather than teaching. For the followers of *Tantrika* sects the giver of a *mantra* was *Guru*.[25]

These secret *mantras* were communicated in the ears of the disciples and were called *bija*, *bijaksara mantra*, or the *Guru-mantra*. It was in these *Pauranika* and *Tantrika* sects that the lineage of guruship began to be established. For the line to continue it was considered essential that the *Guru* be married and have sons. Apparently, it was because of this consideration that the father of Balyogeshwar of the Divine Light Mission married a second wife. His first wife— who was alive—is not worshipped because she is not the "mother of God" or the "divine mother."[26]

The *Upaniṣadic Ācārya-Guru* could teach students of any class (except *Śūdra*) without considering caste or creed. But *Tantrika gurus* could give a *mantra* only to the members of their own sect. Naturally a sectarian mentality developed, each group claiming its *Guru* to be supreme.[27]

Saint Kabir (CE 1440-1518), born in the family of a Muslim weaver, raised the status of the *Guru* more than his predecessors. He was influenced by both the Sufis (Muslim mystics) and Hindu *gurus* (especially Ramananda). These two influences caused him to reject the doctrine of *Avatarā* (incarnation), idolatry, rituals, and the authority of all scriptures, whether Koran or Vedas. He substituted the authority of the *Guru* in place of scriptures or incarnations. He preferred to worship the *Guru* in place of idols.[28] It is further remarked,

> *Guru* and God are both standing, whose
> Feet shall I touch first?
> I shall touch yours O *Guru*, for
> You revealed God to me.[29]

Guruism in India

India achieved political independence in 1947, but because our national leadership was a product of Western Civilization, the cultural dominance of the West continued. Expect in the dress of some of our leaders, we continued,

25 Masih, *The Understanding of Guruship in Neo-Guruism*, 7.

26 Masih, *The Understanding of Guruship in Neo-Guruism*, 7.

27 Masih, *The Understanding of Guruship in Neo-Guruism*, 7.

28 Mangalwadi, *The World of Gurus*, 7.

29 Mangalwadi, *The World of Gurus*, 7.

as many felt, to ape the West. Our language, education, politics, economy, judiciary, science, technology, medicine, and entertainment were all heavily westernized. Perhaps this was inevitable and necessary and, in some cases, even good. No doubt we need much more humility to learn from traditions other than our own.[30]

Political independence gave us tremendous self-confidence. The search for our cultural heritage, which had begun in the previous centuries, became more vigorous. Today, indigenous art, sculpture, music, dance, medicine, and language are being rediscovered, as are those things that are more foundational to culture: philosophy, religion, politics, and education. There are voices asking us to be indigenous. The revival of guruism is an important part of this process.[31]

Many *gurus* consciously seek to mould our culture in the light of their philosophy. Swami Sivananda dedicated his Bliss Divine to "the promotion of a happy new civilization and culture built on the blissful atman that pervades all." Swami Krishnananda entitled his three lectures, given at Allahabad University in November 1960, "Resurgent Culture."[32]

Unquestionably, the trend to incorporate indigenous culture into our social life is a good one, but it can and already has been exploited by evil and selfish forces. The path to cultural awareness should not be followed blindly. The institution of guruism, with its teachings and implications, needs to be understood and analysed. Its strengths should be appreciated and its weaknesses seen. Only then should we accept or reject guruism as a cultural phenomenon.[33]

Understanding the Notion of *Guru*: A Post-modern Approach

Postmodernism refers to the intellectual mood and cultural expressions that are becoming increasingly dominant in contemporary society. We are apparently moving into a new cultural epoch, postmodernity, but we must pinpoint in greater detail what the postmodern phenomenon entails.[34] The early evidences of the basic ethos of postmodernism have been largely negative. This ethos flows from a radical rejection of the Enlightenment mind-set that gave rise to modernity. We can find traces of the postmodern ethos everywhere in our society. It constitutes a radical break with the assumptions of the past.[35]

---

30 Cf. Swami Vivekananda, *Lectures Volume 3* (New York: Deutschland, 1896), 156.

31 Vivekananda, *Lectures Volume* 3, 156.

32 Mangalwadi, *The World of Gurus*, 4.

33 Mangalwadi, *The World of Gurus*, 4.

34 Stanley J. Grenz, *A Primer on Postmodernism* (Grand Rapids, Michigan: William B. Eerdmans Publishing Company, 1996).

35 Grenz, *A Primer on Postmodernism*, 13.

India has a very long tradition of *Gurus*. In few cases, fathers and grandfathers acted as *Guru* to their own children and family members and transmitted to them the knowledge of the *Vedas*. The husbands often acts as *gurus* to their wives and taught them the secrets of liberation. Some of the most prominent teachers of ancient India were Vyāsa Vashista, Bharadwaja, Parasara, Vishwamitra, Ashtavakra, Uddalaka Aruni, Yajnavalkya, Satyakama Jabala, Angirasa, etc.[36]

Many divinities also acted as teachers. Brahmā was the most prominent among them, as the original teacher and transmitter of all the *Vedas*. The Tantra tradition recognizes Śiva as a great teacher and world teacher. He is the teacher of Parvati, who in turn transmits the secrets of transcendental knowledge to chosen disciples. Viṣṇu, Kṛṣṇa are considered universal teachers.[37]

Paying respect to a *Guru*, touching the feet of a *Guru*, serving the *Guru* and taking care of his personal needs, praising and appreciating a *Guru*, seeking the blessings of a *Guru*, remembering and meditating on the name of a *Guru* are part of Hindu spiritualism.[38] Some *Guru* traditions hold that their *gurus* have the power to wash away sins, neutralize past *karma*, pass on spiritual energy to chosen disciples, or grant them liberation. Meditating upon a *Guru*'s name or *Guru*'s image are encouraged in many traditions to seek the *Guru*'s blessings (*Guru anugraha*).[39]

In today's world, the reputation of professionals depends upon the school or the university where they study, but, in ancient India the reputation of students depended upon the *Gurus* who initiated them into the study of scriptures. No one would become a *Guru*, unless they were chosen by their teachers and given the permission to teach on their behalf. The order in which the instruction of a spiritual teacher passed from one teacher to another through success generations is known as *gurukarma*. Thus, in Hinduism the relationship between a *Guru* and his students varies from tradition to tradition. Overtime, the role of a *Guru* has also changed. In olden days, there were no printed texts. If students had to learn anything about the hidden teachings of a sacred text, they had to seek the help and instruction of a teacher. Nowadays most of the texts with numerous commentaries are available in public domain and within easy reach. Therefore, to acquire the knowledge of the scriptures, we may not need the assistance of a *Guru*.

---

36 https://deshika.wordpress.com/2016/04/06/post-modern-perspectives-on-the-guru-disciple-relationship/ (29th August 2019).

37 https://deshika.wordpress.com/2016/04/06/post-modern-perspectives-on-the-guru-disciple-relationship/ (29th August 2019).

38 https://www.hinduwebsite.com/hinduism/concepts/guru.asp (2nd September 2019).

39 John A. Saliba, *Understanding New Religious Movement*, Second edition (New York: Altamira Press, 2003), 91.

Unless a *Guru* manifests in our life, we may consider alternatives and focus our effort on self-purification. It may also be noted that if a *Guru* is god in human form, so are we. We are also an aspect of *Brahman* and possesses the same soul and the same potential to achieve the highest wisdom. Hence, our *satguru* (God) is already in us as our very Self (*Isvara*). If we learn to contemplate establish our mind in *satguru* we may not require any external *Guru*.[40]

In Hinduism, there is a provision to consider a sacred scripture, a deity or the very Self as one's guide and *Guru* and develop a mental and intuitive connection. With the help of contemplation, austerities, and self-purification, one may strengthen faith in personal *Guru* of the subtle realm and seek help either to introduce the self to the *satguru* or lead towards light, knowledge and immortality.[41] In ancient times, the *Guru* worked mainly for *shishyas*, or students, imparting knowledge, serving the people around him/her. Today self-serving *gurus* assume divinity to serve material ends, diminishing the concept of God even as they situate themselves as living gods. They risk becoming corrupted by power.[42]

The concept of *Guru* is far more exalted and profound, because he/she is a role model in almost every aspect of a disciple's life. He/she takes on the disciple's *karmic* debt and leads him/her out of it, to whatever extent possible, not just in one life, but possibly over future lives as well. It is imperative for the *Guru* to ensure the disciple's spiritual transformation. This responsibility is far greater than that of the *Guru* playing the role of a mother or performing the duty of a father.[43] In principle, a *Guru* is not a person but a concept that embodies infinite wisdom and universal knowledge. Thus, in a *Guru*-disciple relationship, the disciple emulates not the person he/she refers to as *Guru*, but his/her *gunas* (qualities). There are several examples in history where a *Guru* has inspired disciples without being physically present.[44]

Conclusion

A *Guru* is one who leads to the path of enlightenment. *Gurus* are guides to self-knowledge. They projects an air of absolute certainly not only about his/her enlightenment but about almost all matters. The guidance by a *Siddha Guru* is singularly directed towards the liberation of the Self from ignorance. Whether

40 https://deshika.wordpress.com/2016/04/06/post-modern-perspectives-on-the-guru-disciple-relationship/ (29th August 2019).

41 https://deshika.wordpress.com/2016/04/06/post-modern-perspectives-on-the-guru-disciple-relationship/ (29th August 2019).

42 Saliba, *Understanding New Religious Movement*, 91.

43 Hingori, *Guru Sūtra*, 10.

44 Hingori, *Guru Sūtra*, 10.

a Guru appears as healer, sage, prophet or guide, his/her role is to catalyse the unmasking of the divinity within humankind by displacing our ignorance with light. A true *Guru* inspires to walk the path of resoluteness and conviction. He/she invokes incredible feelings of strength, divinity, love, acceptance and fullness in the depth of the true Self. A Guru is an embodiment of truth and compassion.

12

A Study on Aloysius Pieris' Living Encounter of Religious Pluralism

Aorenla Longchar

Introduction

Our contemporary world is becoming religiously diverse in variety of ways. Religious diversity is also experienced traditions within the religions. Religious pluralism calls for coexistence, cooperation and respect of all traditions. To recognize the values of other religions is the heart of religious pluralism. This article is an exploration Aloysius Pieris' experiences of religious diversity and his attitude towards other religions. Pieris does not claim himself as religious pluralist, nevertheless he has contributed various features of religious pluralism in his willingness to learn from other religions for building a peaceful society.

Life and The Contribution of Aloysius Pieris

Aloysius Pieris was born in 1934 in Sri Lanka. He is a Jesuit priest who earned a doctoral degree in Buddhist Philosophy from the University of Sri Lanka in Colombo in 1972. Pieris is the founder and Director of the Tulana Research Centre in Kalaniya, Sri Lanka. He earned the first doctorate in Buddhist studies awarded to a non-Buddhist by the University of Sri Lanka. He is viewed as one of Asian Catholic's leading experts on interreligious dialogue. Buddhism in Sri Lanka influenced Pieris very deeply. His dialogue with Buddhism was especially with the Theravada tradition. His experience with Buddhism led him to a deeper reflection in theological understanding, and he assimilated

Buddhist elements into the liturgical celebration of the Mass. His aim was to translate the Christian message within a Buddhist conceptual framework.[1]

Many Christian theologians developed their version of a pluralist option in and out of a long, sincere and penetrating dialogue with people from other faiths. Pieris has also developed a theology of liberation through his encounter with Buddhism in his major work, such as *Asian Theology of Liberation*, *Love Meets Wisdom* and *Fire and Water*. He is regarded as a leading scholar of Asian Liberation Theology and Buddhist-Christian dialogue. His work is a deconstruction of old paradigms and a construction of a truly Asian theology: a holistic, interreligious, and liberative theology, which integrates the best of the liberationist approach and the best of the inculturationist approach into a creative dialogue.

Pieris's Method of Approaching Religion

Pieris' understanding of religion is based on Asian experience. Pieris understand religion in two ways. The first is his method of approaching religion from the history of religions; and the second is his understanding of cosmic and metacosmic dimension of religion from Asian religiousness. Pieris mentions three levels of experiences in religions. These three levels refer to primordial experience, collected memory and interpretation that can be seen in major religions. The primordial experience is the initial experience of individual. For example, the event of Buddha, Jesus and experience of Brahmin and Yahweh. The collective memory is based on the primordial experience and it has a long history to reach the present generation. This experience is kept from age to age and memory is embodied by written records, rites and rituals, life-styles, traditions, festivals, symbols and institutions.[2] The interpretation plays an important role in each religious adherent to shape their religions. For instance, he pointed out that although Christianity was born on Asia soil, when it arrived in Europe, Christianity was Europeanized and in the sixteenth century, Christianity came back to Asia with "one possible interpretation of Christian soteriology."[3] According to Pieris, interpretation is not the explanation of the previous experience to understand new experiences but "utilizing a known vocabulary in a new way to communicate the new experience."[4] For instance, the word Christianity in 'Pentecost' and Buddhism in '*Karma*' has been adopted from past. But, they become new experiences for Christian and

1 Aloysius Pieris, "An Asia Way to Celebrate Eucharist," *Worship*, Vol. 81, No. 4 (2007), 314-328.

2 Aloysius Pieris, *Prophetic Humour in Buddhism and Christianity: Doing Inter-Religious Studies in the Reverential Mode* (Colombo: Ecumenical institute for Study and Dialogue), 108.

3 Pieris, *Prophetic Humour in Buddhism and Christianity*, 110.

4 Pieris, *Prophetic Humour in Buddhism and Christianity*, 108.

Buddhist respectively. Pieris sees 'interpretations' as necessary but he also sees it as danger. So, according to him, interpretation has both positive and negative impacts. He expressed: "It is necessary because, otherwise, a religion cannot become accessible to each successive generation. A religion has to be continually interpreted according to the aspirations, needs, and challenges of each epoch."[5]

Pieris attempts to connect these three levels. There must be an interrelationship between 'primordial experience, collective memory and interpretation' without emphasizing on one level. Pieris criticizes what we have often seen as "only at the level of interpretation without ever touching the first level of experience, which is ineffable and incommunicable but realizable. Moreover, he points out that "one cannot penetrate into the first level of the core experience unless it is mediated by the collective memory of that experience."[6] In brief, we cannot separate these three levels because all of them are very important in the relationship among religions. The core experience of a religion is preserved and protected not only by the basic beliefs and practices that perpetuate its memory, but also by means of "interpretations" that grow around that religion.

Pieris' View on Interreligious Dialogue

One of Pieris' great contributions to theology is that he reconfigures interreligious dialogue at the centre of the liberation theological project. He brings together liberation in Asia with the religions through the model of symbiosis. Pieris develops the notion of basic human communities. These communities are interreligious communities working for justice; and it is in their 'ongoing liberative praxis' that adherents find the uniqueness of their own religious traditions.[7] Here, there is no room for the traditionally understood categories of inclusivism, exclusivism and pluralism. Instead, Pieris uses the categories of syncretism, synthesis and symbiosis.

Syncretism is a 'haphazard mixing of religions', where the interaction actually changes the meanings and values of narratives, rituals and symbols. Synthesis is the creation of a third way from the integration of two or more religions, which destroys the uniqueness and identity of those original religions. However, in basic human communities, symbiosis occur and, 'each religion, challenged by the other religion's unique approach to the liberationist aspiration of the poor... discovers and renames itself in its

---

5 Pieris, *Prophetic Humour in Buddhism and Christianity*, 109.

6 Aloysius Pieris, *Love Meets Wisdom: A Christian Experience of Buddhism* (New Delhi: Intercultural Publications, 1990), 120.

7 Aloysius Pieris, *Fire and Water: Basic Issues in Asian Buddhism and Christianity* (New York: Orbis Books, 1996), 158.

specificity in response to the other approaches.'[8] Pieris further says that basic human community is not a group that has come together for interreligious dialogue. The origin and development, and the culmination of the activities of a basic human communities is ideally the total liberation of nonpersons and nonpeoples. It is within the process of this ongoing liberative praxis that each member of the basic human communities discovers the uniqueness of his or her religion.[9]

The symbiotic liberationist approach is essential, and Pieris vigorously critiques academic interreligious dialogue. Pieris argues that each religion constitutes irreducible differences; therefore the goal in an interreligious encounter is neither syncretism nor synthesis but rather symbiosis. Pieris avoids the terms "syncretism," and "synthesis" in interreligious encounter because they tend to imply the violation of the unique individual identity of each tradition and because they gloss over differences. Syncretism, as Pieris identifies, is an unsystematic way of mixing of religions according to the preference or convenience of a person or group. Similarly, Pieris call synthesis, the creation of something altogether new out of two religions (or more) which destroys the uniqueness and identity of the original religions.

Dialogue with Religion

As observed, Pieris highlights multifaceted religiousness as the specific character that defines Asia within other poor countries in the Third World. He sees other religions as significant and positive elements within one single but progressive economy of God's design of salvation. For Pieris the primary focus of any genuine inter-religious dialogue, that takes place in the basic human communities, is our common calling to God's Reign for which there are many names according to various religious traditions. This common calling implies a return to the liberative core of one's own religion while mutually confirming the common liberative orientation of one another's religion. It is a common call to all religionists for a radical conversion or transformation of the whole universe in its present age with its complex mixture of good and bad, into another age, namely into the reign of God. In the liberative praxis this conversion is not only a turning towards God, but also a turning towards the poor (Mk. 10: 23-25). For Pieris, it is in the context of liberation (dialogue with the poor) that a true conversation between religionists could take place.[10]

---

8 Pieris, *Fire and Water: Basic Issues in Asian Buddhism and Christianity*, 161.

9 Pieris, *Love Meets Wisdom: A Christian Experience of Buddhism*, 3.

10 Aloysius Pieris, *An Asian Theology of Liberation* (New York: Orbis Books, 1988), 107.

Diologue with Culture

Pieris says that for the Church to be truly inculturated, it must be rooted in the liberating aspects of poverty and religiousness. The two-fold process of inculturation and liberation entails, in short, proclaiming to the poor in their own language, the Good news that Jesus is the incarnation of the covenant between the God and the poor.[11] For the success of incultration and liberation, Pieris asserts that the first and most important thing is to initiate a constructive dialogue between two parties. The Church must not simply placate the poor with one-sided promises of a 'future world' or an 'a-cosmic Absolute', but should also be attentive to their material spirituality. Inculturation is the process of local Christian Churches getting involved in the people's struggle for full humanity which eventually gets its roots deeply embedded into the life and culture of the people, most of whom are non-Christians. For Pieris inculturation and liberation, rightly understood, are two names for the same process. He also asserts that inculturation and liberation are two integral dimensions of Asian inter-religious dialogue. At the same time, interreligious dialogue and inculturation which has nothing to do with the poor cease to be ministries of God's Reign.[12] Pieris believes that an authentic Christian theology must search for the Asian face of Christ, which unites the liberating aspects of religion and poverty. The churches' mission in Asia is therefore to discover what is liberating in the religiousness and poverty of the poor by participating in their lives, by being immersed in the local population's struggle for humaneness, and by becoming rooted in the culture of the people.[13]

Pieris' Approaches to Other Religion

Each religion is a singular phenomenon and represents, in a way, a judgement passed on every other religion.[14] When we look at Pieris' ideas towards other religions, we can see every religion has its significant language. It is the uniqueness of each religion. Communicating among religions is like a language game which cannot be seen from a nominalistic perspective. It is not just merely communication. Pieris proposes that this language is "the specificity of self-communicative event" and it is "a specific mode of experiencing reality."[15]

Pieris reduces all given Christian approaches to other faiths to two models: either the "Christ-against-religion" model (neo-orthodox, evangelical, as well as Latin American liberation theologies) or the "Christ-of-religions"

---

11 Pieris, *An Asian Theology of Liberation*, 38.

12 Aloysius Pieris, *God's Reign for God's Poor: A Return to the Jesus Formula* (Kelaniya: Tulana Research Center, 1998), 68.

13 Pieris, *An Asian Theology of Liberation*, 124.

14 Pieris, *Love Meets Wisdom: A Christian Experience of Buddhism*, 17.

15 Pieris, *Fire and Water: Basic Issues in Asian Buddhism and Christianity*, 183.

model (Catholicism's anonymous-Christian theory as well as India's and the World Council of Churches' cosmic Christology). Both approaches conceal a "crypto-colonialist theology of religions ... that keeps our revolutionary rhetoric from resonating in the hearts of the Third World non-Christian majorities."[16] For Pieris the basis and framework for Christian mission and religious encounter should not be Christology (presupposing Christ to be either against or already within other religions) or theology (exploring whether/how other religions recognize God). Rather, Christian approaches to other faiths should be grounded in soteriology, in the "ineffable mystery of salvation," which for Pieris is the divine urge and impulse to liberate and generate "a new humanity."

All religions, including those of the East, share in and contribute to this liberating mystery, which is the only real "absolute" in religious encounter. Mission and dialogue should be based on collaboration with other believers in this mystery. Theological clarifications about the uniqueness of Jesus can follow.[17] Pieris' attitude toward other religions is very relevant for religious pluralism. He accepts the uniqueness of each religion.

Pieris's View on Theology of Religion

Theology of religions is mainly concerned with one's attitude towards other religions. Pieris preferred syncretism, synthesis and symbiosis models instead of using threefold typology—exclusivism, inclusivism and pluralism. The reason is the perception of their own religion as exclusively salvific; the inclusivists who situate the Salvific Absolute in their own religion, but hold it to be secretly operative in other religions, which thus become indirectly salvific. The third school—pluralism—attributes to each religion its unique role in salvation, rejecting as almost irreligious in any attempt at co-opting the other's religion to one's own paradigm of soteriology. For Pieris, "many Asian theologians who condemn both exclusivism and inclusivism as imperialistic get easily thrown into the third slot. They are labelled pluralists,"[18] He argued that that theology of religions based on the mentioned above does not make sense in the Asian context. He says-

> I am embarrassed when I am asked in the classrooms and in public forums whether I am an inclusivist or pluralist. The reason is not that I dismiss the paradigm wherein the three categories

16 Aloysius Pieris, "The Place of Non-Christian Religions and Cultures in the Evolution of Third World Theology," in *Irruption of the Third World: Challenge to Theology,* edited by Virginia Fabella and Sergio Torres (Maryknoll: Orbis Books, 1983), 133-134.

17 Pieris, "The Place of Non-Christian Religions and Cultures in the Evolution of Third World Theology", 144.

18 Pieris, *Fire and Water: Basic Issues in Asian Buddhism and Christianity*, 155.

> (Exclusivism, Inclusivism and Pluralism) do not make sense. For, our starling point is not the uniqueness of Christ or Christianity, or of any other religion. A *fortiori* such as a concern would never be a hidden agenda in any interreligious dialogue that may engage us. Furthermore, interreligious dialogue itself is not a conscious target pursued as something desirable per se, as it is a luxury which the urgency of the socio-political crisis in Asia would not permit.[19]

Pieris acknowledged that his theology is inspired by two fundamental experiences in Asia: his immersion in Buddhist studies and his exposure to Asia's massive poverty. For Pieris, Christianity will achieve real inculturation in Asia and become of Asia only by receiving a double baptism: at the "Jordan of Asian Religiosity" and on the "Calvary of Asian Poverty." The first baptism aims to enter the deep encounter with Asian religiosity and learn from it; meanwhile the second is the option of the Church toward the poor and oppressed people in Asia.[20] First of all, Pieris offers a "core to core" dialogue, a "*communicatio in sacris*" in which Christianity's teachings will be enriched by Buddhism's teaching and *vice versa.* Secondly, Pieris also insists strongly on the uniqueness of religious traditions, yet he aims for a "symbiosis" of mutual work and instruction, a symbiotic multiple belonging.

Towards A Liberative Theology of Religions

Pieris' places himself in the Asian context and holds that authentic theology is always a theology of liberation. According to Pieris there cannot be non-liberational theology. As Pieris always claims, he never invented but *discovered* a theology through a ceaseless baptism into the twofold Asian reality, namely, *many poor and many religions*, the situation he finds himself in. He believes that in order to be an authentic religion, it must have "liberative experience." Pieris conceived a new perspective for Asian Christology based on Asian experiences. For Pieris, two Asian realities, i.e., poverty and religious pluralism, represented the major challenges for Christianity in Asia. He portrayed Jesus as an "Asian Guru" who identified himself with the poor and brought them together to struggle for liberation. He upholds a liberative Christology. He is very positive about religion unlike Marx and others who viewed religion as an obstacle for liberation. He sees in Asian religions the potential for liberation. He has observed that the Basic Christian Communities have revolutionized

19 Pieris, *Fire and Water: Basic Issues in Asian Buddhism and Christianity*, 155-156.

20 Aloysius Pieris, "Two Encounters in My Theological Journey," in *Frontiers in Asian Christian Theology: Emerging Trends*, edited by R. S. Sugirtharajah (New York: Orbis Books, 1994), 141-146.

the ecclesiology in the Asian Churches where inculturation and liberation are conceived as twins in the same womb of praxis.[21] Pieris says,

> ... inculturation is the by-product of an involvement with people rather than the conscious target of the program of action. For it is people that create a culture. It is therefore, from the people with whom one becomes involved that one understands and acquires a culture.[22]

Pieris also realizes the weaknesses of liberation theology and inculturation. Liberation theology tends to neglect Asian religiosity as a means for liberating Asian people. On the other hand, inculturation is not involved in addressing social and political problems. Pieris said that "inculturation is the by-product of involvement with a people rather than the conscious target of a program of action."[23] Inculturation does not have a program for overcoming poverty and injustice in Asia. Hence, he proposed an Asian liberation theology that seriously view Asian religiosity as a means for liberation in the context of social and political circumstances. Pieris believed that Asian religions have a soteriological seed which they are not conscious. Jesus can be understood in the Asian context only if Christianity dares to adopt an Asian soteriological understanding and reflect the essence of liberation. Therefore, for Pieris, "an Asian theology of liberation lies hidden there, waiting to be discovered by those ready to sell all things."[24]

Liberation from poverty, injustice, oppression and discrimination has become one of the tasks for Christian mission. Liberation theology has been seen in different names such as Black theology, Feminist theology, Latin America liberation theology and Asian liberation theology. The reason for these different names is due to the movements that depend on different historical and contextual backgrounds. According to Pieris, Asian religiousness and poverty are the reality of Asia.[25] Asian religiousness is based on cosmic religiosity. So, Pieris said that we should not talk about religion only from metacosmic religiosity. He attempts to point out Asian religiousness is very relevant with a "Semitic approach to human liberation." He stresses that "liberation in the Bible is a religious experience (nonpeople struggling to be people) of the poor, for what liberates is the redeeming love of God, and the final fruit of liberation is the saving knowledge of God."[26] Moreover, he said that liberation in the

21 Pieris, *An Asian Theology of Liberation*, 112.

22 Pieris, *An Asian Theology of Liberation*, 38.

23 Pieris, *An Asian Theology of Liberation*, 39.

24 Pieris, *An Asian Theology of Liberation*, 71.

25 Pieris, *God's Reign for God's Poor: A Return to the Jesus Formula*, 69.

26 Pieris, *God's Reign for God's Poor: A Return to the Jesus Formula*, 123.

Bible is "a joint venture of God and the people (poor) covenanted into one indivisible Saving Reality." Pieris believes that authentic Asian liberation theology will encourage churches to be churches of Asia not churches in Asia because a church in Asia is just an extension of Euro-American churches. Local Church of Asia will be able to promote "Basic Human Communities." In these Basic Human Communities, Christian and non-Christians participate and members of these communities work together for fullness of being humanity.

Towards A Theology of Religious Pluralism

Pieris believes that the spirit of cosmic religion is closely related to religious pluralism. To understand that process, he attempted to show or distinguished 'cosmic' and 'metacosmic' dimensions that are integrated in major religions. He insisted that the framework of Asian religions which led to major religions "are composed of two complementary elements: a cosmic religion functioning as the foundation and a metacosmic soteriology consisting the main edifice."[27] He further points out that the religious socialism of the Asian monks is based on the Metacosmic religiousness that point to a salvific beyond attainable within the person through gnosis. Metacosmic religiousness means not the negation of cosmic reality but a 'non-addiction to cosmic needs.'[28] He contend the relationship between cosmic and metacosmic in this way: the metacosmic is the human heart's infinite potentially that must be dreamed by our imagination, grasped by our intuition, strategized by our reason, actualized by our personal and collective effort, but always under the perennial impulse of love. Thus humankind is the experiential link between the cosmos and the metacosmic.[29] Out of his analysis of the cosmic-metacosmic structure of Asian religions, Pieris builds a theory of *enreligionization*,[30] by which he criticizes both the inculturationist disregard for the liberation of the poor and the liberationist prejudice against religions. Through this new concept, *enreligionization*, Pieris promotes an integrationist Christian radical orthopraxis: a participatory experience of other religions in an interreligious liberative praxis for the liberation of the poor. For Pieris, *enreligionization* means to follow the example of Jesus in the way of a participatory discernment, knowing that religion can become enslaving when it deadens the individual awareness of poverty and sacralizes oppressive systems in alliance with power. He holds that the Asian Christians are called to continually discern the liberative elements from the

27 Pieris, *God's Reign for God's Poor: A Return to the Jesus Formula*, 71.

28 Pieris, *An Asian Theology of Liberation*, 43.

29 Pieris, *Fire and Water: Basic Issues in Asian Buddhism and Christianity*, 52.

30 '*Enreligionization*' or '*inreligionization*' is Pieris' own neologism. Although the term itself is only used occasionally, the idea consistently reappears in most of his articles as the basis for his whole theology.

various religious trends in Asia. He asserts that in spite of their negative aspects, all religions have liberative potential at heart; so, *enreligionization* means to enter into 'core-to-core' dialogue with other religions. For example, by participating in the Buddhist rituals and meditations which retain the liberative core experience of *agapeic* gnosis, Christians can recognize their own core experience of salvation as *gnostic* agape. The theory of *enreligionization* is Pieris' answer to the search for a proper Christian engagement with the complex reality of Asia, in which cosmic and metacosmic religions intermingle with socio-economic and political factors.

Pieris realizes the need for restoring the values of religion. Indeed, there is a gap between practice and doctrine among most religionists. Moreover, since religion is a very sensitive thing, we need to be very careful with other religions. He believes that when we deal with other religions, 'fairness' and 'fidelity' are very important. According to Pieris, a Christian 'theology of religious pluralism' has to be a blend of two obligations: fidelity to what is unique in Christian faith, and fairness towards other religionists' distinctive otherness.[31] Pieris opts for a pluralistic approach based on the foundation for an interreligious theology of religion. He suggests that the poor are God's people regardless of their religious affiliation, so that interreligious alliances can be formed in which the liberating elements from all religions should be employed in service of a common practice.

Pieris focuses on building the Church of Asia through "the Jordan baptism" to be truly inculturated with the Asian religions. It means that interreligious engagement is not much about intricate doctrines and histories, but it is about concrete relationship. One cannot build relation only through texts and theories, but it is possible only under the tutelage of an experienced guide, through a baptism in the Jordan, through tradition, rites and practices. IN this context, Pieris calls interreligious dialogue a *communication in sacris*—a religious communication through the total immersion in the religious practice and learning the language. However, true interreligious dialogue is when one penetrate the experiential level to the core level and build "core to core dialogue."[32] Pieris points out his immersion in Buddhism brought him to experience the necessity of a "core to core" dialogue between Christianity's *agape* and Buddhism's *gnosis* and vice versa. Love (*agape*) and wisdom (*gnosis*) are not mutually exclusive; rather *agape* and *gnosis* are each by itself

---

31 Aloysius Pieris, "Towards a Theology of Religious Pluralism: Fidelity and Fairness in Inter-faith Fellowship" in *Towards A Planetary Theology: Along the Many Paths of God* edited by Jose Maria Vigil (Canada: Dunamis Publishers, 2010), 123.

32 Frederix Glorieux, "Does Christ Have an Asian Face? An Analysis of Aloysius Pieris' Theology of Religions," *Louvain Studies* 30 (2005), 336.

inadequate to experience and express the Ultimate and therefore need each other.[33]

Towards A Mutual Co-Existence of Religions

Pieris says that each religious tradition is a singular phenomenon and is in a way a judgment passed on every other religion and is therefore in their nature to provoke comparison and mutual criticism, confrontation and reciprocal correction.[34] Pieris applies the dialogical integrationist approach to the study of his radical ecclesiology and Christology. In his search for an Asian way of doing theology, Pieris discovers the importance of the Church's humble immersion into the religious experience of the non-Christian poor. To him, this vision will only be possible when the Church becomes a communion of the basic human communities or the Kingdom communities, the locus of the twofold liberating praxis: the *gnostic* detachment and the *agapeic* involvement. Pieris calls this a 'Christopraxis' from which his liberation Christology of religious pluralism has been derived. He emphasizes that the salvific meaning of Christ is not to be drawn from metaphysical speculation but to be discovered in the process of liberating praxis, which is always 'interreligious' in Asia. He promotes a symbiotic model of interreligious collaboration for the liberation of the poor, which does not dilute the unique identity of each religion. Thus, in his ecclesiology and Christology, Pieris integrates theory with praxis and Christianity with other religions in the holistic vision of God's Kingdom which is already present and operative among the poor in Asia.

Conclusion

In recent decades a number of methods have been formulated to address issues associated with Christian theology of religions that attempt to articulate the understanding of other religions while maintaining the integrity of Christian claims. Pieris attitude towards other religions is relevant in religious pluralism. He accepts the uniqueness of each religion; rejects syncretism and theology that ignores the poor. Religious Pluralism portrays a world that has moved "beyond mere toleration" toward the active engagement with religious difference. Interreligious dialogue is the practice of religious pluralism. It is a tool for reconciliation, mutual understanding and mutual enrichment among religions. It will help not only learning other religions but also enhancing one' own religion. Authentic dialogue has no place for a hidden agenda in

33 Peter C. Phan, "Multiple Religious Belonging: Opportunities and Challenges for Theology and Church," in *Being Religious Interreligiously* (New York: Orbis Books, 2004), 78.

34 Aloysius Pieris, "Western Christianity and Asian: A Theological reading of Historical Encounters," *Dialogue*, New Series VII 2 (1980), 49.

each side. Religious tensions among different religionists can be reduced by authentic dialogue. Moreover, dialogue can promote a spirit of cooperation. But, Dialogue is not an end in itself, nor is there any preoccupation about one's religious identity or uniqueness. Dialogue for dialogue's sake is pointless as it becomes mere intellectual exercise. .

13

Islāmic Studies: A Post-Modern Approach

Pamhor Thumra

Introduction

The paper on Islāmic Studies: A Post-Modern Approach attempts to analyse the approaches, prospects and challenges of Islāmic studies in the post-modern period with special reference to the contribution of Henry Martyn Institute, Hyderabad, in Islāmic studies. The article discusses two important paradigms of Islāmic studies. It relates to the approach of Islāmic in the late modern period, followed by the trends of Islāmic studies in the post-modern period marking a significant change in the approach to Islāmic studies. It further discusses the future direction of Islāmic studies in relation to the approaches, prospects and challenges of Islāmic studies in contemporary India.

Henry Martyn: A Brief History

The Henry Martyn Institute was established in commemoration to Henry Martyn's contribution towards Indian Muslims. Born in Truro, Great Britain in 1781, Henry Martyn came to India in 1806 at the young age of 25. The same year he reached Serampore, West Bengal and worked as a Military Chaplain of the East India Company.[1] He spent much time in learning Hindustani language

1 Wilma S. Stewart, "Henry Martyn and Serampore," in *The Bulletin of Christian Institutes of Islāmic Studies* LIII/1 (April 1964), 13.

for mission towards the Muslims.[2] He was engaged in preaching Christianity to the Muslims and translation of the Bible, besides other activities. During this period, Persian was one of the important languages used by the Indian Muslims. It was important for him to obtain a translation of the New Testament in Persian in order to reach out to the Indian Muslims. By the end of March 1811, at the age of 30, he set out for Persia. He finally reached Persia on 21st May. It was here in Shīrāz (Iran), Martyn sat down for his translation works. During this period, he had dialogues with Muslim scholars on Christianity. On the 24th of February 1812, he finally completed the translation of Persian New Testament. Unfortunately, on his way to Constantinople on the 14th October 1812, he passed way due to prolonged sickness and ill health at the age of 32.[3]

The Henry Martyn Institute and Islāmic Studies

The Henry Martyn Institute—which was initially a School—was established in the early 1930 at Lahore[4] (present day Pakistan). The name was suggested by L. Bevan Jones "after the pioneer missionary among Muslims in India."[5] The Henry Martyn Institute has been engaging in the study of religions[6]—especially Islāmic studies,[7] interfaith dialogue, and Christian-Muslim relations.

---

2 George Koovackal, "Henry Martyn Institute of Islāmic Studies" (Master Thesis, Aligarh Muslim University, 1981), Appendix No. 1.

3 John Elder, "Henry Martyn in Iran," in *The Bulletin of Christian Institutes of Islāmic Studies* LIII/1 (April 1964), 23-24, 32.

4 With the collaboration of inter-denominational missionary societies, the Henry Martyn School of Islāmic Studies was founded on 27th January1930 with Mr. Bevan Jones as the Principal, and L.E. Brown and J.A. Subḥān as the Staff members. Andreas D'Souza, "Introduction," in *From Converting the Pagan to Dialogue with Our Partners: HMI's Fifty Works of Evangelism and Interfaith Relations*, edited by Andreas D' Souza (Hyderabad/New Delhi: HMI/ISPCK, 2009), xiii-xvi; see also the work of T.I. Chinniah, "An Examination of the History of the Henry Martyn Institute of Islāmic Studies and Its Evaluation" (B.D. Thesis, Senate of Serampore College, 1975), 16-28.

5 John A. Subhan, "Henry Martyn Institute of Islāmic Studies, Hyderabad," in *Al-Basheer: The Bulletin of Christian Institute of Islāmic Studies* 1/2 (April-June 1972), 18; David T. Lindell, "Henry Martyn Institute of Islāmic Studies," in *From Converting the Pagan to Dialogue with Our Partners: HMI's Fifty Works of Evangelism and Interfaith Relations*, edited by Andreas D' Souza (Hyderabad/New Delhi: HMI/ISPCK, 2009), 27; Subhan, "Henry Martyn Institute of Islāmic Studies, Hyderabad," in *Al-Basheer*, 13; Diane D' Souza, *Evangelism, Dialogue, Reconciliation: The Transformative Journey of the Henry Martyn Institute* (Hyderabad: Henry Martyn Institute, 1998), 7.

6 This paper specially focuses on HMI in relation to Islamic Studies. It may be stated that apart from the study of religions, HMI is involved in praxis oriented programmes and researches.

7 The Institute since its establishment was a centre for Islamic Studies. After the Institute's affiliation to the Senate of Serampore University in recent years, the study of religions has been extended to Hinduism and others.

Later, the Institute was moved to different parts of India until it finally settled at Hyderabad in 1970. In HMI's 89 years of service, it has undergone tremendous change in approaches to the study of religion and interfaith relations.[8]

The Early Thrust for Evangelism

The approach to the study of religion, especially Islām in the modern period was overwhelmingly evangelism oriented. For instance, many Christian missionaries who came to India and encountered with Indian Muslims at the beginning of the 20th century felt the need to learn Islām. This mission towards Indian Muslims was one of the bases for founding Henry Martyn School. Different missionary conferences voiced the need for mission among Muslims: the Cairo Mission Conference in 1906; Edinburg Conference in 1910; Lucknow Conference in 1911; and the National Christian Council (NCC, now known as National Council of Churches in India) in 1924 and 1926. The NCC proposed to open courses on Islāmic Studies in Arabic, Islāmic History, Theology, Law, Culture, and Arts—including language studies on Persian, Pushtu, and Urdū. These courses were open for those missionaries and clergies who were interested in works among Muslims. The approach to the study of Islām can be understood by studying the aim and objective at the founding of this School. It attempts to "... use every means to enable the messengers of the Gospel in India to commend Christ acceptable to Muslims."[9] The approach was therefore apologetic in nature and missionizing in outcome. It further adds

> The members of the staff were to undertake the study of various phases of Indian Islām, publish the results of their studies for the benefit of workers in the field. Produce Christian literature suited to the needs of the day, and to constitute themselves into a teaching body, both for missionaries from the West who desire to devote themselves to work among Muslims and for the training of Indian clergy, ministers and other workers...[10]

In the event of the registration of HMI under the Company's Act, Madras, the Board of Management Committee underlined the objectives of HMI:

> To assist the church and other institutions to realize and fulfil their evangelistic obligations to Muslims by fostering an adequate and sympathetic understanding of Islām.

---

8 Souza, *Evangelism, Dialogue, Reconciliation*, 3.

9 The proceedings of the 3rd meeting of the NCC, 1929, cited by Souza, "Introduction," in *From Converting the Pagan to Dialogue with Our Partners*, xvi.

10 Chinniah, "An Examination of the History of the Henry Martyn Institute of Islāmic Studies and Its Evaluation," 67.

To conduct Islāmic studies and the comparative study of religions in such theological colleges or seminaries of the churches in India, willing to cooperate.

To organize seminars and conference for the study in the practical issues of evangelism and questions relating to life and development in contemporary Islām in India.

To direct and assist in elementary studies of Islām for the local congregation.

To develop and maintain libraries to be made available to staff and students for study and research.

To publish books and reporters, periodicals, bulletins, pamphlets, tracts, handbills and other publications for use among staff and students and others.[11]

The aforementioned objectives further translate that the School attempts to study Islām and comparative study of religions by fostering a sympathetic attitude towards Islām and Muslims. Nevertheless, this sympathetic approach was grounded in the zeal and burden to bring the Muslims to the Christian fold.

In the initial days of the School, students were taught in the comparative study of Islām and Christianity. Their main activities remain evangelism. For example, John A. Subḥān edited the bi-monthly journal *Ukhuwwat* in Urdū for the presentation of the gospel to the Muslims.[12] Meanwhile, the School had extension department carried out for course lectures on Islām to different colleges such as Bishop's College, Kolkata, and Serampore College, Kolkata. J.W. Sweetman and J.A. Subḥān went to different part of North and South India for seminars and lectures on Islām and Christianity. Students from many part of India and abroad came to participate in the school. Some of the prominent participants were Rev. M.G. MacLeod the Principal of Westminster in Oxford and Dr. Wilfred Cantwell Smith who was the Director of Islāmic Studies at McGill University, Montreal, Canada.[13]

The Study of Islām in Post-Modern Era: A Dialogical Approach

If the early period of HMI's engagement in Islāmic studies was primarily evangelism, the 2nd half of the 20th century was an era of dialogue. However,

11 Chinniah, "An Examination of the History of the Henry Martyn Institute of Islāmic Studies and Its Evaluation," 67-68.

12 Subhan, "Henry Martyn Institute of Islāmic Studies, Hyderabad," in *Al-Basheer*, 19; Chinniah, "An Examination of the History of the Henry Martyn Institute of Islāmic Studies and Its Evaluation," 30.

13 Subhan, "Henry Martyn Institute of Islāmic Studies, Hyderabad," in *Al-Basheer*, 20-22.

the shift from evangelism approach to dialogue was not a sudden change. The 50s and 60s were the intervening decades as HMI responded to the call of the Church for interfaith relations and reconciliation. When the School became Institute in 1960, the objective of the Institute still reads as "to assist the Church to fulfil its evangelistic obligation by fostering among the Christians an adequate and sympathetic understanding of Islām"[14] In 1947, an article written by John Ṣādiq—the then NCC Secretary—"Plea for a Fresh Approach to Muslims," appeared in Bulletin of the Henry Martyn School of Islāmic Studies on the need to see Christian evangelism, not as an aggressive attack on Muslims and their religion but a relation to the Muslim word shaped by "a spirit of guidance, humility and understanding love."[15] This article along with many others signifies the change in the Institute's attitude and approach in the study of Islām and their approach towards Muslims.

Ian H. Douglas[16] initially introduced the concept of dialogue in the Bulletin of HMI. He said that "even if Christian-Muslim meeting is a long way off, there is a real hope of true dialogue here and there at the highest intellectual level. And the preparation of Christians in study conferences under able leadership increases the possibilities."[17] Douglas in his editorial in Bulletin of the Henry Martyn Institute of Islāmic Studies, 1960, expresses the need for relations between religions.[18] In John Carman's review of Kenneth Craqq's *Call of the Minaret*, the former asked if Craqq's call—to be understanding of Muslims—can be extended to the Hindus and Buddhist.[19] He suggested bracketing all theological judgment about Islām. From 'comparison' HMI began to engage Muslims towards a sincere effort for dialogue.

The change in approach to the study of Islām led to numbers of seminars for Christian and Muslim relations. This trend became an integral part of the Institute's objective. Dialogue with Muslims was an approach discussed by Kenneth Cragg in Christian Institute for the Study of Religion and Society (CISRS) and HMI joint collaboration in 1960. In what was once a one-sided Christian study of Islām often with a missionizing and superiority complex,

---

14 Koovackal, "Henry Martyn Institute of Islāmic Studies," 92.

15 John W. Sadiq, "Plea for a Fresh Approach to Muslims," in *Bulletin of the Henry Martyn School of Islāmic Studies* XXXIII (Jan-March 1947), 3-4; Souza, *Evangelism, Dialogue, Reconciliation*, 8-9.

16 He was the Director of the Institute from 1962-1967.

17 Christian W. Troll, *Christian-Muslim Relations in India: A Critical Survey* (Bangalore: Association for Islāmic Studies, 1980), 17.

18 Ian H. Douglas, "Contiguity and Constraint," in *The Bulletin of the Henry Martyn Institute of Islāmic Studies* ILVIII/1 (Jan-March 1960), 1; also see, Souza, *Evangelism, Dialogue, Reconciliation*, 14.

19 John Carman, "Craqq's Call to Understanding," in *Bulletin of the Henry Martyn School of Islāmic Studies* ILVII (July-Sept 1959), 26.

the approach to the study of Islām became a collaborative effort whereby both Muslims and Christians actively participate together towards understanding Islām. For instance, a seminar on "Faith and Works" held on October 19-22, 1965 with the Islāmic Institute (Delhi) in Nagpur had Christians and Muslims presentations on interfaith dialogue. It was a first of its kind. It became a meeting point for Muslims and Christians—and a new chapter in the relation of these communities. A similar programme was held in Hyderabad in which John Taylor, Reader of the Islāmic Studies at the Selly Oaks Birmingham and Rev. Fr. Dr. Wijngaards gave speeches on the need for Christian-Muslim relations. In this seminar, Dr. Syed 'Abdul Laṭīf presented a paper on common grounds between Christianity and Islām and Prof. Yūsuf-ud-Dīn, Head of the Department on Comparative Religion at Osmania University lectured on "Christianity and Islām—the Need for Better Understanding." He underlined on the need for relationship between Christians and Muslims.[20] The approach for interfaith relations became a collaborative joint effort of both Christians and Muslims.

A dialogue soon followed in a seminar in Rajpur in 1968 on "Muslim-Christian Seminar" and the themes presented were on "The Crisis of Relevance," "Islām in the Modern World," "Religion in the Modern World," "Christian Faith and Secular Life," "The Relevance of Islām to the Modern World," among others by both Christian and Muslim Scholars. In 1968, Ian H. Douglas' "Muslim-Christian Seminar, Rajpur, March 1968" which appeared in The Bulletin of Christian Institute of Islāmic Studies (1969) asserts that dialogue is not a compromise of the gospel but an "expression of loyalty" whose purpose is "to come together as strong men [*sic*], convinced that God is with both of us."[21]

The period from 1970 saw increased attention on Christian-Muslim dialogue: there were dialogues on themes such as "Christian Witness Among the Muslims" in 1971 and in 1975 there was a seminar on "Christian-Muslim Interaction in India" where the participants were scholars of both Muslim and Christian communities. This was followed by dialogue on "Mosque and Church: Their Contribution to Inter-Religious Harmony and Reconciliation" jointly sponsored by Indian Institute of Islāmic Studies (IIIS) in New Delhi, Catholic Bishops' Conference of India (CBCI) and HMI in 1978. In 1980—HMI's Golden Jubilee— a Delhi seminar was jointly organized by HMI,

---

20 Subhan, "Henry Martyn Institute of Islāmic Studies, Hyderabad," in *Al-Basheer*, 22-23. "Editorial," in *The Bulletin of the Henry Martyn Institute of Islāmic Studies* LV/1 (April 1966), 1; Chinniah, "An Examination of the History of the Henry Martyn Institute of Islāmic Studies and Its Evaluation," 86; Souza, *Evangelism, Dialogue, Reconciliation*, 16.

21 Ian H. Douglas, "Muslim-Christian Seminar: Rajpur, March '68," in *The Bulletin of Christian Institute of Islāmic Studies* III/1 (July 1969), 20-28.

Dialogue Commission of the CBCI and the Jamia Millia Islāmia on the theme "Religious Education in Secular India."[22]

The Institute opened up new partnership for dialogue with Islāmic study centres. One such partnership was with the Indian Institute of Islāmic Studies in New Delhi (IIIS). The IIIS and HMI seminar on "Mosque and Church: Their Contribution to Inter-Religious Harmony and Reconciliation" had papers from Syed Vaḥīduddīn, former Head of Department of Philosophy at Delhi University who points out the Qur'ānic basis for interfaith dialogue and Ziāul Ḥasan Fārūqī, the former Principal of Jamia Millia Islāmia who calls for the need on the part of the religious community to open up for dialogue. Z.H. Fārūqī asserts the importance of an objective study of religious tradition—a reversal of traditional exclusivist attitude and an increased effort for relationship.[23]

This seminar also observed that Christian institutes have incorporated and studied a number of subjects for Islāmic studies. Prof. Iqbāl Ansārī, Director of the Institute of Islāmic Studies at Aligarh University expressed the need to incorporate the study of Christian teachings or religions as the Christians or other religious adherents see it. It was observed that Madrasa syllabus does provide a study on Christian faith though within the Islāmic framework.[24] Some of the commitments of the seminar was "fostering the teaching of Islām in Christian institutions of religious learning and *vice versa*; to check, in a scholarly manner, any educational material as to its fairness in dealing with matters pertaining to either Christianity or Islām"; and also "to initiate and foster theological thinking about central questions touching the faith and ethical teachings of both religions."[25] Thus, it may be observed that from the 1930s till the 1950s the approach of the School remained evangelistic. But since the 1960s to the present, HMI has been consciously working towards an objective and dialogical approach to the study of Islām in particular and religion in general.

Prospects and Challenges of Islāmic Studies: Future Directions

The study of Islām is dynamic—it is a continuous study gathering to the changing needs of the particular community and the society at large. One of the issues or difficulties often expressed in Islāmic studies is the space of critical interpretation. This includes a historical-critical interpretation of the Qur'ān, the Sunna of the Prophet, Islāmic Jurisprudence, and other critical study in relation to Islām. It remains to be seen as to how far post-modern approach to the study of religion which critically analyses 'conventional established

22 Koovackal, "Henry Martyn Institute of Islāmic Studies," 70-74.

23 Troll, *Christian-Muslim Relations in India: A Critical Survey*, 31-33.

24 Troll, *Christian-Muslim Relations in India: A Critical Survey*, 33.

25 Troll, *Christian-Muslim Relations in India: A Critical Survey*, 34.

truth' work in the study of Islām. Islāmic studies cannot rest on conventional explanation with little scope on the part of the reader for re-interpretation. This amounts to monolithic understanding of religion.

The future directions of Islāmic studies in India cannot ignore the theological and philosophical inquiries of the people. If Islām has to remain relevant to the Muslims, the religious leaders and the educated Muslims must gather to the intellectual needs of the Muslims. It cannot afford to ignore the social, economic, religious, educational, and political realities of the Muslims. Islāmic studies must answer to these issues.

The Rediscovery of Philosophical Inquiry

While the scope of Islāmic studies has incorporated many areas of Islāmic studies, subsequent attention may be made in the subject of philosophy. Islāmic scholars, especially in the medieval centuries, have been the main proponent on the study of philosophy and relative and comparative study of philosophy. Early Muslims' study of Greek philosophy in the medieval period is unparalleled in the history of the world. In the Islāmic East, especially in the Abbasid period (750-1258), a major study of Greek philosophy took place. The Mu'tazilites, followed by early philosopher such as Al-Kindī (d.866), Al-Fārābī (d. 951), Ibn Sīnā (d. 1037) among others, worked upon the interpretation of the nature of reality. In the Islāmic West, there were philosophers like Mālik ibn Wuhayb (d. 1130), Ibn Bājjah (d. 1138), and the famous Ibn Rushd (d. 1198), among others.

The science of philosophical inquiry is indispensable in Islāmic studies, apart from the theological interpretation of the religious text. Further studies on the rediscovery of the philosophical inquiry into the nature of Islām, its revelation, and the texts which are the basic fundamental of religions are indispensable in contemporary Islām. It is an attempt to present Islām both theologically and philosophically viable. Philosophy, which is identified as *ḥikma* (wisdom), is an important element in Islām. Al-Kindī, one of the early Islāmic philosophers says that it is the knowledge of the reality of things; a knowledge of the truth.[26] Seyyed Ḥossein Naṣr viewed that philosophy is deeply rooted within the worldview of the Qur'ānic revelation. One of the important Islāmic philosophers to be studied in our times is Ibn Rushd. He was both a rational philosopher and also a devout chief religious head of Cordoba (Spain).[27]

---

26 Seyyed Hossein Nasr, "The Meaning and Concept of Philosophy in Islām," in *History of Islāmic Philosophy*, part I, edited by Seyyed Hossein Nasr and Oliver Leaman (London: Routledge, 1996), 25.

27 Seyyed Hossein Nasr, "Introduction," in *History of Islāmic Philosophy*, part I, edited by Seyyed Hossein Nasr and Oliver Leaman (London: Routledge, 1996), 16.

It is a matter of fact that philosophical inquiry into the nature of religions—to a large extent—made way for theological interpretation after the Medieval Muslim history. One witnesses this phenomenon after the death of Ibn Rushd in the Islāmic West. It would not be out of context to assert that philosophical inquiry into the nature of religion to a large extent in many parts of Islāmic societies—including India—have witnessed less interest. There is a dichotomy between reason and faith, or reason and revelation. There has always been a school of thought which opines that philosophy and revelation are unbridgeable; that Islām is a revealed religion and philosophy is a foreign science mostly inspired by Greek philosophy.[28]

There are many discourses in Islām which is highly philosophical, thereby necessitating a rational response. Philosophy should, in this sense, give another approach of reasoning. In this context, the thesis of Ibn Rushd in his *Decisive Treatise* (*faṣl al-Maqāl*) is an important example. In his defence of philosophy in the study of religion, he provided philosophical reasoning in what was a theological debate in relation to the knowledge of particulars,[29] on God and the eternity of the world,[30] the soul in relation to life after death[31] and on the existence of God.[32]

It is important to re-assert Ibn Rushd's thesis that Islām and philosophy are not incompatible; that Islām is a rational system of belief requiring rational arguments. It is important to re-establish the Qur'ānic injunction which obligates the study of philosophy; that the Law recommended its study.[33] For instance, the Qur'ānic injunction in 59:2 reads "... reflect you have vision"; 7:185 "have you not studied the kingdom of the heavens and the earth and whatever things God has created?" among others. It is important to focus on what Ibn Rushd said in his *Decisive Treatise* that "truth does not oppose truth but accords with it and bears witness to it;"[34] that such study does not contradict the Scripture. The study of philosophy in Islāmic studies is important because both Scripture and philosophy are sources of the same truth, which is factual, descriptive and about an objective world.[35] For this reason, it has been observed

28 George F. Hourani, *Reason and Tradition in Islāmic Ethics* (Cambridge: Cambridge University Press, 1985), 6.

29 Averroes, *Decisive Treatise and Epistle Dedicatory*, translated by Charles E. Butterworth (Utah: Brigham Young University Press, 2001), xli, 12.

30 Ibn Rushd, *Faslul-al-Maqal*, translated by Hamid Naseem Rafiabadi and Aadil Amin Kak (New Delhi: Sarup and Sons, 2003), 17-20.

31 M. Saeed Sheikh, *Islāmic Philosophy* (London: The Octagon Press, 1962), 135.

32 Majid Fakhry, *Averroes: His Life, Work and Influence* (Oxford: One World, 2001), 29.

33 Averroes, *On The Harmony of Religion and Philosophy*, translated by George F. Hourani (Oxford: E.J.W. Gibb Memorial Trust, 1961), 44, 84.

34 Averroes, *Decisive Treatise and Epistle Dedicatory*, xxvi.

35 Averroes, *On The Harmony of Religion and Philosophy*, 22-23.

that the philosophical approach to the study of Islām cannot be reduced to the issue of faith and reason or between religion and philosophy. Seyyed Ḥossein Naṣr observed that Islāmic philosophical study is Islāmic in nature, because, philosophy functions in a universe dominated by the Qur'ānic revelation and the manifestation of the divine principle. For example, an Islāmic inquiry into the nature and knowledge of God philosophize the unity of God within the language of Islāmic idea and concept.[36]

The Call for Ijtihād

Intellectual freedom is an important aspect of Islāmic studies. Ijtihād is the way forward in Islāmic studies. However, this is easier said than done. Wilfred Cantwell Smith's remarked that Muslims are "too bewildered to ask systematic questions about its own"[37] stands true even today to a large extent. The wave of a critical study of religious traditions has scarcely impacted the Indian landscape. While a historical-critical study of religion is encouraged, it becomes much more complex when an individual belonging toacertain religious group does a criticalstudyof anotherreligion. It is, for this reason, Aṣaf A. A. Fyzee once remarked that it is the Muslims who can criticize Islām; that Muslims can tell fellow believers on how to be a better Muslim and to reform Islām.[38]

'Irfān A. 'Umar's study of Maulānā Waḥiduddīn Khān's renewal of the 'Spirit of Islām,' reiterates the imperative of ijtihād. Critique—based on sound reasoning and argument—for Khan is an important requirement for the renewal of Islām.[39] Ijtihād by its very definition implies a conscious effort in presenting the message of Islām in every generation. It is for this reason a mujtahid is tasked with interpreting the message of Islām in changing contexts and situation without altering the core principle of Islām. It is an adaptation based on the principle of interpretation.[40] It is a call for a critical view of blind

---

36 See, Oliver Leaman, "Introduction," in *History of Islāmic Philosophy*, part I, edited by Seyyed Hossein Nasr and Oliver Leaman (London: Routledge, 1996), 1-3; also see, Nasr, "Introduction," in *History of Islāmic Philosophy*, 11, 17-18.

37 Wilfred Cantwell Smith, "Universities Studies of Religion in a Global Context," in *Study of Religion in Indian Universities* (A Report of the Consultation held in Bangalore in September, 1967), 81.

38 Cited by Mushir-Ul-Haq, *Islām in Secular India* (Simla: Indian Institute of Advanced Study, 1972), 79-80.

39 Irfan A. Omar, "Ijtihād as intellectual Jihād: Renewal of the 'Spirit of Islām' in Maulana Wahiduddin Khan's Thought," in *Journal of the Henry Martyn Institute* 37/1 (Jan-June 2018), 2.

40 Waheedulla Hussaini Quadri Multani, "Significance of Ijtihād (Reasoning) in Islām," in *Journal of the Henry Martyn Institute* 35/1 (Jan-June 2016), 86. Omar, "Ijtihād as intellectual Jihād: Renewal of the 'Spirit of Islām' in Maulana Wahiduddin Khan's Thought," 7.

following (*taqlīd*)—towards a jihād (striving) for the best. Because, when *taqlīd* gains more prominence than ijtihād, the Sharī'ah losses its dynamism and hence the Muslim community is stagnated[41] in terms of interpretation. Ijtihād is reading of the past with a fresh eye, revisiting the interpretation and reasoning in the light of the present context.[42]

Khān pointed out the rift between what is understood as a religious and secular dimension. In this case, many Muslims live with this dichotomy of religious life often opposing the national, cultural identity of the society. It is in this context that the case for harmonizing the rift between the religious and secular factor have to be pursuit by the scholars in Islāmic studies. This according to Khān has been poorly responded by the 'Ulamā'.[43]

The case for ijtihād in Madrasa education is another important issue brought forward by Khān—which according to him—has failed to instil independent reasoning to the students. The issue of being resistant to change or the fear of upsetting the 'status quo' is another issue. It is for this reason, Khān says that in most of the peoples' mind they are unwilling to see and adapt to the change around them; that they are unable to provide a sustainable and meaningful response to the ever-growing changes.[44] Maulānā Waḥīduddīn Khān says that the 'Spirit of Islām' would mean addressing the issue in which Muslim live in—a response to the signs of the times.[45] In response to the ways of doing ijtihād in the present context, Maulānā Khān mentions three ways of understanding jihād: 'Jihād of the Pen'—which is for the scholars involved in intellectual pursuit; 'Jihād of Compassion'—which is the struggle to witness one's faith to others; and 'Jihād of a Social Activist'—which is a struggle for solidarity as a response to the context of the society transcending beyond religion, nationality, ethnicity, cultures[46] and so on.

41 Multani, "Significance of Ijtihād (Reasoning) in Islām," 89; Mushir-Ul-Haq also assesses that while the Qur'ān and Ḥadīth is considered as the source of law, the main contention between the modernist and fundamentalist Muslim have been on the issue of the sole right of the 'Ulamā' to interpret the Sharī'ah. See, Haq, *Islām in Secular India*, 64-65.

42 Omar, "Ijtihād as intellectual Jihād: Renewal of the 'Spirit of Islām' in Maulana Wahiduddin Khan's Thought," 9; Multani, "Significance of Ijtihād (Reasoning) in Islām," 88.

43 Omar, "Ijtihād as intellectual Jihād: Renewal of the 'Spirit of Islām' in Maulana Wahiduddin Khan's Thought," 11.

44 Mushir-Ul-Haq had also voiced similar concern in Haq, *Islām in Secular India*, 38-39.

45 Omar, "Ijtihād as intellectual Jihād: Renewal of the 'Spirit of Islām' in Maulana Wahiduddin Khan's Thought," 11-12.

46 Omar, "Ijtihād as intellectual Jihād: Renewal of the 'Spirit of Islām' in MaulanaWahiduddin Khan's Thought," 14.

Gender Egalitarian Readings of the Text

One of the specific areas relating to gender[47] and the need for Ijtihād is the thrust for re-reading and re-interpreting the Qur'ānic text in relation to women. This has become a crucial issue in India when Muslim women have often been branded as being looked down, treated as inferior, abused and oppressed by patriarchal hegemony. The contextual reading of the Qur'ān based on the context in which the texts were revealed and interpreted is important. It is important, because, unless it is done so, the ethical and legal aspect of the Qur'ān will become obsolete and irrelevant.[48] It is to avoid a literalist understanding of the text. It is important to clear the air of doubt that has marred Islām as gender-unjust. As a matter of fact, the Qur'ān espouses an egalitarian society. However, Qur'ānic texts have been to a large extent corrupted by the patriarchal interpretation.

The egalitarian text of the Qur'ān must become a central part of Islāmic studies. The assertion that woman and man are equal; that they are treated equally in the presence of God does not need further substantiation. For instance, women are equal to men in the quest forknowledge; she is also entitled to freedom of speech, choice, and association. The relation between husbands and wives is mutual and equal. Women are granted full rights to determine, collect and keep her *mehr*; they are economically independent and may possess her own property.[49] Both men and women are regarded as God's *khalīfah*.[50] These are some of the themes that would be crucial in presenting a gender egalitarian reading of the Qur'ān and thereby reiterating the important place of women in Muslim society.

There are however texts which have been misinterpreted and misrepresented by patriarchal interpretation. Qur'ānic texts such Qur'ān 2: 228 which seems to mention menfolk in a higher degree than women; the issue of witness (2:282); separation from men not of their kin (33:33) have been construed as texts which are oppressive to women. It further includes texts which have often been misconstrued for women domination like Qur'ān 4:34 (men as in charge of women) and Qur'ān 4:3 (the issue of polygamy). These are some of the texts that have been used and misused for ulterior motive. The re-interpretation of these texts in their proper contexts and its intended

---

47 Gender in this paper refers primarily to women.

48 Abdullah Saeed, *Interpretation the Qur'ān: Towards a Contemporary Approach* (London: Routledge Pubs., 2006), 2-3.

49 Ruth Roded, "Women and the Qur'ān," in *Encyclopedia of the Qur'ān*, edited by Jane Dammen McAuliffe (Leiden: Brill Pubs., 2006), 527.

50 Amina Wadud, Towards a Qur'ānic Hermeneutics of Social Justice: Race, Class and Gender," in *Journal of Law and Religion* 12/1 (1995-1996), 48.

meaning is essential on the part of Islāmic scholars to clear the misconceptions and misrepresentation of the texts.

One of the contemporary female voices in the interpretation of the Qur'ān is Āmina Wadūd, an Afro-American Islāmic scholar. She calls for female voices in the re-reading of the texts in the light of gender experiences. She was of the view that the traditional interpretation of the Qur'ān has to a large extent perpetuated violence against women and limited the role of women. It is for this concern that she adhered to a gender-inclusive reading of the Qur'ān. She viewed that the patriarchal interpretation of the text is done by men from the perspective of men and therefore is not infallible.[51]

Social, Economic and Educational Response

Islāmic studies must answer to the contextual issue of the community. In the Sachar Committee Report,[52] the Muslims in India is reported to have identity-related concerns. It was noted that Muslims were branded as 'anti-national' and as being 'appeased.' The degree of suspicion associated in public spaces with wearing a burqa', the beard, topī, etc—such marker of identity—has been frown upon as something foreign.[53] There is also the issue of gender-identity where Muslim women were subjected to discrimination often with a religious colouring.[54] It was reported that there is security related issue in the event of communal violence, whereby Muslims have often been the target for interrogation or branding them as perpetrators of violence, or as anti-national.[55]

Contextual Islāmic studies have to ponder on the reason why Muslim in India faces identity crisis. What would define a person to be an Indian and that too Indian Muslims? Could this be the case of a preconceived, prejudiced stereotypical idea of the Islāmophobes or a perceived dichotomy between India's

---

51 Asma Barlas, "Amina Wadud's Hermeneutics of the Qur'ān: Women Rereading Sacred Texts," in *Modern Muslim Intellectuals and the Qur'ān*, edited by Suha Taji-Farouki (Oxford: Oxford University Press, 2006), 104.

52 This is a report of a high level committee constituted by Dr. Manmohan Singh to study the social, economic and educational status of the Muslims in India. This Committee was headed by Justice Rajindar Sachar and the ad hoc members were Saiyid Hamid, Dr. T.K. Oommen, M.A. Basith, Dr. Rakesh Basant, Dr. Akhtar Majeed, Dr. Abusaleh Shariff, Member-Secretary. In short this committee came to be known as the Sachar Committee. The committee covered the states of Andhra Pradesh, Karnataka, Uttar Pradesh, Rajasthan, Jammu & Kashmir, Assam, West Bengal, Delhi, Kerala, Madhya Pradesh, Gujarat, Bihar and Maharashtra. The finding of the study was presented to the Prime Minister on 17th November 2006 and was tabled in Parliament on 30th November 2006. See, Rajindar Sachar, *Social, Economic and Educational Status of the Muslim Community: A Report* (New Delhi: Government of India, 2006), iii-iv.

53 Sachar, *Social, Economic and Educational Status of the Muslim Community*, 11-12.

54 Sachar, *Social, Economic and Educational Status of the Muslim Community*, 12-13.

55 Sachar, *Social, Economic and Educational Status of the Muslim Community*, 13.

secularism and Islāmic values? The allegations of religious fundamentalism, terrorism and extremism, as Muslim 'identities' have done much harm to the Muslim society. It is the prerogative on the part of the community and the study of Islām to counter such allegations. It is crucial to underline, as part of Islāmic studies, the teachings on peace and universal humanity. In the case of Indian Muslim women, Islāmic studies must dig into the issue as to why Muslim women are often portrayed as inferior and discriminated in spite of the fact that Islāmic teachings value the place of women in the society. Taking these social realities of the Muslims in India, it is crucial on the part of the Muslim intellectual, religious leaders to respond to these concerns. Islāmic studies must remain contextual to the social issue of the people without which religion will fail to have an impact on the life of the adherents.

It is important to point out the prerogative of Islāmic studies to address the issue of economic constraints among the Muslims. According to the Sachar Committee Report, Muslims in India are economically constrained which in turn highly impacted the socio, economic and educational status of the Muslims. The concentration on informal sectors, with a very low percentage of employment, less access to government employment and participation, among others, needs a conscious response on the part of the Muslim community. For instance, according to the Report in 2006, the committee out of their study reports that the presence of Muslims has been found to be only 3% in the IAS, 1.8% in the IFS, and 4% in the IPS. The share of Muslims in the employment sector in various departments is low at all levels. The same is the case for Muslims' representation in the Universities and in Banks.[56]

Islāmic studies cannot ignore the realities of Muslims in relation to educational status. It must address the issue behind Muslim educational stagnation. Citing again the report of Sachar Committee, it is reported that Muslim educational status is a matter of great concern. It reported that the literacy rate among Muslims is below the national average; that most Muslim children are school dropouts. It is reported that the representation of Muslims in the top Medical colleges is about 4% of students—most of them were known to be studying at the UG level namely in MBBS, Dental, Nursing, etc.[57] The issue gets even more complex with madrasa education. The process of 'modernizing' madrasa education is another great concern. The issue of mainstreaming madrasa education to a variety of subject areas and the issue of employability[58] all needs a credible response. This was also the issue raised by

56 Syed Zafar Mahmood, "Summarised Sachar Report on Status of Indian Muslims," (13th December 2006) http://www.milligazette.com/dailyupdate/2006/200612141_Sachar_Report_Status_Indian_Muslims.htm (14th August 2019).

57 Sachar, *Social, Economic and Educational Status of the Muslim Community*, 69-70.

58 Sachar, *Social, Economic and Educational Status of the Muslim Community*, 17-18.

Maulānā Waḥīduddīn Khān in which he mentioned the need for independent reasoning and being adaptive to change. Khān therefore asserts, as mentioned above, that the 'Spirit of Islām' would mean addressing the issue in which Muslim live in—a response to the issues of our times.[59]

Abjuring the Definition of Religion

Another important trajectory in the post-modern period may be further discussed in relation to W.C. Smith's approach to the study of religion, especially Islām, and the need for sustained effort for a dialogical approach to the study of religion. Smith attempted a sympathetic study of religion and Islām in particular. In his study of Islām, he analysed concepts such as 'faith,' 'religion' and 'cumulative tradition.' Smith in his book *The Meaning and End of Religion* distinguished 'faith,' 'religion' and 'cumulative traditions.' He calls for abjuring the definition of religion which means to remove the intellectual spectacles through which one sees religious life. It is a call to discard that intellectual spectacle that divides religion in terms of theological and religious traditions. This approach is important in order to be free from monolithic understanding of religion and thereby allowing a maximum variety of expressions. He calls for faith which has the capacity to orient one's life that transcends beyond the mundane life. This approach of study does not exclude the personal, inward and hidden aspects of human life—which is faith. For him faith is the crux of religious reality.[60]

Smith approach to the study of religion and Islām in particular is on the basis of faith. Smith was knowledgeable of the limitation human society imply on religion whereby the society is segregated into different religious groups such as Christianity, Hinduism, Sikhism, Islām and others. This narrow segregation calls for abjuring—meaning to renounce—this term which will open up a wider and deeper nature of faith. Because, faith is the feeling of the wholly other; it is between the individual and numinous, while religion is the external expression. Smith's approach to the study of religion is "the attempt genuinely to understand one religious movement involves one in a

---

59 Omar, "Ijtihād as intellectual Jihād: Renewal of the 'Spirit of Islām' in Maulana Wahiduddin Khan's Thought," 11-12.

60 Seyed Mostafa Rokhsefat, "Wilfred Cantwell Smith's Contribution to the Study of Islam" (Master of Arts in the Philosophy of Religion, Faculty of Religious Studies McGill University, February 1994), 70, 88; Wilfred Cantwell Smith, *The Meaning and End of Religion* (Minneapolis: Fortress Press, 1963), v-vi; also see, W.C. Smith, "Comparative Religion: Whither—and Why?" in *The History of Religions: Essays in Methodology*, edited by Mircea Eliade and Joseph M. Kitagawa (Chicago: The University of Chicago Press, 1959), 34.

requirement to understand all, and to understand religious diversity as a fact of human life, and the long term shift in categories as a fact of human thinking."[61]

Dialogue of Life

Dialogue between religions based on faith is a sustained effort. While we have discussed the call for interfaith dialogue in the post-modern era, dialogue is not a onetime effort—it is a sustained pruning. Dialogue here does not mean comparison. One cannot compare or even engage relatively on doctrinal, theological and religious experiences from one to the other. It is not possible to compare the nature of revelation in Islām and Christianity in spite of their proximity. Because, all religions are unique in their own ways.[62] Dialogue here does not mean searching for a universality of religions. Such attempts for universality, according to Paul Tillich, would destroy religion from its depth. Joachim Wach further commented that each religion has to be understood from its own context without looking for 'universal keys.'[63] Furthermore, dialogue is not an attempt to hammer out a typology of religions irrespective of their relativity. For instance, this can be said of the Semitic or Indic religions. Because, every religion's inner experience cannot be substituted by another experience. In other words, the plurality of revelations cannot be reduced to singularity.[64]

In the context of pluralistic India, the objective study of religion and interfaith dialogue towards interreligious relations at a time when Indian society has been marred by religious fundamentalism, communalism, intolerance, and bigotry is the need of the hour. It is significant to reiterate the appeal of Professor Ziāul Ḥasan Fārūqī of Jamia Millia Islāmia in the Tughluqabad seminar of 1978 on the theme "Mosque and Church" in which he made a strong plea to open up for dialogue and do away with traditional attitudes. His call for a change of traditional exclusive attitudes enumerates dialogue on both the intellectual and practical aspects. It is a call for dialogue with people of another faith which entails listening to each other's experiences. He based such interfaith relation on shared action on the principle of *ma'rūf*—which is good, beautiful and just. This shared action is a united effort "for a just social order, against all kinds of injustices, social, economic and political, from co-

61 W.C. Smith, *On Understanding Islam* (Hague: Mouton Publisher, 1981), 41.

62 N.N.N. Raman, *Methodological Studies in the History of Religions—With Special Reference to Hinduism and Buddhism* (Shimla: Indian Institute of Advanced Study), 2-3.

63 Refer, Paul Tillich, "The Significance of the History of religions," in *History of Religions: Essays on the Problem of Understanding*, edited by Joseph M. Kitagawa (Chicago: Chicago university Press, 1967), 253; Joachim Wach, Sociology of Religion (Chicago: University of Chicago Press, 1944), 4. Raman, *Methodological Studies in the History of Religions*, 3.

64 Raman, *Methodological Studies in the History of Religions*, 3.

operating in doing things that make life good and beautiful."[65] In the intellectual level, it is important to inculcate the study of different religious experience in the syllabus of the students. Professor Iqbāl Anṣārī of the Institute of Islāmic Studies in Aligarh, rightly pointed out the need to study another religion as the adherents see it and not from one's own framework.[66]

No religion can claim absolute truth in a pluralistic society. Exclusivist and inclusivist view of religion breads a 'holier than thou' attitude; while a pluralist view of religion ushers goodwill in the society. Thus, interfaith dialogue and relations are important directions for Islāmic studies. In this regard, it is important to reiterate the Qur'ānic injunctions and examples set by Prophet Muḥammad. The Pact of Medina which the Prophet drew up after his migration from Mecca to Medina in 622 CE is an important source of dialogue with people of another faith. This is an institution of peaceful relations between the Muslims and non-Muslims. It guarantees religious, cultural and political rights based on the principle of plurality and freedom of religion. It is important to reiterate the Qur'ānic principle of plurality in 5: 42-44 (Torah for the Jews and Qur'ān for the Muslims); 5: 256 (non-compulsion in religion); 2: 62 (rewards not in the name of religion but good deeds and submission to God), among others, as the basis of dialogue.

Conclusion

The future direction of Islāmic studies in terms of its approaches, prospects and challenges is a response and a continuous entelechy to the changing context of the society. This dynamics works in philosophical, theological, juridical, social, religious, economic and other concerns. It may be reiterated again that Islāmic studies must response to these concerns lest it become obsolete. The approach forward is a philosophical inquiry into the nature of Islām; the need for intellectual reasoning based on ijtihād; and interpretation of the text from the voice of the margins. The approach of Islāmic studies is a respond to the social, economic and educational realities of the Muslims society. In the context of plurality of cultures and religions, Islāmic studies cannot be done in isolation. Narrow intellectual spectacles divides people along religious lines but the inner experiences unites. The approach to the study of Islām is not a call for universality of religions but experience of pluralities. This study is dialogical in approach—dialogue with what is good, beautiful and just, and a dialogue of life. Dialogue is grounded in the foundation of sacrifice—sacrifice for the betterment of one's neighbours.

65 Troll, *Christian-Muslim Relations in India: A Critical Survey*, 32-33.

66 Troll, *Christian-Muslim Relations in India: A Critical Survey*, 33.

14

Anekântavâda: A Method for Religious Pluralism

Otoka S

Introduction

Anekântavâda (Relative Pluralism) refers to the Jain's view of multifaceted nature of reality. Jain seers taught that reality could be understood only if a person was all-knowing, but since human being possesses only limited or partial knowledge and therefore understanding the concept of reality in its fullness is not possible for any worldly beings. This view is wonderfully illustrated through the parable of the blind Men and an Elephant. Being blind they had to rely on the sense of touch. Where each of them touched the different parts of an Elephant's body and gave their own description about an Elephant from their relative point of view, but nobody could describe the totality. And therefore, to arrive at the complete picture all view must be taken into account. The principle of *anekântavâda* is vitally important, globally relevant principle, even to those who do not fully embrace a Jain path as a way of life. In other word, one does not need to be a Jain in order to learn valuable lessons from Jainism.

Anekânta doctrine has remained more or less obscure to the contemporary mind. It will certainly be philosophically fruitful to explore this area of Indian philosophy. The Jainas used their method *syâdvâda* 'seven-fold prediction' and *nayavâda* 'standpoints' in order to defend their *anekânta* philosophy. This is an approach which affirms the relativity of perspective but avoid a sceptical relativism that would deny the possibility of ever grasping the truth at all. The challenge of religious diversity in India is not a new phenomenon. And therefore this article attempts to understand the doctrine of *anekântavâda* as an approach for religious pluralism.

Origin

The origin of *anekântavâda* can be traced back to the teaching of Mâhavîra, the 24th Jain *Tîrthankara,* who used it effectively to show the relativity of truth and reality. Taking a relativistic viewpoint, Mâhavîra is said to have explained the nature of the soul as both permanent from the point of view of underlying substance, and temporary, from the point of view of its modes and modification. The dialectical concepts of *syâdvâda* (conditional view points) and *nayavâda* (partial viewpoint) arose from *anekântavâda,* providing it with more detailed logical structure and expression.[1]

Historical Development

The Principle of *anekântavâda* is the foundation of many Jain philosophical concepts. The development of *anekântavâda* also encouraged the development of the dialectics of *syâdvâda* (conditioned viewpoints), *saptibhangî* (the seven conditioned predictions), and *nayavâda* (partial viewpoints).[2] To provide a general chronological frame for Jainism in relation to other discourses, the development of dialogical approach can be divided into four stages, which is distinguished on the basis of the different main partners of communication. Stage one is the stage of origination when communication took place within the evolving Jain community and was also mainly addressed to the Jain community. During the second stage, communication about *anekântavâda* was part of Indian discourse about how to achieve the ultimate goal in life. Stage three, beginning in the late 19th century, sees communication shaped by the colonial powers and the encounter with the West that costly occurred on unequal terms. Stage four is characterized by the global network of communication, which is accompanied by a slowly waning Western dominance and an increasingly global audience.[3]

1 Ratan Singh, *Jainsim Philosophy and Culture* (New Delhi: Global Publication, 2011), 79.

2 Singh, *Jainsim Philosophy and Culture*, 87.

3 Melanie Barbato, *Jain Approach to Plurality* (Netherlands: Koninklijke Brill NV, Leiden, 2018), 4.

Terminology

The Sanskrit compound *an-eka-anta-vâda* literally means "doctrine or non-exclusivity or multiple viewpoints, *an* 'which *is not', eka* 'one', *vâda* 'viewpoint." It is translated into English as "scepticism" or "non-absolutism."[4]

Meaning of Anekântavâda

Anekântavâda is known as the teaching of plurality, or the doctrine of non-one-sidedness. Also known as the teaching of many-sidedness, many-pointedness, and doctrine of may fold aspect, non-radicalism, non-absolutism, non-equivocality and relative pluralism. According to classical Jain philosophy, this many-sidedness applies to both existence and truth; thus, *anekântavâda* has both an ontological and an epistemological aspect. Concerning ontology, *anekântavâda* states that every object has an infinite number of attributes. Concerning epistemology, it claims that in any one statement or conceptualisation one can only grasp a limited amount of attributes, while other, equally existence aspects are neglected. Epistemological discourses on *anekântavâda* developed two central theoretical concepts: *Nayavâda* and *Syâdvâda,* or as one Indian scholar has said, the "the bird of *anekânta* flies on the wings of *Nayavâda* and *Syâdvâda.*"[5] And therefore, it is very clear that one cannot talk about *anekântavâda* without taking into consideration the concept of *Nayavâda* and *Syâdvâda. Anekântavâda* and its corollary teachings are thus means for the Jain to deal with plurality both on ontological and epistemological levels. This can also be used in a complex philosophical debate; however for Jains the concept is nothing but a set of belief that includes respect for others.

Anekântavâda encourages its adherents to consider the views and beliefs of their rivals and opposing parties. Proponents of *anekântavâda* apply this principle to religion and philosophy, reminding themselves that any religion or philosophy-even Jainism-which clings too dogmatically to its own tenets, is committing an error based on its limited point of view.[6]

Jain Doctrine of Relativity

The Jain doctrine of relativity can be understood in three different concepts; *Anekântavâda Nayavâda* and *Syâdvâda.* These concepts help one to understand the viewpoint of others. Although, it might appear as three different concepts however they are closely knitted with one another. *Nayavâda* and *Syâdvâda* are seen as a reflection or a supporting doctrine of *Anekântavâda.*

---

4 Singh, *Jainsim Philosophy and Culture*, 79-80.

5 Barbato, *Jain Approach to Plurality*, 3.

6 Singh, *Jainsim Philosophy and Culture*, 80.

Anekântavâda

Anekântavâda is one of the most important fundamental doctrines of Jainism. It is known as the principle of pluralism and multiplicity of viewpoints, the idea that truth and reality are perceived differently from different point of view, and that no single/partial point of view can be regarded as the complete truth. Jains contrast all attempts to proclaim absolute truth with *adhgajanyâyah,* which can be illustrated through the parable of the "blind men and an elephant". In this story each blind man touched different parts of an elephant (trunk, leg, ear, etc.). All of them claimed to have understood everything and explain the true appearance of elephant according to their experience, but they could not succeed due to their limited perspective, in fact all their explanation was just a part of truth within the larger truth. The principle is more formally stated by observing that objects are infinite in their qualities and modes of existence, so that they cannot be completely grasped in all aspects and manifestation by the finite perception.[7]

However, philosophically there is always a problem in attempting to synthesise the opposing viewpoints, and Jain philosophers knew about such problems. In order to get rid of the problem the idea of "relative pluralism" was developed (synthesis of two doctrines): the doctrine of 'standpoints' (*Nayavâda*) and 'relativity' (*Syâdvâda*). Relative Pluralism is considered as the fundamental mental attitude which sees 'reality' differently from different viewpoint being a partial expression of reality. There is a famous story told of Mâhavîra, "when he was on the middle floor of his home he was 'downstairs' according to his father who was on a floor above, and 'upstairs' from the point of view of his mother on a lower floor, but both parents we right from their different points of view." The relativity of viewpoints brings together such differing viewpoints into a single logical expression.[8]

Syâdvâda

The concern of the Jain tradition are not confined to the realm of philosophy in the sense of inquiry into the nature of reality, but extend to the realm of 'meta-philosophy' as well-to reflection upon and discussion of what constitute the proper nature of philosophical discourse. This brings us to *syâdvâda,* translated literally as the 'maybe doctrine', but more accurately as the 'doctrine of conditional or qualified assertion', the doctrine of the proper formulation and analysis of philosophical claims in light of the philosophy of relativity.[9] The Sanskrit etymology root of the term *syâd* is 'perhaps' or 'maybe' but

7 Singh, *Jainsim Philosophy and Culture*, 79.

8 Natubhai Shah, *Jainism: The World of Conquerors*, Vol. I (Great Britain: Sussex Academic Press, 1998), 114.

9 Jeffery D Long, *Jainism: An Introduction* (London: I.B. Tauris, 2010), 143.

in the context of *syâdvâda,* it means 'somehow' or 'from a perspective'. *Syâdvâda* is a theory that explains how statements should be formed, namely in a non-absolutist manner: for each subject of thought or discussion, ideally the predication should be conditioned by the use of particle *'syâd'* (from a certain perspective) in order to show that no statement can possibly capture the whole range of attributes that any object can possesses.[10] *Syâdvâda* provides an expression to *anekânta* by recommending that the epithet *syâd* be prefixed to every phrase of expression. However, *syâdvâda* is not only an extension of *anekânta* ontology, but a separate system of logic capable of standing on its own. *Syâdvâda* is also known as *saptibhangînaya* or the theory of seven conditioned predictions. They are:[11]

1. *Syâd-asti*—somehow it is,
2. *Syâd-nâsti*—somehow it is not,
3. *Syâd- asti-nâsti*—somehow it is and it is not,
4. *Syâd-asti-avaktavyah*—somehow it is and it is indescribable,
5. *Syâd-nâsti-avaktavyah*—somehow it is not and it is indescribable,
6. *Syâd- asti-nâsti-avaktavyah*—somehow it is, it is not and it is indescribable,
7. *Syâd- avaktavyah*—somehow it is indescribable,

Each of these seven propositions examines the complex and multifaceted nature of reality from a relative point of view of time, space, substance and mode. Hence it is obvious that the knowledge which the seven conditioned of predictions leads to, must be the highest ideal of knowledge. A knowledge from which the defects have vanished altogether and in which the ideal element is grasped in its purity and entirety, in its coherence and harmony. It is the only adequate form of knowledge, because it has the characteristics of necessity i.e. the constituent elements of it are apprehended, not as isolated or independent terms or notions but as a related to or flowing out of each other so that one being given, the others must necessarily follow and the whole body of knowledge constitutes one organised system.[12]

Nayavâda

Nayavâda is also seen as an expression of *anekânta,* it is the theory of the partial standpoints or viewpoints. *Nayavâda* is a compound of two Sanskrit words, *naya* 'partial viewpoint' and *vâda* 'school of thought or debate'. An

10 Barbato, *Jain Approach to Plurality*, 3.

11 Satischandra Chatterjee and Dhirendramohan, *An Introduction to Indian Philosophy* (Calcutta: University of Calcutta, 1954), 85-87.

12 P.C. Nahar and K.C. Ghosh, editors, *An Encyclopaedia of Jainism* (Delhi: Sri Satguru Publications, 1996), 105-106.

object has infinite aspects to it, but when an object is described in practice, it is described only from a relevant aspect and ignores the irrelevant ones. This does not deny the other attributes, qualities, modes and other aspects; they are just irrelevant from a particular perspective. *Nayavâda* holds that all philosophical disputes arise out of confusion of standpoints, and the standpoints one adopts are, although one may not realize it, "the outcome of purpose that one may pursue."[13] It is the theory that there are various perspectives from which reality can be perceived, depending on which aspect of reality is in the forefront of the observer's mind.[14]

This doctrine is illustrated with the example of the golden crown. A golden crown comes into the possession of a king. His son, the prince, wants to keep the crown, but the queen wants it melted down and made into necklace. The king agrees to the wishes of his wife and the crown is melted down. The queen is delighted to have a new necklace. The prince is disappointed that the coveted crown has been destroyed. The king, however, is indifferent, for the amount of gold in question has remained the same.[15]

This shows an analytical process of ontological investigation helping one to dive deep into the net-work of inter-related parts of the things known through the ordinary means of knowledge and select, as well, one or the other attribute from the innumerable attributes, the aggregate of which makes up the being and expression of the said known things with a view of interpreting and understanding the selected attribute for a correct and complete conception of the ontology of the same. Thus a *naya,* it is clear, predicates one of the innumerable attributes of a thing without denying the rest.[16]

Anekântavâda: The Ontology of Relativity

Anekântavâda is an ontological doctrine. Its fundamental claim, as it eventually came to be understood by the tradition, is that all existent entities have infinite attributes. As Haribhadra says, "Existence is characterized by emergence, perishing, and duration. On account of this, it is said that the entities have infinite attributes and is the object of an instrument of knowledge."[17]

This idea stems from the ontological realism that characterizes the Jain's position. Reality is essentially as we perceive it. However, our perception of reality is never an absolute and for which contradictions are apparent such as, continuity and change, emergence and perishing, permanence and flux, identity and difference-reflects the interdependent, relationally constituted nature of

13 Singh, *Jainsim Philosophy and Culture,* 82.

14 Barbato, *Jain Approach to Plurality,* 3.

15 Long, *Jainism: An Introduction,* 143.

16 Ghosh, *An Encyclopaedia of Jainism,* 79-80.

17 Long, *Jainism: An Introduction,* 141.

things. Reality in simple term can be understood as a synthesis of opposites. It is therefore consistent with the nature of reality to affirm contrary attributes of any given entity. The number of possible predictions which can validly be made of an entity is heightened to infinite by the fact that, Jainism affirms a definition of an entity which includes within itself the entity's relations, both of being and of non-being, with every other entity constituting the cosmos.[18]

Traditional Basic Postulates of *Anekântavâda*

Every object or entity that we know is endowed with more than one attributes, seeming to be contradictory sometimes. But, it is a conglomerate of attributes. The seemingly contradictory attributes are nothing but complementary parts of the whole in the multifaceted reality. There is no way that the entity or object could be described as a whole until it is integrally studied with respect to all its aspects. *Anekântavâda* is an integrated form of different partial truth about the reality. And therefore, ones description about the reality in no ways reflect the ideal truth however, the truth with respect to some realistic and for which every description may represent a partial or relative truth. It is quite possible that different observer under different conditions may have different explanation about the same phenomena. Human's languages are not capable of describing that multifaceted reality, and therefore adding prefix *syâd* (May be) before one's statement could be a proper way of describing about the reality from one's point of view.[19]

Gandhi on Anekântavâda

The principle of *anekântavâda* also influenced Mohandas Karamchand Gandhi to adopt principles of religious tolerance, *ahiṃsâ* and *satyagraha.* One of the highest concentrations of Jains in India is in the region of Gujarat, the western coastal region in which Gandhi was born and raised. Jain ideals and practices have long exerted an influence upon the Gujarati Hindu *Vaiṣṇava* community, of which Gandhi was a member, and Jain monks were frequent visitors to the Gandhi's household when he was still a boy. Indeed, before he undertook his first journey abroad to London, his family permitted him to do so only after he took a vow 'not to touch wine, women and meat', a vow administered by one Bacarajī Svāmī, a jain monk.[20]

It has been noted that Gandhi, as a synthesizer of *āstika* and *nāstika* religion, has taken the *advaita* concept of *āstika* religion and gave a new hermeneutic to have a pluralistic inclusivism, so that it can accommodate all

18 Long, *Jainism: An Introduction,* 141.

19 N. L. Jain, "Anekântavâda and Conflict Resolution," in *Jain Studies,* edited by Colette Caillat and Nalini Balbir (Delhi: Motilal Banarsidass Publishers Private Limited, 2008), 69-86.

20 Long, *Jainism: An Introduction,* 169.

religions of lower and higher. Gandhi also finds *nāstika* literature pointing to a pluralistic approach; which not only tolerate other religions but gives equal for other religions. Jain concept of *anekântavâda* is one such. Gandhi by his own confession subscribed to the Jain concept of *anekântavâda*. In a couple of significant statement he affirms his faith in the *anekântavâda* of Jainism.[21] "I am an *anekântavâdi*. This is the most important thing that I have learnt from Jain philosophy. It is implicit in Vedanta Philosophy, while in Jain it is explicitly stated…"[22]

It was Jain philosophy that allowed Gandhi to conceive of ultimate reality pluralistically, in both personal theistic and impersonal *advaitic* terms. Most importantly, from Gandhi's perspective, it was Jain philosophy that allowed him to exercise not only tolerance but empathy for the positions of those with whom he disagreed.[23]

Intellectual *Ahiṃsâ*

Jinas theory of relativity has frequently been characterized and promoted as 'Intellectual *ahiṃsâ*'. Which can be understood as a practice of non-violence extended to the realm of philosophical discourse, and may even be considered as a charity towards other philosophical positions and their possible insights into the character of reality. It is rooted in the fact that reality is multi-faceted (*anekânta*) and thus amenable to multiple, non-exclusive perspectives, and that non-violence (*ahiṃsâ*) is an essential components of the Jain path to liberation.[24] According to some scholars, this logical method recognizes that everybody has only a limited perspective on the truth. At the same time, since this method recognizes that all perspective bear within themselves some level of truth, it is a highly tolerant method for treating non-Jain philosophical perspectives. Rather than rejecting other perspectives out of hand, the Jains recognize that they have some grasp of the truth, and therefore are to be separated and tolerated. This tolerance is rooted in the Jain ethical imperative of *ahiṃsâ*. Just as all living beings are to be treated with respect and non-violence, so the Jains adopted the stance that the perspectives of all beings are to be treated with respect and nonviolence-in this case, intellectual nonviolence.[25]

21 P.L. John Panicker, *Gandhi on Pluralism and Communalism* (Delhi: ISPCK, 2006), 190-191.

22 M.K. Gandhi, *Khadi: Why and How*, edited by Bharata Kumarappa (Ahmedabad: Navajivan Publishing House, 1955).

23 Long, *Jainism: An Introduction,* 170.

24 Long, *Jainism: An Introduction,* 154.

25 John E. Cort, "Intellectual Ahiṃsā Revisited: Jain Tolerance and Intolerance of Others", in *Philosophy of East and West,* Vol. 50, No. 3 (Honolulu: University of Hawai'i Press, July, 2000), 324-347.

The concept of *anekântavâda* allows Jains to accept truth in other philosophies from their own perspective and thus inculcate tolerance for other viewpoints. *Anekântavâda* is non-absolutist and stands firmly against all dogmatisms, including any assertion that Jainism is the only correct religious path. It is thus an intellectual *ahiṃsâ,* or *ahiṃsâ* of the mind. Singh agrees with Burch that "Jain logic is intellectual *ahiṃsâ.* Just as a right-acting person respects the life of all beings, so a right-thinking person acknowledges the validity of all judgments. This means recognizing all aspects of reality, not merely one or some aspects, as is done in non-Jain philosophies."[26]

Religious Pluralism

Religious Pluralism is a term widely used in recent times, to find ways to confront communalism, conflict and discord among religious groups and help them overcome these, and enable the people to move toward attaining meaningful relationships among them. Pluralists work on the premise that all religions, more or less, are of the same virtue, and therefore, it is important that each religion should deal with other as if they are on a level playing field. S.J. Samartha define religious pluralism as "a part of the larger plurality of races, people and cultures, or social structures, economic systems and political patterns of language and systems, all of which are part of the total human heritage." Further, he affirms: "how different religions respond to the Mystery of Ultimate Reality in different ways, it is important because it touches ultimate questions about human life and destiny."[27] However, M. Stephen opines that pluralism is not just about the celebration of diversities of life or about a peaceful co-existence between religions, rather pluralism is engaging oneself in action that are guided to promote life in its fullness for all people. Thus religious pluralism is an attempt towards creative living of religious by way of mutually engaging in serving others, appreciating, criticizing and transforming each other in order to make life meaningful to everyone.[28] In religious pluralism cultural and religious traditions are woven together in such a way that, while every culture and religion keeps its uniqueness, it is also enriched by other cultures and religions.[29]

Any religious institution that claims "we alone possess the Truth; we alone possess access to salvation" errs gravely. The Truth, the Divine, and the power of the Divine cannot be possessed. To make such a claim is, at best,

26 Singh, *Jainsim Philosophy and Culture,* 92.

27 S. J. Samartha, *One Christ-Many Religions: Towards a Revised Christology* (Bangalore: SATHRI, 1992), 4.

28 Harsha K. Kotian, *Christo Normative Pluralism: A critical Appraisal of the Works of Stanly Jones, Stanley Samartha and Paul Knitter* (Delhi: ISPCK, 2011), 3.

29 Ambrogio Bongiovanni, Leonard Fernando, and Victor Edwin S.J., eds., *Dialogue in A Pluralistic World* (Delhi: ISPCK, 2013), VII.

the sin of pride, the sin of confusing oneself and one's human instrument with the divine. Such claim is no more than a cynical arrogation of power by mere human institution putting itself in the place of divine. We cannot possess the truth. All religions are but forms attempting to manifest the vast emptiness.[30]

It is the understanding of most pluralist that all religions have more or less the same liberative potentialities and they are self-contained system capable of leading their adherents towards salvation. It is felt so, because all religions seek to encounter the same Ultimate Being even thought they perceive it differently.[31] Pluralists think that the one-way road as the road to destruction.[32] Knitter in his book *"No Other Name?"* states that "they who know one, know none."[33] Samartha opines that "since God or the Mystery is so profound a being, it is impossible to experience the profoundness of the divine or to express the extent of God in one set of symbols, form or formula of faith."[34] Pluralist, therefore, want to propose many way of salvation. Instead of claiming that Jesus/Muhammad/Buddha/Krishna/Mâhavîra and so on, is the only road and liberator, they insist on equal recognition and respect for other religions, other lords and other saviours. They admonish world religion to consider that in a world of religious diversity, any claim of superiority of their religion embodies the myth of religion uniqueness. Therefore, any religious assertion "outside one's religion there is no liberation" reflect an exclusivist faith, which hinders a meaningful relationship with other faith. According to Samartha, such claims amount to theological violence against neighbours of other faiths and are dangerous to communal harmony and world peace. [35] Pluralists, therefore, urge the religions to make a "paradigm shift" in its thinking and thus in its theology by replacing their centrality or the part of experience about an elephant with the totality of an Elephant (Centrality of God). Which John Hick might term it as a "Copernican Shift"

For the Dalai Lama, religions are tools and accordingly people differ in significant ways from each others. Some religions might be best for some people, while other religions might suit other people best.[36] Every individual has their way of understanding religion; some people might be fascinated by

---

30 Sallie King, "A Pluralistic View of Religious Pluralism," in *The Myth of Religious Superiority: A Multifaith Exploration*, edited by Paul F. Knitter (New York: Orbis Books, 2005), 88-104.

31 Kotian, *Christo Normative Pluralism,* 5.

32 Paul F. Knitter, *No Other Name? A Critical Survey of Christian Attitudes toward the World Religions* (Philippines: Claretian Publications, 1985), 6.

33 Knitter, *No Other Name,* 2.

34 S.J. Samartha, *One Christ-Many Religions: Toward a Revised Christology* (New York: Orbis Books, 2014), 4-5.

35 Kotian, *Christo Normative Pluralism,* 6.

36 King, "A Pluralistic View of Religious Pluralism," 88-104.

some religions, while for some people they are amazed by other religions. And this is so, because every individual responds to the reality according to their own relative point of view and according to their own experience, however, reality is same for everyone.

Issue of Religious Fundamentalism

Claim of religious superiority all too easily, if not invariably, become calls to religious violence. Exclusive claims to absolute truth have exacerbated the division of the human community into rival groups, and have repeatedly been invoked in support of oppression, slavery, conquest, and exploitation.[37] In recent years there has been an increased rupture in harmonious living. Communities have been set against each other on the basis of caste, language, ethnicity and especially religion. The other is projected "as an enemy" to be avoided and abhorred. The increased communal conflict and violence in the past few years is causing irreparable damage to the beautiful fabric of humanity.[38] Fundamentalism and communalism have blinded people from seeing beyond his/her perspective. In a recent incidence Imran Ismail Patel, a hotel employee was allegedly trashed by a group of men and was forced to chant 'Jai Shri Ram' in Aurangabad city of Maharashtra.[39] Similarly a painful incident is about a 24-year-old Muslim man Tabrez Ansari, he was beaten up on a suspicion of theft and was forced to chant "Jai Shree Ram" on 18th June, 2019.[40] The haunting is the story of fifteen-year-old Junaid Khan, returning home on a crowded train after buying new clothes for Eid, who was stabbed repeatedly because he was Muslim and thrown off the train to bleed to death on the tracks.[41] The case of a dairy farmer, Pehlu Khan, transporting cattle legally with a license, was beaten to death on 1st April 2017 while his tormentors filmed his pleas for mercy on their mobile phones. In 2015, when a Muslim man, Muhammad Akhlaq, father of the serving Indian Air Force havildar, was lynched by a mob in Uttar Pradesh on suspicions of having killed a cow, the authorities launched a forensic investigation into whether the meat in his

---

37 Paul F. Knitter, ed., *The Myth of Religious Spirituality* (New York: Orbis Books, 2005), X.

38 Bongiovanni, *Dialogue in A Pluralistic World*, VII.

39 Maharashtra: "*Mob forces Muslim man to chant Jain Shri RAM, Hindu couple comes to rescue*", in https://www.indiatoday.in/crime/story/maharashtra-man-beaten-refusing-chant-jai-shri-ram-1571412-2019-07-19 (News Paper: India Today, July 20, 2019). Accessed on 16-08-2018, 08:00 pm.

40 *"Muslim man beaten up on suspicion of theft, forced to chant Jai Shree Ram, succumbs to injuries,"* in https://www.indiatoday.in/india/story/jharkhand-muslim-man-lynching-jai-shree-ram-jai-hanuman-1554634-2019-06-23 (News Paper: India Today, June 23, 2019). Accessed on 16-08-2019, 08:30 pm.

41 Shashi Tharoor, *Why I Am A Hindu?* (Faridabad: Thomson Press India Ltd., 2018), 183.

refrigerator was beef (it was not), he died of natural cause a few weeks later.[42] The mentioned incidents reflects the bitter reality of religious intolerance, and the reason is because we tend to reduce everyone into our limited mental universe, where we are like a frog in the well thinking we have the absolute authority over reality.

The Importance of Relative Pluralism

The awareness of the existence of many standpoints make relative pluralism necessary; the standpoints are partial expressions of truth, while relative pluralism aims at the complete truth. Relative Pluralism aims to unify, co-ordinate, harmonise and synthesise individual, and even conflicting, viewpoints into a comprehensible whole. It is like music, which blends different notes to make perfect harmony. Relative pluralism teaches tolerance, co-existence and respect for others, necessary in creating a harmonious society. Some philosophical, religious and political system claims to interpret reality in its entirety, while containing only partial versions of the truth, but they cannot do full justice to the manifold nature of the world in which we live, as judgments about the world must necessarily vary according to the observer's perspective. Relative pluralism seeks to provide a solution to the intellectual chaos and confusion stemming from the ambiguous and metaphysical contradictions of differing philosophical systems. The doctrine of relative pluralism frees one from spurious thinking such as the belief that any one faith is nearer to the truth than others. It is an understanding, which urges us to study different religious, opinions and schools of thought and is a basis for sound thinking. *Anekantadristi* (infinite vision) respects the thoughts of others and as a result one's own opinions will be accorded their worth.[43]

Anekântavâda: A Philosophy of Religious Pluralism

Long in his book *Jainism: An Introduction*, opines that adopting the Jain philosophy of relativity according to one's own version, could justify drawing inspiration from a wide and diverse range of sources, by incorporating the insights of other's sources into one's own view. The scriptures of different religious traditions such as: The *Bhagavad Gita*, The Bible, The Quran, Torah, Tolstoy, Theosophy, all of these can become resources where one could tap for ideas and embrace as elements in one's own in this constantly growing and changing worldview. This could be seen as an intellectual expression of pluralism of one's own desire 'to take the whole world in the embrace of his/her love.' *Anekântavâda* allows one to embrace the truth in the belief of others; it enabled a person to see truth in other person, and also enables a

42 Tharoor, *Why I Am A Hindu?* 250-251.

43 Shah, *Jainism: The World of Conquerors*, 114.

person to make other's truth as his/her own truth, without contradicting or sacrificing any of the truths he already held.[44] The Jain doctrines of relativity are an important cornerstone of the claim that this is a tradition with universal relevance; for one does not necessarily have to be a Jain to adopt the Jain pluralistic method.[45]

In a context like India where religion plays a very decisive role in moulding the mindset of the people, the question of an appropriate approach to religion is crucially important. The most important question in the multi-religious context of India is how people of different faiths can live together in harmony and peace. In a religious pluralistic context such as India, where conflicting truth claims compete with each other for superiority and identity and religious diversity raises number of issues. But, the theory of *Anekantavad*a seems to offer paradigmatic significance. It provides axiom that, truth is many sided and relative. No group or proposition can claim monopoly on truth. Not only does it de-absolute truth, it offers a relational view of reality and provides an epistemology for dialogue. It employs *anekantadristi* (infinite vision) perspective for an integral approach to religious.[46]

Anekântavâda as a theory might sound irrational for some group of people; this group of people are the one who are not interested in any manner to involve in any kind of mutual understanding with the people of other faith. However, on the other hand there are bunch of people who sees this theory as a perspective for developing a relation between different religious groups. It may take time for the former to really understand and see it as a new perspective, for some of them they may never embrace this theory and the reason may be because the theory originates from Jainism, but if the word Jainsim is clouding one from accepting *anekântavâda*, there's never going to be an objection, because according to this theory anybody can formulate the theory from its own relative point of view.

Anekântavâda as a Method for Religious Pluralism

Indian society as we read in history, encompasses many things and was capacious to all kinds of faith, its eclectic thoughts and the concept of unity in diversity were the essence of Indian society in the past history, even today India is known for its "unity in diversity" because of its nature of plurality. However, they have been altered by religious intolerance, hatred, violence, disrespect, in the recent days by some few groups of people, probably the self-centered and the egoistic people who cannot think beyond the boundary of their faith. And the society that we have today does in no way reflect the past glorious Indian

44 Long, *Jainism: An Introduction,* 170.

45 Long, *Jainism: An Introduction,* 171.

46 Panicker, *Gandhi on Pluralism and Communalism,* 220.

history. Our society is now vulnerable to inequality, intolerance, oppression of minority in the name of religion by the religious fundamentalist, where the minorities are chivied in the name of religion; the rights, the burden and the cry of the minorities are all deafed by religious intolerance and where the Majority are trying to impose their religious teachings in every sphere of life. The concept of *anekântavâda* becomes relevant in respecting the view of every individual without objection, by giving special concern and showing equality to every religious tradition and by respecting their claims about the reality.

Jain philosophy in general and *anekântavâda* in particular can provide a solution to many problems that we face today in the name of religion. The important essences that are enshrined in Indian Constitution such as, democracy, freedom of speech and secularism are all implicitly an attitude of *anekântavâda.* The Jain doctrine with its emphasis on *ahiṃsâ* and *anekântavâda,* is capable of solving religious intolerance, hatred, violence and so on. Ignoring the life and views of others, rooted in dogmatic and ill knowledge and disrespecting the legitimate claims of others, leads to violence and destructive behaviour. *Anekântavâda* has a larger role in our context today, as it is designed to avoid one-sided error, reconcile the contradictory viewpoints, accept the multi-faceted nature of reality, and respect the relative truth of the observer.

Conclusion

Jainism has given a unique concept of nature which is not found in any other thought. A deep conceptual doctrine, *anekântavâda,* stating that the nature is multidimensional, multifaceted, having infinite modes of manifestation, all existing at once i.e. at the same time. Everything we think, see or imagine is a manifestation of the same Ultimate Truth, although on the face of it, some facets may even appear mutually contradictory. It is not merely a doctrine but it is also a physical reality, a true and complete description, depending on what is being observed. It also has application in day to day life for harmony and understanding at personal, societal, national, and spiritual levels.[47]

It has been pointed out that an object or reality cannot be fully comprehended by worldly beings because of its multi-dimensional aspect of reality, as ordinary humans cannot rise above the limitations of their senses; their understanding of reality is partial and is valid only from an observer's point of view. This is why Jainism points to the fact that reality may be comprehended from different 'angles', and every standpoints are important for understanding the theory or relative pluralism, which brings out the relativity of descriptions or accounts of the world, both concrete and abstract. In fact there can be infinite number of the standpoints. The idea of pluralism which

47 Narendra Bhandari, *Jainism The Eternal and Universal Path for Enlightenment* (Ahmadabad: RISSIOS), 33.

says that all religions, more or less, are of the same virtue and that different religions respond to the Mystery of Ultimate Reality in different ways, points towards *anekântavâda* theory especially the parable of the blind men and an elephant. It is certain that every religion has their own way of experiencing the Mystery of Ultimate Reality, although the source of their manifestation is one but different religion has expressed the experience according to their own perspective and understanding just like the story of the blind men and an Elephant. And all their expression stands valid and true simply because all of their expression is nothing but a partial truth about that one single reality. Every individual should know that, we have a limited perception; and our perception is not enough to know everything that roams around this planet. Moreover the mystery of God's relationship with every individual shows that everybody experience the same reality in different ways, and that is enough to invite everyone to be in good relationship with one another amidst our differences. In our ordinary epistemological states we are like the blind men taking our single way of knowing reality to be absolute, and thus getting into endless arguments with each other. The Jain *anekântavâda* offers a way out of such endless debate.

15

Contribution of Vijayanagara Empire towards Bhakti Movement of Haridāsas

Baila Chanakesavalu

Introduction

Haridāsa movement is a less popular Bhakti movement which began in Karnataka. Though it was less popular, its roots could be traced by studying the history of Vijayanagara Empire which emerged to revive the Sanatana Dharma. The growth of the movement during thirteenth to fifteenth century can be understood by understanding the historical and religious settings of the Haridāsas.

The Vijayanagara Empire

The history of Vijayanagar has been considered the glorious chapter in the history of Independent Hindu South India during fourteenth century.[1] Historian Suryanath U. Kamath mentions about the rise of Vijayanagara Empire as follows:

> After the fall of Karnataka's royal dynasties, the Hoysalas and the Seunas, and the other dynasties of South India like the Kakatiyas of Warangal (Orangal) and the Pandyas of Madurai, a sort of political vacuum was created in south India. The Vijayanagara Empire came

---

1 K.A. Nilakanta Sastri, *The Illustrated History of South India* (New Delhi: Oxford University Press, 2009), 167.

into existence to fill this vacuum. It also played a historic role in protecting the Hindu religion and culture in south India. They had their capital at Vijayanagara (modern Hampi near Hospet in Bellary district).[2]

Historian N Venkata Ramanayya writes that two copper-plate grants (inscriptions) both dated in 1336 CE, attribute the foundation of the Vijayanagara to Harihara I.[3] In the context of the distressing social and economic conditions that prevailed in Dakkan and South India on account of the Muhammadan occupation, the Vijayanagara Empire devoted and dedicated to the restoration and maintenance of Hindu independence and culture.[4] Two theories: Telugu/ Warangal origin[5] and Karnataka origin give accounts of the origin of Sangama brothers—the founders of the Empire. But the Telugu origin theory lacks support of contemporary records. The Sangama brothers having matrimonial relationship with Hoysalas support prove their Kannada origin.[6] Their devotion towards Karnataka deities and respect towards Kannada language proves their Karnataka origin.[7] Historian Suryanath U Kamath, identifies Harihara, Bukka, Kampana, Marappa, and Muddappa, the sons of Sangama, as founders of Vijayanagara Empire in 1336 CE.[8]

The founders of Vijayanagara Empire were interested in religious matters. The guidance of Vidyāraṇya, the head of the Sṛngeri Monastery in founding the

2 Suryanath U. Kamath, *A Concise History of Karnataka* (Bangalore: M.C.C Publications, 2012), 157.

3 N. Venkata Ramanayya, *Vijayanagara Origin of The City and The Empire* (New Delhi: Asian Educational Services, 1990), 48.

4 Konduri Sarojini Devi, *Religion in Vijayanagara Empire* (Bangalore: Sterling Publishers Private Limited, 1990), 11.

5 The Historians who support Telugu origin theory argue that "Harihara and Bukka, the founders of the Empire, were officers at the court of the Warangal. After the first fall of this Kakatiya capital, they fled and took service under the ruler of Kampila. When Kampila was attacked by the army of the Sultan, he had them converted to Islam. Later, the Delhi Sultan appointed them governors over the southern provinces. In the south, they met sage Vidyāraṇya and under his influence, were reconverted to Hinduism. They revolted against the Delhi Sultan and founded the new Hindu Empire of Vijayanagara". Kamath, *A Concise History of Karnataka*, 158-159.

6 *Kamath, A Concise History of Karnataka*, 158-1-9.

7 "The Sangama Brothers had great devotion for the Karnataka deities like Virupakasha of Hampi or Kesava of Beluru. This also indicates that they originated from the Kannada Country. They signed even their Sanskrit records in Kannada letters as "Shrivirupaksha". Many of their titles were in Kannada language and were used in the same form even in Sanskrit, Tamil and Telugu records. These titles were "Bhasege tappuva rayaraganada," "Moorurayaraganda" "Arirayadatta" and so on. They have not assumed any such titles in Telugu language" Kamath, *A Concise History of Karnataka,* 158-159.

8 Kamath, *A Concise History of Karnataka,* 158-159.

empire is a clear sign of religious intervention in ruling.[9] Emphasis is not laid on Harihara I who did not show any interest in religion. After Harihara, Bukka ruled the empire. During his reign a notable event gives a hint to understand the emperor's attitude towards religion and religious minorities in settling a dispute between Śrī Vaiṣṇavas and Jainas.

Nilakanta Sastri's arguement gives a clue about the task of preserving the Hindu social and political order in their empire by emperors of Vijayanagara.[10] The emperors of Vijayanagara prioritized the task of preserving the Hindu social and political order from being destroyed by Islam.[11]

Social Conditions

The society was divided into a number of castes and sub castes.[12] Casteism seems to have prevailed in the society of Vijayanagara Empire. Each caste had an elder to look after the affairs of their own community. Caste groups had separate settlements of living in quarters of their own and follow their own peculiar customs and habits.[13] Caste differences and untouchablity were rigid and the state helped these elders to enforce caste regulations and untouchability was the undivided part of the society.[14] People of all castes had opportunity to work in Army.[15] A Vīragallu (herostone) which commemorates heroic death of a soldier reveals death of a low caste soldier from Mādara caste.[16] Barbers enjoyed a special patronage from Rāmarāya. Suryanath Kamath notes that "in the local assembly of every place, leaders of all castes had representation."[17] Outcastes were identified with tilling the land and menial work and lived in hamlets at a distance from the village proper.[18] Village schools were run by village teachers under the shade of tree or in verandahs of temples. Learning Sanskrit was not possible to lower strata of society because it was monopolised by Brahmins. The condition of women was good during Vijayanagara Empire. Though they were confined to their homes, they were also performing many public functions including clerks and guardians in the palace.[19]

---

9 Devi, *Religion in Vijayanagara Empire*, 11

10 Sastri, *The Illustrated History of South India*, 203.

11 Sastri, *The Illustrated History of South India*, 203.

12 Kamath, *A Concise History of Karnataka*, 180.

13 Sastri, *The Illustrated History of South India*, 209.

14 Kamath, *A Concise History of Karnataka*, 180.

15 Sastri, *The Illustrated History of South India*, 208.

16 Kamath, *A Concise History of Karnataka*, 180.

17 Kamath, *A Concise History of Karnataka*, 180.

18 Sastri, *The Illustrated History of South India*, 210.

19 Kamath, *A Concise History of Karnataka*, 180.

Economic Condition

Agriculture was the main source of economy in Vijayanagara Empire. The majority of the population lived in villages depending on agriculture as their main occupation.[20] Rice, wheat, jowar, cotton, sugar cane and pulses were grown on large scale along with plantations of betel leaves, coconuts and areca.[21] The village was a settlement of peasants and its assembly an association of landlords.[22] Irrigational facilities were maintained well by the empire, large tanks and canals were built in and around Hampi.[23] Sharing the common land of village with artisans of the village was practised.[24] Weaving of cotton textiles, carpentry and coir work were popular professions; women were also involved in spinning and earned their own wages which improved the economic condition of the families.[25] The rise of feudatory powers increased export trade with new towns. Malenadu and coastal sides were famous for producing spices which heightened the commerce. Surynath notes that "The imperial capital was a great centre of world trade."[26] Public works, like building of forts, canals, huge temples and quarrying of stones elevated their economic conditions.

Religious Conditions

Vijayanagara Empire restored Hindu religion under their royal patronage by understanding that they have to protect the Hindu religion. Konduri Sarojini Devi notes that the "object of the Vijayanagara Empire was the preservation of Hindu Dharma and tradition, Vedic religion and varṇāsrama-dharma against the onslaughts of Islam."[27] Suryanath thus comments about religious conditions during the beginnings of the empire:

> The Empire which had come into existence after the destructive campaigns of the Delhi sultans took upon itself the duty of protecting Hindu religion. 'Gobrahmana Pratipalanacharya' (Protector of cows and the seekers of truth), 'Hindurayasuratrana', Vaidikamarga samstapancharya' are some of the titles of the emperors, indicating the objectives of the empire. As true Hindus,

20 Sastri, *The Illustrated History of South India*, 210.

21 Kamath, *A Concise History of Karnataka*, 181.

22 Sastri, *The Illustrated History of South India*, 214.

23 Kamath, *A Concise History of Karnataka*, 181.

24 Sastri, *The Illustrated History of South India*, 214.

25 Kamath, *A Concise History of Karnataka*, 181.

26 Trade in jewellery and precious stones was going on a scale that stunned the foreign visitors towards the empire of Vijayanagara. Kamath, *A Concise History of Karnataka*, 182.

27 Devi, *Religion in Vijayanagara Empire*, 16.

the emperors protected and patronised all religions including Islam and Christianity. Mangalore had four mosques, and many coastal towns had flourishing settlements of Muslim traders as at Honavar and Mangalore.[28]

The emperors who dedicated themselves for the restoration of Hindu religion patronising other religions is remarkable. Sangama brothers were followers of Śaiva sect, but Harihara had high regard for Advaita Gurus of Sringeri maṭha. Though founders of the empire were Śaivas they accepted Varaha or Divine Boar as their royal insignia.[29] Irrespective of caste and religion, the empire appointed people for high offices. Saints of many religions found patronage under Vijayanagara Empire. A unique record of the reign of Harihara II dated CE 1377 throws light on the revival of Dharma by the Vijayanagara rulers.[30]

Religious tolerance also had a prominent place in the religious history of Vijayanagara Empire. Suryanath quotes the statement of Barbosa: "The King allows such freedom that every man [*sic*] may come and go and live according to his own creed without suffering any annoyance and without enquiry, whether he is a Christian, Jew, Moor or Heathen."[31] All types of religion were favoured under the Rāyās of Vijayanagar, and many temples of South India were restored.[32] All great leaders of the respective religious sects of the empire received state patronage.[33]

Krishnadevarāya (1509-29)

The reign of Krishnadevarāya was the period of Vijayanagara's great success. He is known as an incarnation of the Lord Kṛṣṇa. His coronation was celebrated a fortnight later on Kṛṣṇa Janmastami, the birthday of Lord Kṛṣṇa, to convey the incarnation of Krishnadevarāya.[34] Suryanath Kamath notes, that "Krishnadevarāya, the most able among the emperors of Vijayanagara, has been called the *greatest among the rulers of South India.* He was an able administrator, valiant conqueror, great scholar and religious minded monarch."[35] During his period army was victorious and Vijayanagara city

28 Devi, *Religion in Vijayanagara Empire*, 178.

29 Kamath, *A Concise History of Karnataka*, 178.

30 Devi, *Religion in Vijayanagara Empire*, 17.

31 Kamath, *A Concise History of Karnataka*, 179.

32 Sastri, *The Illustrated History of South India*, 281.

33 Kamath, *A Concise History of Karnataka*, 179.

34 Sastri, *The Illustrated History of South India*, 177.

35 Kamath, *A Concise History of Karnataka*, 167.

was prosperous.[36] He patronized all religious sects.[37] Sastry notes that "His religious orthodoxy was also shown by the capture from the Udayagiri and re-erection in Vijayanagar of a fine image of Balakrishna."[38] The sage Vyāsarāya, a well-known Haridāsa, composed songs celebrating the occasion.[39]

Krishnadevarāya was known as the most liberal minded emperor in the history of Vijayanagara Empire, but he expressed his love towards varṇāśramadharma in his work *Āmuktamālyada*.[40] The emperor was a gifted scholar and wrote the Telugu work *Āmuktamālyada* and the Sanskrit play *Jāmbavatī Kalyāṇam*.[41] *Jāmbavatī Kalyāṇam* describes the marriage of Śrī Kṛṣṇa with Jāmbavatī and was very popular during celebrations of the Caitra or spring carnival of Śrī Virūpākṣa, the tutelary deity of the Vijayanagara Kings. *Āmuktamālyada*, emperor's Telugu work deals with Vaiṣṇavism in general and the Viśiṣṭādvaita school of Rāmānuja in particular.[42] Being a keen observer of people's faith and practices, Krishnadevarāya contributes to the religious literature.

Religious Background

Religion and religious saints have played a role in Haridāsa movement of Karnataka during the Vijayanagara Empire. Existence of various religions in the empire might have given broader understanding to Haridāsa movement.

Vaiṣṇavism

Karnataka has been the home of many religions namely Śaivism, Vaiṣṇavism, Buddhism and Jainism, these religions flourished in Karnataka.[43] The emphasis here on Vaiṣṇvism is because the Haridāsas sprung from this tradition, during Vijayanagara Empire. Vaiṣṇavism was very popular in the Vijayanagara Empire, and several factors contributed to the popularity of the faith.[44] The Rāyas of Vijayanagara were great patrons of Vaiṣṇavism.[45] The Supreme deity Viṣṇu is a divinity of the highest rank in Hinduism.[46] "The word Viṣṇu is

36 Sastri, *The Illustrated History of South India*, 177.

37 Kamath, *A Concise History of Karnataka*, 168.

38 Sastri, *The Illustrated History of South India*, 179.

39 Sastri, *The Illustrated History of South India*, 179.

40 Devi, *Religion in Vijayanagara Empire*, 19.

41 Kamath, *A Concise History of Karnataka*, 168.

42 Devi, *Religion in Vijayanagara Empire*, 29.

43 Kamath, *A Concise History of Karnataka*, 148.

44 Devi, *Religion in Vijayanagara Empire*, 79.

45 Sastri, *The Illustrated History of South India*, 179.

46 J. Gonda, *Aspects of EarlyViṣṇuism* (Delhi: Motilal Banarsidass Publishers, 1993), 1.

derived from the root 'viṣ' and it means to pervade."[47] Konduri Sarojini Devi highlights about Mukti aspect of Vaiṣṇavism:

> The Vaiṣṇava concept of God as Saguṇa Brahman and as one possessing a celestial body of unsurpassable beauty and endowed with auspicious qualities was within the comprehension of the common man (sic) who, obviously, could not grapple with the metaphysical abstractions involved in the Advaita concept of Nirguṇa Brahman. Moreover, the concept of Saguṇa Brahman enabled the easy establishment of a kind of personal equation between man (sic) and God. The Śrī Saṁpradāya aspect of Vaiṣṇvism, associating as it does, Lakṣmi or the Goddess of wealth, with her Divine consort, Lord Viṣṇu, in granting Mukti to the spiritual aspirant, had a great appeal to the imagination of the unsophisticated as well as the intellectual. Again the Visiṣṭādvaita doctrine of prapatti or salvation through self-surrender, the idea that man (sic) could attain Mukti by complete self-resignation to God on one's mere desire was certainly more appealing and attractive than the alternatives of strict monasticism, rigorous austerities, rigid discipline and the like which characterised the way to salvation offered by the other Darsanas.[48]

In this light, great importance was given to Haridāsa tradition and their dāsas had a great appeal since dāsa and dāsa-dāsya bhakti suggested the vision and contemplation of God in every atom of God's creation and the significance and purpose of each and every self.[49] Partaking of the Naivedya by the Vaiṣṇava devotee gave him a priviledge of feeling which was not in practice of Śaivism. Royal patronage was also an important factor for the popularity of Vaiṣṇavism. Vaiṣṇavism flourished during the reign of Saḷuvas who were, the second dynasty of Vijayanagara Empire. Influence and relationship of Vijayanagara rulers with Tamil country is also an aspect of popularity of the faith.

Śaivism and Lingayatism

Śaivism was the most popular religion in the early rulers of Vijayanagara Empire. Sangama brothers, the founders of Vijayanagara Empire, were Śaivites. Details about all schools of Śaivism were mentioned in contemporary records.[50] Śiva is the central figure in Śaivism. Śiva's origin could be traced

47 S. Robertson, *Bhakti Tradition of Vaiṣṇava Āḷvārs and Theology of Religions* (Kolkata: Punthi Pustak, 2006), 13.

48 Devi, *Religion in Vijayanagara Empire*, 79.

49 Devi, *Religion in Vijayanagara Empire*, 79.

50 Devi, *Religion in Vijayanagara Empire*, 49.

to Vedic times. It is understood that "In spite of the fewer hymns devoted to Śiva, there is no reference to the worship of linga or phallic in the Vedas."[51] Pāsupata school of Śaivism was founded by Lakuliśā who was considered an incarnation of Śiva.[52] About the origin of Śaivism, it is stated that "in the religious world, the Saiva system is the heir to all that is most ancient in South India; it is the religion of the Tamil people, by the side of which every other form is comparatively foreign and recent origin."[53] In different schools of Śaivism, Pāsupata School emphasises five categories propounded by the founder. They are Kārya (effect), Kāraṇa (cause), Yoga (meditation), Vidhi (religious practices), Duḥkhānta (dissolution of the sorrow).

In Karnataka, Lingayatism supports Bhakti movement. It is difficult to see the early history of this sect. The vague early history of the sect has led most scholars to conclude that it was founded by Basava, the minister of Kalacuri King Bijjala (1162-1167 CE).[54] However, this is far from the truth, for none of the books on Vīraśaivism, either in Kannada or in Sanskrit, ascribes the foundation of the sect to Basava.[55] A critical examination of the theology and metaphysics of the sect suggests that it is very ancient.[56] Only on the basis of Basava Puraṇa and some other books, some scholars believe Basava to be the founder.

The Lingayats, 'wearers of the linga', or Vīraśaivas, 'heroes for Śiva', seem to have had some connections with the Kalamukha order.[57] There are some scholars who interpret the term to mean a "brave or virile follower of Siva," that is, vira (brave) and Saiva (follower of Siva).[58] However, there are some texts which explain the term to mean a follower of Śiva who takes supreme delight in knowing the fact that the ultimate goal of human life consists in realising the unity between Śiva and the individual soul (jivatman).[59]

---

51 Robertson, *Bhakti Tradition of Vaiṣṇava Āḷvārs and Theology of Religions*, 22.

52 Devi, *Religion in Vijayanagara Empire*, 49.

53 Robertson, *Bhakti Tradition of Vaiṣṇava Āḷvārs and Theology of Religion*, 22.

54 S. C. Nandimath, *A Handbook of Virasaivism*, 2nd ed. (Delhi: Motilal Banarasidass, [1942]; 1979), 1.

55 Nandimath, *A Handbook of Virasaivism*, 1.

56 Nandimath, *A Handbook of Virasaivism,* 1.

57 Gavin flood, *An Introduction to Hinduism* (NewYork: Cambridge University Press, 1996), 171.

58 Moti Lal Pandit, *Saivism: A Religio-Philosophisal History* (New Delhi: Theological Research and Communication Institute, 1987), 102.

59 Pandit, *Saivism: A Religio-Philosophisal History*, 104.

Buddhism

The influence of Buddhism was not widespread during Vijayanagara Empire, except in few places such as Kancīpuram, Nāgapaṭṭanam and Kaḷāvati.[60] This may be inferred from the existence of sculptures of Buddha and ephigraphs registering grants of villages for the worship of Buddha.[61] Konduri Sarojini Devi notes about the incarnation of Viṣṇu as Buddha and writes as follows:

> Buddha was considered to be an avatar or incarnation of Viṣṇu, a viewpoint supported by Bhāgavata Purāṇa, the Varāha Purāṇa, the Agni Purāṇa, and the later purāṇas. A contemporary literary work Āmukta Mālyada, also includes Buddha among the incarnations of Viṣṇu. According to one legend, Lord Viṣṇu assumed the avatar of Buddha and destroyed three cities of Tripurāsura with the help of his son, Manmatha. Another version credits Śiva with the destruction of the cities of Tripurāsura. The former version namely that Viṣṇu performed the great feat of destruction appearing as Buddha suggests that Buddha was not only accepted as the Supreme Being-Incarnate but was also credited with possessing the supernatural and miraculous powers of God.[62]

Buddhism flourished as a Śramana movement to counter the sacrificial nature of Hinduism. Because of its nature, Buddhism attracted many people and rulers. But the Bhakti movement originated to counter the rapid growth of Buddhism and Jainism.[63]

Jainism

Jainism had more influence on the life of people, particularly in Karnataka.[64] Jaina authors have made striking contributions to Kannada and Tamil literature. The reason behind the influence of Jainism on people is its affinity with Hinduism. Sastry notes that "Jainism had much more in common with Hinduism than Buddhism, and many popular beliefs and practices were common to both the systems."[65] Many historians note that settlement of a dispute between Śrīvaiṣṇavas and Jainas took place during the reign of Bukka, in which assurance was taken from Śrīvaiṣṇavas that they will protect the Jainas who were in minority.[66] During Vijayanagara period, Jainism was an

60 Devi, *Religion in Vijayanagara Empire*, 188.

61 Devi, *Religion in Vijayanagara Empire*.

62 Devi, *Religion in Vijayanagara Empire*.

63 Robertson, *Bhakti Tradition of Vaiṣṇava Āḷvārs and Theology of Religion*, 24.

64 Sastri, *The Illustrated History of South India*, 283.

65 Sastri, *The Illustrated History of South India*, 283.

66 Kamath, *A Concise History of Karnataka*, 162.

anti-Vedic movement; it came closer to theistic religions due to the changed environment, especially in Karnataka.[67]

Jainism came to Karnataka along with a Mauryan King and received ample support from all the kings of Karnataka.[68] The Satavahanas, the Kadambas, were the first patrons of Jainism in Karnataka. Later Chalukyas, Rashtrakuṭas and Hoysalas extended their willingness to patronize Jainism in Karnataka.[69] The religious tolerance of Karnataka rulers and especially Rāyas of Vijayanagara made possible the co-existence of religions in their empire.

Viṣṇu or Kṛṣṇa as Hari

It is noted that "The culmination of Vaiṣṇava Bhakti is found in the Kṛṣṇa cult, which is a point where various cults converge."[70] Kṛṣṇa is considered as an incarnation (avatara) of Viṣṇu.[71] Mahabharata depicts him as conqueror and protector of the whole earth by residing in Dvārakā. Robertson mentions that "Long before the beginning of the Christian era, Kṛṣṇa was identified with Viṣṇu, Nārāyana and Vāsudeva."[72] This idea connects the worship of Vedic God Viṣṇu and the cosmic god Nārāyana of the Brahmāṇas and the identity of Vāsudeva Kṛṣṇa with Viṣnu and Nārāyana.[73] R. G. Bhandarkar mentions that "The worship of Vāsudeva must be regarded to be as old as Panini."[74] J Gonda suggests that Kṛṣṇa was identified with Viṣṇu because, the benevolent Viṣṇu always was the deliverer of humankind in distress and great helper of the other gods against asuras.[75]

Hari means "tawny, pale or reddish yellow, fallow etc" and used as the Vedic term applying to fire, the sun, lightning.[76] The term Hari serves as a substantive to indicate a tawny horse, Agni, Soma, the pressing stones, the sun, and lightning.[77] As a divine name Hari also occurs in connection with Indra, Soma, and various other beings including demons that belong to Viṣṇu.[78]

67 Devi, *Religion in Vijayanagara Empire*, 161.

68 R. S. Mugali, *The Heritage of Karnataka* (Mysore: Geetha Book House Publishers, 1990), 101.

69 Mugali, *The Heritage of Karnataka*, 101.

70 Robertson, *Bhakti Tradition of Vaiṣṇava Āḷvārs and Theology of Religion*, 19.

71 Gonda, *Aspects of EarlyViṣṇuism*, 157.

72 Robertson, *Bhakti Tradition of Vaiṣṇava Āḷvārs and Theology of Religions*, 20.

73 Robertson, *Bhakti Tradition of Vaiṣṇava Āḷvārs and Theology of Religions,* 20.

74 Ramakrishna Gopal Bhandarkar, *Vaisnavism, Saivism and Minor Religious Systems* (New Delhi: Asian Educational Services, 1983), 4.

75 Gonda, *Aspects of EarlyViṣṇuism*, 159.

76 Gonda, *Aspects of EarlyViṣṇuism*, 107.

77 Gonda, *Aspects of EarlyViṣṇuism*, 107.

78 Gonda, *Aspects of EarlyViṣṇuism*, 107.

Madhvacarya used this term Hari to address the supreme soul that is God. The Haridāsas who were influenced by Madhvic teachings dedicated their songs to Hari and preached the same.

The Bhakti Tradition

The paper thus far has discussed and analyzed the historical and religious back ground which supported Bhakti and Bhakti movement led by Hari dāsas in Karnataka. The above mentioned religions contributed to the Bhakti movement. Lingayatism flourished from Śaivism and Haridāsa movement from Vaiṣṇavism. These movements impacted contemporary societies very much to arouse mood of Bhakti in devotees. In light of Haridāsa movement it is important to understand Bhakti. Bhakti tradition of Hari dāsas has its background in general Bhakti movement.

Roots of Bhakti Movement

The History of Bhakti Movement can be divided into four periods, Upanisidic Period, Religio-philosophical Period, Acharya Period (eighth to thirteenth centuries), and Period of Saints (thirteenth to sixteenth century).[79] Bhakti has its roots in Upanishads. The origin of Upanishads goes back to the Aryan settlement in India on the plains of the Ganges and Jamuna.[80] Even though Upanishads show variety of religious beliefs, they show a ray of Bhakti also in them. The Bhakti, which emphasizes belief in a Personal God, also exists in Upanishads. This Doctrine is found in two of the later Upanishads, The Katha and Svetasvatara.[81] The author of Svetasvatara Upanishad says thus about Bhakti:

> There is a God of grace who is the creator of the world. He exercises choice, electing those to whom He would like to reveal himself. He lives within the human heart and yet is different from it. The human soul and the Divine soul are like two people drinking together; the orders of the righteous world, that is, are subject to the requirements of a moral universe. This Divine being cannot be reached by mere learning. He can only be reached by that complete surrender to Him, which in after ages is described as Bhakti. Such a yielding up of the human soul to God results in genuine peace and joy.[82]

---

79 A. P. Karmarkar, and N. B. Kalamdani, *Mystic teachings of The Haridāsas of Karnāṭak* (Dharwar: Karnatak Vidyavardhak Sangha, 1939), 4.

80 Appasamy, *The Theology of Hindu Bhakti*, 9.

81 Appasamy, *The Theology of Hindu Bhakti*. 9.

82 Appasamy, *The Theology of Hindu Bhakti*. 9.

Bhagavad Gita was also a real source of inspiration for Bhakti during the religio-philosophic period. "The wave of the Bhagavad Gita period lasted till about the 8th century CE. The religion propounded in the Gita was going on hand in hand with those of Śaiva, Buddhist, Jaina and other religious systems."[83] "It was in this period that the Vaiṣṇavite works, the Pancharātra Āgama, the Nārada Bhakti Sūtra and the Śaṇḍilya Sūtra as also the Śaiva Āgamas and the Tantras came into existence."[84] Period of Acharyas also contributed to the development of Bhakti. During this period systematic and logical exposition of different branches of philosophy was studied. After the period of the Bhagavad Gita, the wave of devotion began with the Śri-Vaiṣṇavas in the south under the leadership of Rāmānuja.[85] The great Madhva almost brought it to perfection by propounding his own theory of dualism in the Kannada country. The Haridāsas were the direct followers of Madhva.[86]

Bhakti in Karnataka

Bhakti played important role in the religious culture of Karnataka.[87] R. S. Mugali notes thus about Karnataka's religious scenario:

> The earliest phase of the religion of ancient Karnataka was theism and animism, which have not altogether disappeared from the life of the masses even today. Next, the Aryans introduced his (sic) Vedic faith, modified by the cult of Bhakti. The spread of Jainism somewhat arrested its growth for centuries together. But, it leapt into prominence with the successive rise of the different religious schools like those of Rāmānuja, Basava and Madhva. The Harihara cult of Bhakti and the Bhāgavata tradition of the Smārta sect also grew in importance within the general enlivening atmosphere of Bhakti, created by the great schools mentioned above.[88]

The Dāsas and Śaraṇas of Karnataka, of whatever caste, creed or sex they might be, impressed on the orthodox society the significance and the value of inner culture rather than that of outward form.[89] Mugali notes that teaching of the Bhakti in the language of the people originated at first in the south in the

83 Kalamdani, *Mystic teachings of The Haridāsas of Karnāṭak,* 6.

84 Kalamdani, *Mystic teachings of The Haridāsas of Karnāṭak*, 7.

85 Kalamdani, *Mystic teachings of The Haridāsas of Karnāṭak,* 7.

86 Kalamdani, *Mystic teachings of The Haridāsas of Karnāṭak*, 7.

87 Mugali, *The Heritage of Karnataka*, 115.

88 Mugali, *The Heritage of Karnataka*, 115.

89 Mugali, *The Heritage of Karnataka*, 119.

Tamil land and then spread in Karnataka through the Vachanas of the Vīraśaiva mystics and the songs of the devotees.[90]

In North Karnataka during the middle part of 12th century a great revolution took place. This revolution became a Vīraśaiva movement which gave much importance to Bhakti. Many mystic saints such as Allamaprabhu, Basava, Chennabasava, Siddharama, Akkamahadevi were part of this movement and invoked a great measure of Bhakti in devotees of the movement. They shared their Bhakti experience in a common platform which was known as Anubhava mantapa.

Likewise in 13th century through the leadership of Vedantic teacher Madhva near Uḍupi in south Kanara, Dvaita doctrine flourished. This doctrine emphasised on devotion to Viṣṇu as the highest deity. Some of his successors propagated his thoughts in Sanskrit. Devotees of this faith were disciples of Madhva's successors. Puraṅdaradāsa and Kanakadāsa popularised the school of Bhakti through the institution of Dāsakuṭa, composed of Haridāsas or servants of God, singing songs in simple and racy Kannada.[91]

Growth of Bhakti Movement

Few reasons could be considered for the growth of Bhakti movement in Karnataka and Southern part of India. In consideration to this Robertson mentions that "The main reason cited by many scholars is that it curtailed the growth of Buddhism and Jainism and gave impetus for the renaissance of Hinduism in the form of Bhakti saints.[92] He adds that "One such view is that *bhakti seems to have been Hinduism's method of defense against other religious systems which threatened to eliminate all that is most characteristic of Hinduism, and to deprive its votaries of those things in Hinduism which most bring comfort and consolation to ordinary men and women.*"[93] The social conditions of the time were the reasons for the growth of Bhakti movement. Negative attitudes of Jainism towards religion and women was also another reason pointed out for the growth of Bhakti movement especially in south India.[94] Bhakti cult showed that human beings were eligible for emancipation if they were pure in mind word and deed.[95] Inclusion of the people from lower strata of society was another important reason for the growth of Bhakti movement.[96]

90 Mugali, *The Heritage of Karnataka*, 123.

91 Mugali, *The Heritage of Karnataka*, 100.

92 Robertson, *Bhakti Tradition of Vaiṣṇava Āḷvārs and Theology of Religions*, 10.

93 Robertson, *Bhakti Tradition of Vaiṣṇava Āḷvārs and Theology of Religions*, 10.

94 Robertson, *Bhakti Tradition of Vaiṣṇava Āḷvārs and Theology of Religions*, 10.

95 Mugali, *The Heritage of Karnataka*, 119.

96 Robertson, *Bhakti Tradition of Vaiṣṇava Āḷvārs and Theology of Religions*, 11.

Simplifying the religious teachings in vernaculars rather than Sanskrit was another reason which contributed to the growth of Bhakti movement. The unconditional grace of the Supreme God which is available unto common man or woman by Bhakti was also a reason to the growth of Bhakti movement. Acceptance of all without the discrimination of the caste, without the linguistic barriers, and the choice of personal God appealed the mass.

Dāsa Bhakti

Bhakti movement allows various forms of Bhakti. Bhāgavata Purana mentions various types of Bhakti. Haridāsas emphasized on Dāsa Bhakti, because this "Dāsa Bhakti suggested the vision and contemplation of God in every atom of God's creation and the significance and purpose of each and every self."[97] Konduri Sarojini Devi states with reference to the Bhāgavata Puraāa and Sanḍilya sūtra, these different kinds of Bhakti or devotion for obtaining happiness in this life: "Sankīrtana (singing the glories of the Lord); Smarana (meditation); pāda-seva (worshipping the holy feet of the Lord); Sravana (listening to stories or songs in of the Lord); Arcana (offering different kinds of service); Vandana (bowing to the Lord in prayer); Dāsya (serving the deity in many different ways); Dāsa-dāsya (serving the devotees of the Lord)."[98] These are few among the suggested ways of Bhakti. This highlighted in Puraṅdaradāsa's lyric saying "Dāsana Maḍiko enna sāsira nāmada Venkaṭa ramaṇa" which means "make me your salve O thousand named Venkataramana."

Hari Dāsaru

The Haridāsas[99] were saints of the Madhva Sampradaya who preached the Bhakti to Lord Hari with their mystic experiences during thirteenth century CE onwards.[100] "Dāsakūṭa or the order of Dāsas was composed of saintly souls belonging to different communities."[101] Karmarkar and Kalamdani mention about the non-recognition of Haridāsas as follows:

97 Devi, *Religion in Vijayanagara Empire*, 79.

98 Devi, *Religion in Vijayanagara Empire*, 108.

99 Another important group that propagated Bhakti in Karnataka constitutes Haridāsas who were votaries of the Dwaitha religion ushered in by Madhvacharya. The Dāsakūṭa component of this school lead by Puraṅdaradāsa and Kanakadāsa has preached the tenets of Bhakti within the parameters of their philosophical beliefs. Their Kīrtanas were eminently successful in merging of literature and music in the service of Bhakti. Here again Sanskrit was pushed to the background. Some of the devotional lyrics by these servant and singing saints and their successors have lasting merits. http://www.Classicalkannada.Org/index English html. Accessed on 13.09.2013.

100 Devi, *Religion in Vijayanagara Empire*, 144.

101 Devi, *Religion in Vijayanagara Empire*, 114.

Even Sir R.G. Bhandarkar has not referred to the Viṭṭhal cult which originated and flourished in Karnaṭak since the thirteenth century A.D. (cf. His work: *Vaiṣṇavism and Śaivism*). Not to mention the efforts made by Dr. Kittel and Rice, it may be asserted that only in recent years some efforts have been made to furnish a historically correct account in connection with the Haridāsas. The late R. B. Narasimhachar has given a brief survey of these Haridāsas in his "*Karnaṭak Kavicharite*". Mr. Belur Keshavadas of Mysore, in his recently published work '*Sri Karnāṭak Bhakta-Vijaya*' vols I&II, has given a detailed account of the various historical incidents and miraculous deeds in the lives of some of Haridāsas.[102]

Haridāsas in Karnataka flourished during the Vijayanagara period and had the privilege of royal patronage. But when it comes to the general assessment of Bhakti movement in India and in Karnataka, the role of Haridāsas were less identified. It is observed that "The Haridāsas of Karnataka were thus the first to develop the cult of devotion to Viṭhala and make it a living faith in the Vijayanagara Empire."[103]

102 Kalamdani, *Mystic teachings of The Haridāsas of Karnāṭak*, 9.

103 Devi, *Religion in Vijayanagara Empire*, 144.

16

Revisiting Religious Fundamentalism, Globalization and Empire: A Christian Response

Ravela Jeeva Kumar

Introduction

I am much privileged to present this paper[1] in honor of Rev. Dr. Tadivaka Swamiraju on the occasion his 60th Birthday. Swamiraju ayyagaru teaches in the Department of Religions (Specialization in the area of Hinduism) at Andhra Christian Theological College, Hyderabad. I had the privilege of being his student during my BD studies at ACTC. He blends both spirituality and philosophy in his contemplations. He always thinks of the church as progressive and inclusive community. He is very constructive and organized at the work place. He is a serious academician, writer and a humble servant of God. I pray and wish that God's amazing blessings be upon him on this occasion and make him a blessing to the generations to come. This paper examines the religious fundamentalism as a threat that perpetuates disharmony to a society. It also

1 This is a revised version of the paper presented in the National Colloquium organized by SATHRI at Henry Martin Institute, Hyderabad held from 9-11 August, 2016. The author acknowledges the encouragement of UTC doctoral friends in presenting this paper and also would like to thank Rev. Fr. Jerry Kurian for the suggestions to the paper. Also, the author acknowledges the contribution of Ms. Zubeno Kitahn to the core of the paper in its initial stage.

proposes various probable views to demonstrate Christian commitment as a response to religious fundamentalism in our context.

Religions can provide a discreet contemplation to promote harmony and wellbeing in society. The reality of diverse religions and religious ideologies cause either social tensions or sociable environment among people as it depends how religions are being used in a society. Nevertheless, the present world witnesses that religious ideology has unfortunately become a source of conflict and violence. Religious fundamentalism emerges out of certain religious ideology that disturbs serenity and harmonious life of the society and causes human destruction. Perhaps one can interpret that the history of religions is replete with disharmony and bloodshed. India is known as a land of diverse religions, multiple cultures and languages. A wide range of faiths maintains a beautiful sustenance of religiosity of people in this country. This multiple religious environment exposes to a variety of spiritualities which have probable chances to create vivid notions about God, salvation and social welfare of all. Of course, it can also lead to disputes over theological notions of divinity and humanity.

It is observed that in Indian society very often ruling power of the state reasons divisive politics and religious intimidation which perturb the socio-economic life of the citizens. Few fundamentalists and their cultural organizations collaborate with political power and create a sense of fear and terror as they deeply commit to restore the culture and glory of their religious faith which they believe is at the verge of losing its sanctity. These organizations work as vertebrae for various political parties messing up the notions of culture and nationalism. They also endorse fanatic views in the name of religion and culture by denying safe space to the minorities in the country. Owing to the fact that fundamentalism raises intolerance among the citizens, the present Indian society faces innumerable conflicts and riots. At this point it is inevitable to understand the issues of religion, state and the evil nature of fundamentalism that obstructs humane environment in our society. It is indispensable to reflect upon the space which the religions occupy in the life of human society, religious fundamentalism and the nexus between religion and state. It is to fathom the role of religion that has to promulgate peace and justice against the notion of religious fundamentalism.

This paper is an attempt to unpack the nexus between religion and state in the context of religious fundamentalism and its negative consequences in our society. While dealing with such an intrinsic topic, the following questions are imperative to respond from Christian point of view. What is the stand of a Christian against the fanatic view of religion? What is the response of the church to a situation where and when State, aided by certain religious ideology becomes silent at the issues of religious fundamentalism and violence? How can Christian theology embedded in the gospel of Jesus Christ address the issues of fundamentalism and religious violence?

Religion and Fundamentalism: An Overview

Religions deliberate about the existence of God and God's actions in the world. The notion of religion develops a position of self-human consciousness which affirms a body of truths about God and it is a human duty that can be discovered by natural reason.[2] The major theistic traditions such as Judaism, Christianity and Islam claim the existence, nature and activities of God and understanding of God as eternal, all-powerful, all-knowing, the creator and sustainer of the universe and the proper object of human obedience and worship.[3] Particularly philosophers of religion examine those claims whether 'the conception of the object of human religious activity is coherent and such a being of God really exists.'[4] Therefore the notion religion implies to the existence and nature of God asserts revealing power of the divine that empowers human to experience unique relationship with God who is omni sense, omnipotent and omnipresent.

Fundamentalism arises when there are diverse opinions of people about certain issues. Most probably it emerges in the sphere of religions when people follow certain doctrines as part of their conventional spiritual practices. Fundamentalism desires to go back to basics and reemphasize the very idea of 'what is said' in the religious teachings which according to fundamentalists is a revelation of God to the ancient people. Even fundamentalists go to the extent of creating violence and injustice to the communities and justify it as it is the will of God to do so.[5] Particularly fundamentalists do not accept and receive modern way of interpreting the scriptures and the fusion of science and reason in understanding the meaning of life and God in religious scriptures. In this process, they cannot accept modern interpretation of those revealed teachings. For the reason that they fear of those modern hermeneutics that exacerbate the essence of original teachings handed down from generations to generations. When radical views which modernity brings out, come to dominate over the teachings of religion, the followers of that religion cannot tolerate any kind of alteration in its interpretation of teachings but resist the dominance of modernity. In other words, fundamentalism, does not welcome modern thinking of religious teachings but follow the old teachings even in modern days.

2 W. J. Wainwright, "Natural religion," in *The Cambridge of Dictionary of Philosophy*, ed., Robert Audi (Cambridge: Cambridge University Press, 1995), 521.

3 Philip L. Quinn, "Philosophy of Religion," in *The Cambridge of Dictionary of Philosophy*, ed., Robert Audi (Cambridge: Cambridge University Press, 1955), 607.

4 Philip L. Quinn, "Philosophy of Religion," 608.

5 Aloys Otieno Ojore, "Religious Fundamentalism," *AFER* 1 (2001), 257.

The mid of 19th century witnesses the birth of fundamentalism in all the religions across the world espousing certain way of belief system, which is being endorsed by the teachings of religions. In the history of Christianity, the Protestant movement of North America played a vital role in rising fundamentalism as a movement based on the ideas of dispensationalism. Dispensationalism rejected the liberal interpretation of the scriptures advocated by modern theologians and initiated a committed reading of the Bible, interpreting the word of God based on the division of history into period of time and dispensations that are named as seven.[6] The dispensationalists who upheld literal meaning of the biblical teachings believed in the structured periods of time and went to the extension of anticipating the second coming of Christ. They labelled themselves as fundamentalists as they believe in the basics of scriptures. The Calvinists, Presbyterians and Calvinistic Baptists were groups who took up this movement to the level of convincing new believers to grasp the word of God as it is written. The movement of fundamentalists had spread across Europe and America promulgating the literal meaning of salvation, fellowship and second coming of Jesus Christ by the beginning of 20th century.[7]

In the recent years, Islamic fundamentalism has been a global threat to peace, security and human rights in the world thereby the exchange of knowledge, cultural investigations to redefine politics and the spirit of nationalism have become crippled. Islamic fundamentalist believes in violence and brutality in order to disseminate their fundamental views that continue to terrorize people in many incidents and much of bloodshed is the result. Although the roots of Islamic fundamentalism go back to the first centuries of Islam it dawns few decades ago when Ruhollah Khomeini came to power in Iran in 1979.[8] Mohammad Mohaddessin is of the opinion that the regime of Khomeini transformed the idea of creating a global Islamic rule from an unachievable ideal to an achievable goal by many fundamentalist groups being aided by the global Islamic nations.[9] Consequently, it led to the emergence of

---

6 The seven periods of time developed by dispensationalists were very much rampant during the 20th century in the spirit of protestant movements. According to them the seven are named as Innocence (the Garden of Eden), Conscience (Adam to Noah), Human Government (Noah to Abraham), Promise (Abraham to Moses), Law (Moses to Christ), Grace (Christ through the present to the Judgment of the world) and the Kingdom or Millennium. This belief system stems from a small British sect called "Plymouth Brethren' which rose up in Ireland and England during 1820's. Ernest R. Sandeen, *The Origins of Fundamentalism: Toward a Historical Interpretation* (Philadelphia: Fortress Press, 1968), 4.

7 Sandeen, *The Religious Fundamentalism: Toward a Historical Interpretation*, 5-6.

8 Mohammad Mohaddessin, *Islamic Fundamentalism: The New Global Threat* (New Delhi: Anmol Publications, 2001), xxi.

9 Mohaddessin, *Islamic Fundamentalism: The New Global Threat*, 41.

various Islamic fundamentalist groups who deteriorate the healthy relationships among the nations with their violent attacks and brutal killings.

Fundamentalism in India is rampant as it negates the reality of existence of multiple religions in the country. Perhaps it is the Hindu fundamentalism that tempts and causes cultural riots and communal violence in Indian society. The beginning of 20th century developed various socio-political and religious situations in India. As India was under British rule struggling to get independence, the national congress party, particularly under the leadership of Nehru and Gandhi, was busy in spreading the spirit of nationalism among the people of the country. On the other hand, Hindu religious ideologues fabricated the spirit of nationalism based on the Hindu religious views which caused much tension and communal riots. One can witness that such a religious fanaticism led to the division of the country into two nations as India and Pakistan. The Hindu religious fundamental view has become widespread with a book entitled '*Hindutva: Who is a Hindu*' written by Vinayak Savarkar, a Brahmin in 1923. This book interprets 'Hinduness' in a peculiar way arguing Christianity and Islam as foreign religions and they have holy locations outside India thereby it is meaningless to sustain those religions in the land of India.[10] This eventually led to emerge the modern Hindu fundamentalist movement known as Hindutva. The Hindutva fundamentalism becomes extreme and labels Christianity and Islam as threat to Hinduism and cultural nationalism which is the main essence of Hindu movement. Moreover, it denies the freedom of religion and human rights of minorities.[11] Such a religious fundamentalism, in fact, regulates political agenda which in most of the cases becomes threat to the minority religions particularly in the context of existence of multiple religions. Indian society experiences such fundamentalism at the moment in which the State with the ideology of a particular religion brings out the notions of culture, language and nationalism eventually targets and seizes the religious freedom of citizens. Denying a safe space to the people of other faiths has been a phenomenon in Indian context. Hinduism as a dominant religion in India with its plethora of organizations like Hindutva, Rashtriya Swayamsevak Sangh (RSS), Vishwa Hindu Parishad (VHP) etc. spreads hatred and discrimination against the minority. It also promotes division among people of the country galvanizing cultural nationalism against the interest and perception of non-Hindu religious communities.

---

10 Mary Ann Lind, "Hinduism, Fundamental," in *Encyclopedia of Fundamentalism*, ed., Brenda E. Brasher (New York: Routledge, 2001), 224.

11 S. Robertson, *Freedom of Religion: A Human Rights Issue* (Bangalore: BTESSC/SATHRI, 2007), 6-16.

The Nexus between Religion and Empire

It is a reality even in the days of antiquity that religion supports empire or empire exists with the support of religion and making it as part of state administration. The bilateral relationship between religion and empire is obvious which could be seen in the history of religions. The ancient Egyptian and Israelite kingdoms believed that kings are the representatives of God on the Earth as the kingship was not a secular but a religious office in the ancient west Asia.[12] The Hebrew Bible witnesses that there was violence and bloodshed when state uses religion to support its political authority (I Kings Chaps. 16-18).[13] The notion of divine emperor was also strong in the Middle East during the early church period and emperor sanctions the *modus operandi* of the political matters with aid of religion. Hence, it is imperative to detect the nexus between religion and empire in the past and present in order to underline the negative consequences that have surfaced out of such a merger of both. The history of Christianity informs us that Christianity had been declared as a religion of the empire as soon as the early church grew and multiplied in many parts of Asia and Middle East. In the fourth century Constantinople safeguarded Christians from the threats of state military forces and Theodosius in the later fourth century made Christianity the official religion of the empire.[14] The Catholic Church in Europe with the help of empire invaded the Islamic nations in the medieval period to uproot Islam in many countries in the Middle East and reclaimed the Holy places of Jerusalem and other cities as they were related to the faith traditions of Christianity. These invasions were known as religious crusades led by European churches against Muslim states in the history. This was one of the examples to understand that the Church utilized the power of empire in accomplishing what they have aimed in terms of religious establishments. Probably, these religious invasions would inform the exclusivistic and truimphalistic attitudes of Christianity in the medieval period.

After Islam was founded in the seventh century as religion, it became a state religion in many empires. It was a state religion during the Ottoman Empire in the Middle East as well as in several other empires and it intervened in and influenced the state policies in many Islamic nations.[15] On the one hand, in some countries few Islamic religious groups opposed the state for using

---

12 John Bright, *The History of Israel*, 3rd ed. (London: SCM Press, 1981), 221-223.

13 R. Jeeva Kumar, "Ecclesiology in the Context of Religious Fundamentalism: An Old Testament View," in *Ecclesiology: The Continuing Possibility of Renewal—Festschrift to Bishop Dyvasirvadam on his 60th Birthday*, ed., Ch. Vasantha Rao and Vinod Victor (Delhi: ISPCK, 2012), 102-106.

14 Scott A. Merrimann, *Religion and the State: An International Analysis of Roles and Relationships* (Santa Barbara: ABC-CLIO, LLC, 2009), xvi.

15 Merrimann, *Religion and the State: An International Analysis of Role and Relationships*, 41-43.

Islam to develop the notion of nationalism. Pakistan is going through this kind of struggle. On the other hand, some groups supported the state to increase power in order to ensure that Islam was supported by state for its dominant existence. Afghanistan is a prime example where several Islamic groups support the state to use the power of the state to achieve political means aiming Islamic teachings to be promulgated. Of course, both Christianity and Islam allowed other religions to exist in their states but imposed varying degrees of penalties upon the minority religions. Though some states recognized and accepted religious freedom of all by the end of the eighteenth century, religion and state help and sustain each other's position in their existence.[16]

On careful examination of the nexus between religion and state in India it is apparent that Hinduism had sustained its hegemony with the help of the state. Long back ago, the Vedic Hinduism established and sustained caste system imposed religious hegemony on Dravidians the original inhabitants of the Land. Although Jainism and Buddhism emerged as counter movements against such a heinous religious structure of Hinduism, down the years Hinduism with its dominating principles was able to destroy these religions and converted them into Hinduism.[17] At the same time, the emergence of Hindu fundamentalists, particularly in the beginning of the 20th century, permeated the politics and began to utilize the power of state. Thus, religion and state are intertwined with each other in many instances to establish the state that implements the teachings of religion. Prior to the world wars the majority of nations across the globe experienced colonial regimes and religious conversions and invasions alongside. After the collapse of Empire in many nations, states have taken formation. In the context where states have been created by the people replacing the rule of empires, the notions of democracy and secularism have been continuously thrived to sustain states. States have been formed not with the religious interest but with the secular position and ideology. Under the influence of modernism and liberalism all the nations adopted secular view of state to govern its people beyond religious influence. However, religion still becomes a tool in the hands of rulers to establish a new way of cultural life and cultural nationalism by taking aid from religions in all possible ways. It is very startling to understand that religion and politics are intersecting at various points in terms of framing rules and laws that lead a society. Robert Pope argues that religion aided by the state and its political agenda provides a secular space to emerge religious fundamentalism with the support of political realm. He says,

---

16 Merriman, *Religion and the State: An International Analysis of Roles and Relationships*, xvii.

17 David G. Bradley, *A Guide to world Religions* (New Jersey: Prentice Hall, 1963), 104ff.

> Fundamentalisms become most significant when they enter specifically into the political arena. Whether they do so explicitly, in the form of a recognizable political group or implicitly in the form of influence exercised as a consequence of conviction, politics is still the place where fundamentalisms become public, where they are seen to be most effective and most dangerous. As a result, any discussion of religious fundamentalism must at some stage turn to its relationship with the political realm.[18]

It is clear that by utilizing state and its political space religions promote fundamentalism influencing political arena to introduce and implement what religions is seeking among the people. The present post-modern society experiences integration of religion and politics that capture the power to establish a culture that would define nationalism. Such sort of power drawn by merging religion and politics determines to construct human made neo-cultural lifestyle. The question of religion's role in politics and society has intensified with the emergence of modernization and secularization as they influence the social life of citizens in such a way that it directs them to embrace a new way of life which is against the teachings of religions. Some western sociologist in the 1950s predicted the death of religion. They postulated that as human beings discovered the delights of consumerism, there is far less interest in traditional matters like religion. Triumph of modernism will leave no room for "superstition."[19] This global economic system is largely driven and exported by the West along with its political institutions, technologies and culture with little or less regard to how these impositions may be received or to the reactions that may provoke.[20]

There is a strong nexus between globalization and religious fundamentalism. The consequence of globalization is seen in its overarching and driven motive of free market capitalism which is spread to virtually every country of the world. Freidman defines globalization as "the inexorable integration of markets, nation-states and technologies to a degree never witnessed before—in a way that is enabling individuals, corporation and states to reach around the world further, faster, deeper and cheaper than ever before."[21] This system is "hegemonic" because of "its control and dominance

18 Rober Pope, "Battling for God in a Secular world: Political and Fundamentalisms," in *Fundamentalisms*, ed., Christopher H. Partridge (Cumbria: Paternoster Press, 2001), 183.

19 http://www.global-directions.com/articles/religion/religiousfundamentalism.pdf (accessed on 17/10/16).

20 M.J. Stevens, "The Unanticipated Consequences of Globalization: Contextualizing Terrorism," in *The Psychology of Terrorism* 3 (2002): 32 (31-56).

21 T. Freidman, *Understanding Globalization: The Lexus and the Olive Tree* (New York: Anchor Books, 2000), 9.

by powerful individual, national and multinational corporations whose policies, plans and actions are threatening cultural and biological diversity and promoting rise of global monoculturalism."[22] Globalization has become a source of global injustice, inequity, corruption and violence turning "human beings and their cultural activities and creation into commodities for profit."[23] In this regard, according to many religious adherents, fundamentalism is the only way to challenge modernity and globalization. On the other hand, the present age witnesses the technological innovation and digital life generating technological supremacy over the entire humanity across the globe in the name of globalization. The mode of information and technology has become the source of power controlling systems of communication and various media. Such a technological supremacy evolves as a digital empire or media empire and with its unending power structures it assists fundamentalism in order to control socio-cultural life of humans. One needs to discover how this digital age and digital power contributes fundamentalism due to which malicious consequences are rampant in our social and religious contexts.[24]

At the same time, religious fundamentalism infringes the secular space and commits to change the secular face of the state into religious one. Jonathan Fox opines:

> In order to defend against modernity, fundamentalists try to create a separate social and political space with special behavior, language, music, body language, dress, and hairstyles to differentiate members from outsiders. They create a set of rules that are portrayed as a return to the religious values of the past but are perhaps better described as new creations to replace a lost tradition. This is because modernity has created a new environment in which religion must exist and fundamentalist interpretations of their religions must be innovative to function in modern times.[25]

---

22 Michael B. Salzman, "Globalization, Religious Fundamentalism and the need for Meaning," *International Journal of Intercultural Relations* 3 (2008): 321, (318-327).

23 Wati Longchar, "People's Security and Life: Challenges for Theological Education in Asia," *Yu-Shan Theological Journal* 22 (June 2015): 30, (30-31).

24 http://www.worldfinancialreview.com/?p=209, http://www.theatlantic.com/amp/article/462393/ and https://en.M.wikipedia.org/wiki/Electronic_colonialism (Accessed on 24/10/2016); K. K. Kuriakose, "Globalization, Religion and Nonviolence," in *Religion, Terrorism and Globalization—Nonviolence: A New Agenda*, ed., K. K. Kuriakose (New York: New Science Publishers, 2006), 243-264. Leela D'Souza, "Globalization and Religious Fundamentalist Movements: A Search for Identity," in *Globalization and Social Movements: Struggle for a Humane Society*, ed., P. G. Jogdand and S. M. Michael (Jaipur: Rawat Publications, 2003), 53-77; Peter Beyer, *Religion and Globalization* (London: SAGE, 1997), 70-96.

25 Jonathan Fox, *A World Survey of Religion and the State* (Cambridge: Cambridge University Press, 2008), 23.

Fox's elucidation gives us an idea that state would be influenced or be used as an important tool with strength of religious power that could sprout religious fundamentalism to chase out modernism and liberalism. Religious fundamentalism being aided by certain kind of religious teachings intruded into the politics and started influencing the notion of nationalism. State has become a fertile ground where religious teachings have been sown and later shaped into new forms thereby politics and religion intertwined with each other to grab the political power and to create a type of cultural unity which rather stands as a threat to citizens of the country in Indian context. This trend has convoluted political strategy of religions in the country by means of religious violence has become a natural phenomenon in the recent past. Targeting minority, vandalizing their religious symbols, destroying the holy spaces and impinging the dominant views upon the religious communities are the interests of fundamentalist in Indian situation. Hence, the merge of religion with the power of state leads to increase religious fundamentalism which eventually creates antagonism in Indian society. At this juncture, it would be important to understand the effects of religious fundamentalism and its usage of state apparatus in creating unsociable environment such as violence, cultural riots and tensions in our society. At present, Indian society experiences dominance of religion which uses power of the state to implement whatever they deem as imperative according to the cultural fabric of Hinduism. Such as these raise intolerance and hopelessness among the civil society eventually leading to social disorder, violence and marginalization of various communities.

Effects of Religious Fundamentalism

India has long struggled with religious and communal harmony and has experienced inter-religious violence. Inter-religious disharmony begets violence and hatred.[26] Godhra riots revealed the brutal killings and destruction

26 As Indian society witnessed, late in the 1992, Hindu mobs stormed and destroyed the Babri Masjid, a Muslim mosque built in the 16th century by the Muslim emperor Babar in Ayodhya on the site where his army had torn down a temple thought to mark Lord Rama's birthplace. It is alleged that a previously existing Hindu temple was knocked down and replaced. BJP activists campaigned in the issue managed to gather 200,000 people to demolish the mosque forcibly. In the ensuing violence thousands of people were killed across the country. The BJP state government was dismissed for its complicity in the attacks and failure to control the violence. In 2002, attempts to begin building a Hindu temple on a site led a group of Muslims to torch a train carrying activists, killing 58 people. There followed a long running campaign of anti-Muslim violence centered to state of Gujarat in which around 2,000 Muslims were murdered and 100,000 forced to flee. Mary Pat Fisher, *Living Religions: An Encyclopedia of the World's Faiths* (London: I.B. Tauris Publishers, 1997), 112.

of many people for which fundamentalists were solely responsible.[27] Since 2008 terrorist attacks, Muslim communities have been under undue scrutiny and arbitrary arrests and detentions have been intensified by the government which finds these ways as counter terrorism. Indian Christians, Christian missionary groups and Hindus who convert to Christianity or to another faith have reported more frequent harassment and violence, particularly in states with anti-conversion laws.[28] Religious minority communities in India frequently face several attacks by the religious fundamentalist groups in terms of discrimination and violence against them. Therefore, the sense of intolerance is uncontrolled among the minority communities and they challenge and pressurize the states all over the country to end the activities of those fundamentalist groups. However, the connivance of state and religion supports and sustains such fundamentalist actions which are part of their several political agendas. In July 2012, owing to the communal violence between the Bodos and Muslim settlers more than 80 people had died and over 100 thousand took refuge in the relief camp.[29]

The Muzaffarnagar riot that took place in Uttar Pradesh in 2013 claimed at least 48 lives and injured 93 persons.[30] Since the mid-2014, when the Bharatiya Janata Party (BJP) led by Prime Minister Narendra Modi won a parliamentary majority, religious minorities have been increasingly under attack. Many Christians and Muslims have been assaulted and lost their lives. Places of worship, schools, business and homes have been vandalized and destroyed. St. Sebastian's Church in Delhi was burnt at the end of 2014 and St. Mary's Church in Agra was desecrated in March 2015. A priest was dragged

---

27 The violence in Godra (Gujarat State) began when the Hindu activists went to support a campaign led by the Vishya Hindu Parishad (World Hindu Council, VHP) to construct a temple to the Hindu god Rama on the site of a 16th century mosque destroyed by Hindu militants in 1992. A mob of Muslims in the town of Godhra attacked and set fire two carriages of a train carrying Hindu activists returning from Ayodhya, Uttar Pradesh where 58 people lost their lives (many of them women and children). Owing to the Hindu-Muslim riots following the destruction of the mosque many people lost their lives. Between Feb. 28 and March 2, 2002, a three-day retaliatory killing spree organized by Hindus left hundreds dead and thousands became homeless. It resulted in looting and burning of Muslims' homes, shops, restaurants and places of worship. Many Muslim girls and women were raped in Gujarat before being mutilated and burnt to death. "We Have No Orders to Save You:" State Participation and Complicity in Communal Violence in Gujarat 14/3 (c) (April, 2012), 4 (1-68).

28 Madhya Pradesh, Chhattisgarh, Odisha (Orissa), Arunachal Pradesh, Rajasthan, Gujarat and Himachal Pradesh.

29 Razia, "Communal Riots in India," in *International Journal of Research & Development Organization* 1/12 (December, 2015), 69 (64-70).

30 Razia, "Communal Riots in India," *International Journal of Research & Development Organization* 1/12 (December, 2015), 69.

from his car and beaten mercilessly by a mob outside a police station[31] which indicates the inaction of the state power which was supposed to protect the citizens. The Evangelical Fellowship of India had documented more than 38 incidents between November and December 2014. Catholic communities in India also have documented several incidents between December 2014 and February 2015. In Hyderabad, Catholic Christmas carolers were severely beaten by a mob and a catholic speaker was attacked by Hindu nationalists for displaying images of Jesus in the storefront window.[32]All these instances indicate the vulnerability of religious minorities in India.

Religious fundamentalism creates fear and terror in the minds of the masses. Because of tension and unrest, it also creates psychological distress. The violence and threat against the minority groups create fear especially in those who have experienced violence and assault firsthand and those who have lost members of the family or relatives in such incidences. The plight of the victims of survivors of communal violence, the fear and trauma they experience continue to be a serious concern. In India, although religious freedom is officially respected, in practice it is ignored. Denial of religious freedom is becoming an even more serious problem. Whether it is caused by political ideology, criminality or religious inspired discrimination, numerous believers are being persecuted because of who they are and their willingness to express their faith publicly. Religious fundamentalism leads to religious oppression. Many people from different religious affiliations are affected by persecution, discrimination, harassment, torture and imprisonment. In the recent past, the

31 On 23rd August 2008 Hindu blamed Christians for the death of a Hindu leader, Swami Laxanananda Saraswati, along with five other people at Tumudibandh, Khandamal District in Odisha. They went on rampage, killing 100 persons, thousands injured and over 50,000 forced to flee. Many fled to the forest and thousands took refuge in the camps and found themselves threatened in the camps as well. In spite of the Maoist Naxalite groups prominent in that region admitted responsibility for the murder of Swami and his followers, the state authorities and leaders of certain fundamentalist Hindu organizations blamed Christians for the killings. The minority Christians in Odisha experienced various forms of atrocities including looting, destruction of churches and church-run institutions, brutal killings of priests, nuns, church workers and members of the Christian community. Some Christians were forced to undergo "reconversion" to Hinduism as a pre-requisite to return to their hometown (Statement of religious Violence and Intolerance in India of WCC). Also, see *Christians and the Struggle for Religious Freedom with Persecuted and Forgotten? (2012 update)* eds., John Pontifex and John Newton (Surrey: Aid to the Church in Need, 2012), 40-43. Also, refer (International Religious Freedom, USCCB Fact Sheet, 2016), Department of Justice, Peace and Human Development Office of International Justice and Peace.

32 UNCIRF Annual Report, "India," 150.

religious fundamentalism and religious differences have emerged as a crucial factor in international conflict, national security and foreign policy.[33]

At the present context, religious terrorism is one of the biggest threats. It makes thousands of people scapegoats in the area of global terrorism. Religion has become a divisive force causing social disharmony, religious antagonism, ethnic conflicts, social disorder, instability and mutual discord. Terror in the name of various religious traditions gives birth to new era of terrorism in the history of humankind.[34] At the same time, religious fundamentalism poses a threat to the national economic development. Religious intolerance also has caused a major impediment to the world economy by harnessing instability and economic breakdown in many countries. Conflicts spread more on religious lines in many parts of the world. Religion plays an essential part in issues that govern international relations including security, humanitarianism, intervention, human rights, terrorism, war and peace and political movement.[35] Religion affects the state policies, foreign affairs and decision-making process in many nations. One of the significant factors affecting Indian economy is communal riots.

Control of women's identity, roles, rights and protections, sexuality and bodies remain central to religious fundamentalism. The consequences for victims of violence during conflict are grave and it will affect women for the rest of their lives. During conflict and displacement, women's physical and social vulnerability increases. Violence against women during armed conflicts situations is largely based on traditional views of women as property and often as sexual objects. Women are being attributed as transmitters of culture and symbols of nation or community. Hence, violence directed against women is often considered an attack against the values or honor of a society and therefore a particular potent tool of war.[36] Women's body is used as revenge. The victims of such communal violence experience "emotional upheaval,

---

33 Elizabeth Shukman Hurd, *The Politics of Secularism and International Relations* (Princeton: Princeton University Press, 2007), 1.

34 Arvind Singh, "Religious Fundamentalism, Terrorism and Indo-Pak Relations," in *International Research Journal* 2/3 (September, 2017), 1 (1-4).

35 Abdi O. Shuriye, "The Failed Assumption of Some Social Scientists on the Role of Religion in International Relations," in *International Journal of Humanistic and Social Science* 1/3 (March, 2011), 12 (11-17).

36 During the Gujarat riot it was reported that at least three women were gang raped and many injured. To achieve such overarching control requires the acquisition of political power in ways that threaten democratic and egalitarian process and outcomes. Patriarchal control of women in society at large and in fundamentalist movements is multi-layered. It includes social constructions of women's purity and honour that defines a woman's personal identity along lines of communal identity, whether familial, tribal, ethnic or national. Sylvia Estrada Claudia, "Sanctifying Moral Tyranny: Religious Fundamentalism and the Political Disempowerment of Women," in *Religious Fundamentalism and Their Gendered*

identity crisis, personal and collective insecurity and relational disturbance."[37] These are some of the instances that witness the consequences of religious fundamentalism affecting a wide range of human relationships, economy, politics and even human bodies. Having discussed some of the negative impacts of religious fundamentalism in a multi-religious and multi-cultural context like India, formulating a rational and effective response becomes imperative as a Christian community.

Reclaiming Religions: Its Essence and Effectiveness

It would be a challenging task to talk about the essence of religions in the context of existence of multiple religions as each religion and faith tradition poses certain way of spiritual and theological core. At the same time, one needs to be aware of the fundamentalist view of religions while striving to unearth the significance of each religion as misusing of the religious teachings and misinterpreting the spiritual strands will dilute the spirit of unity of a nation. Consequently, it results in division among communities both religious and ethnic thereby capturing of political power becomes an apparent destination to embark on. The emergence of inter-religious and inter-faith dialogues elicits the significance of each religion in contributing vivid notions of theological content in relation to salvation of the world and the welfare of humanity. The following questions would be appropriate while trying to reclaim the essence of religions. Why do we need to accentuate the essence of religions? What does reclaim the religions mean to the Christian communities in Indian context? What do we need to promulgate in our endeavor to reclaim the religions in a multiple religious context?

The existence of multiple faiths, cultures, and languages titivates Indian spiritual fabric with its vivid notions of spiritualities and faiths traditions. Along with the faith of Hinduism other faiths such as Buddhism, Jainism and Sikhism have originated in this land and Christianity and Islam were brought to this land as foreign missionary religions. There is also a movement among the people who claim unhinduness that is embedded in their culture, spirituality and religious life. These people are mostly from lower strata of the Indian social system, bringing out their cultural, political and religious philosophies and countering the dominant Hindu argument at the issues of Hindu dharma, Hindu culture and cultural nationalism.

Impacts in Asia, eds., Claudia Derichs and Andrea Fleschenberg (Berlin: Fredrich-Ebert-Stiftung, 2010), 19.

37 Joseph George, "Emotional Upheaval and Relational Refugeism in Contemporary Indian Experience: An Intercultural Exploration and Proposal for Pastoral Therapy," in *Intercultural and Interreligious Pastoral Caregiving: The SIPCC 1995-2015, 20 Years of International Practice and Reflection*, eds., Karl Federschmidt and Daniel Louw (Norderstedt: SIPCC, 2015), 10-15.

Kancha Ilaiah asserts that Hinduism promotes spiritual fascism whereas the indigenous religions which are non-Hindu in their nature accentuate spiritual democracy and egalitarian views.[38] The rift between these two ideologies and practices simmer socio-cultural life of people across the country. Hence, it is inevitable to retrieve the spiritual potentialities embedded in all the indigenous religions that can contribute to social welfare and wellbeing of all beyond the dominancy of one religion against others in our society. The long standing indigenous religious traditions being practiced by Tribal communities are other added flavors to the situation of multiple religiosities to this country. However, the history of religions in Indian soil is known for its ambiguous role and oppressive social function as the religious structures are misused and mishandled by the political powers for their own ends and means it eventually cause communal tensions and conflicts. S. J Samartha proposes that a positivistic approach in studying the religions would unravel the significance of religions when multiple religions exist in a society. He says,

> Religions provide strength and resources to fight against injustice in society. There are liberative streams to prophetic movements or voices in every religion. Spirituality for combat has drawn the attention of many in the recent past and religions have been referred to as sources for inner power and perspectives of liberation.[39]

In the context of religious fundamentalism and the collusion of state with certain religious ideology Samartha's idea is very helpful and hopeful to reclaim and reassert the religions in order to promote justice, peace and serenity in our society. Samratha proposed various approaches that unpack the potentialities of religions in Indian context. He argues that Missiological, Phenomenological, Sociological and Dialogical approaches would be very accommodating in bringing out the essence of each religions and their particular view of salvation.[40]

---

38 Ilaiah furiously responds to the issue of cultural nationalism raised by the dominant Hindu fundamentalistic groups in India. He firmly believes that Brahminic ideology, its culture and political philosophy sprout fascist views and they are destructive forces to the entire humanity. But Dalitbahujan religions promote democratic spirituality and productive knowledge. Kancha Ilaiah, *Why I am not a Hindu: A Sudra Critique of Hindutva Philosophy, Culture and Political Economy*, 2nd ed. (Calcutta: Samya, 2009), 113-131. Also see, Kancha Ilaiah, *Post-Hindu India: A Discourse on Dalit-Bahujan Socio-Spiritual and Scientific Revolution* (Delhi: SAGE, 2009), 240-241 and 267-290.

39 S. J. Samartha, "Dialogue in a Religiously Plural Society," in *The Multi-Faith Context of India: Resources and Challenges for Christians*, ed., Israel Selvanayagam (Bangalore: BTTBPSA, 1993), 3.

40 S. J. Samartha, "Dialogue in a Religiously Plural Society," 5-6.

Religion and Spirituality

At the same time, believers of all religions should be able to realize the presence of positive elements in all the religions thereby complimenting each other's religious views would be possible. While one is committed to one's faith, one needs to understand the faith traditions of one's neighbor. When such a contemplation and complementation take place the essence of religions will be unpacked and reclaiming religious would contribute to peaceful and harmonious social life in our society. A religion, in order to be human and to create a harmonious co-existence has to be dialogical and realizes that fundamentalism denies scope for such dialogue. Therefore, beyond fundamentals all religions must enter into dialogue with people of all religions. Harmony and peaceful coexistence in a multi-religious and multi-context like India depend on an ongoing dialogue between various religions and cultures. Hence, it becomes imperative to actively participate in the process of inter-religious dialogue,[41] where a dialogue partner is treated with respect, received with openness and any claim for superiority is to be considered as impediment for the practice of dialogue.[42] The believers of all the religions need to be agents of God's truth and justice learned from their religious resources found within the faith traditions. They are also to play a vibrant role in building peace and harmony in modern India amidst religious fundamentalism. How to eliminate intractable differences, which may destruct humanitarian concerns, should be the spiritual task of all.

Interfaith dialogue is not a "cure all" answer to the questions surrounding religious fundamentalism. However, it points toward relationship, understanding, mutual acceptance, sharing and friendship. In the process, serious disagreements are inevitable, but inappropriate responses to them are not. Interfaith dialogue will be beneficial at all levels and across all segments of religious communities. It helps to learn various religious teachings which would be a powerful tool to step forward in facilitating an understanding and respect for different faith communities. One needs to understand that we cannot reach our common origin and destiny without being in communion with one another as brothers and sisters. It is this common brotherhood and sisterhood that will unite human beings with God and also with one another. While we reclaim the religions, it is our genuine duty to celebrate the adequate and profound spiritual potentialities that each religion has sustained in their course of existence. Moreover, each religion should accept to be reformed and revitalized as per the needs of human society and the entire creation thereby

41 Uma S. Sharma, "Contemporary Religious Fundamentalism," *International Journal of Indian Psychology* 2/3, (April-June, 2015), 33, (31-43).

42 S. J. Samartha, *One Christ—Many Religions: Toward a Revised Christology* (New York: Orbis Books, 1992), 170.

the world can experience the richness of the religions in promoting life in abundance.

While political powers contaminate and misuse the religious ideologies for their own selfish political benefits, it is the responsibility of the believers of each religion to share the spiritual profundity with their neighbors thereby richness of faith would contribute and enhance human relationships beyond fundamentalism. The believers of all religions must be aware of the truth that it is basically a fundamentalist and monologist religion that feeds communalism. Despite differences in approach in seeking the truth, all religions agree on the basic, fundamental values of humanism such as truth, justice and faithfulness. Such a notion is a potential point to discern and move with a positive approach in so doing all the religions may strive beyond the futile cultic practices in order to arrive at humanitarian values. The growing religious extremism and increasing violence against religious minorities in India is putting the credibility of India as a secular and democratic state.

Religion and Social Concerns

The common view of both believers and atheists would be welfare of society in all realms of life. If religions begin to pay attention at the social values and prophetic voices embedded in their religious teachings that strive for equality, justice and human dignity there may emerge a spirituality which could empower all the believers to discover humanitarian values in their faith traditions. Hence, all the religions must focus on the social values such as justice, peace, equality, human rights and sociability while they claim precious teachings of their religions. Consequently, these religious teachings will lead the believers to uphold social transformation and enable them to voice for social justice. Moreover, religions should engage in dismantling the social evils and commit to promote liberation and oppression free society.[43] In our reclaiming of religions we ought to go beyond the traditional interpretations of religions and establish socio-economic ethos, political values and spiritual concerns embedded in each religion that could sensitize believers to stand for justice and peace in our broken world.

When it comes to the Christian mission context, the content of the Christian gospel should be the gospel of love, God's compassion and mercy which can widen and deepen the love of God for all the people irrespective of their faith traditions. Christians should not succumb to the fundamental views of the scriptures rather they must read the scriptures for a set of values can enhance life in all realms. At the same time the gospel should address the social problems such as inequality, injustice and divisive powers that terrorize human society being aided by several faces of social evils and illness. It has

43 John Clammer, *Socially Engaged Religions* (Bangalore: Books for Change, 2010), 1-7.

to take up the praxis of 'love-centered connectedness with others, justice-centered transformation systems and wholeness centered life for humanity' thereby Christian stand will witness its core among all the people.[44]

Christians need to reclaim the gospel values that provide a healthy space to all beyond various human made barriers in order to rediscover and promulgate God's reign in this world. Recently, World Council of Churches has committed to bring out a set of recommendations that could promulgate the Christian witness in a multi-religious world. The document emphasizes the Christian witness by which the Church has been privileged by the power of the gospel. The crux of the recommendations lies in its principles which aim at eliciting the core of Christian understanding of God who does not confine to the four walls of the church rather moves around the life of humans in building the relationships of respect with people of all religions restoring peace and justice.[45] The intention of WCC is very clear that the church needs to uphold its witness at the expense of her experience with God. Such sort of Christian witness needs to be implanted in the hearts of the believers to take forward inter-religious relationships with respect and mutual acceptance of one another.

Perhaps, one can witness and interpret the history of Christianity as a history of imperial and capitalistic powers that operated and spread the Gospel throughout the world promulgating passive spirituality that cannot address the issues of social and political oppression, economic hegemony and cultural subjugation. However, the history of the church in the past can also be viewed as an ideal story that informs the transformation of people and communities with the aim of social reformation and spiritual revolution.[46] The protestant missionaries, though they were unable to eradicate the practice of caste system in the churches, took a bold stand against the caste discrimination perpetrated by the dominant people awakening the Dalit communities to receive the gospel as a means of social dignity, identity and spiritual privilege. Thus, the church has potentiality to promote vigor and valor in the minds of the believers who can modify socio-spiritual structures of our society beyond human made barriers. At this juncture, Christians are required to allow their fundamentalism to be dismantled and should be encouraged to come forward in solidarity with the people of other faiths who suffer at the cost of religious fundamentalism.

---

44 "Mission in the Context of Religious Fundamentalism," in *Doing Mission in India Today*, ed., H. Vanlalauva (Kolkata: SATHRI, 2012), 132-134.

45 "Christians Witness in a Multi-Religious World-Recommendations for Conduct," in WCC Document prepared on 28 June 2011, https://www.oikoumene.org/en/resources/documents/wcc-programmes/interreligious-dialogue-and-cooperation/christian-identity-in-pluralistic-societies/christian-witness-in-a-multi-religious-world, (Accessed on 04/08/2016).

46 John E. Clough, *Social Christianity in the Orient* (New York: American Baptist Foreign Mission Publications, 1914). 1-25.

Conclusion

This paper has attempted to bring out some of the historical situations of religions, religious fundamentalism and the nexus between religion and state. Religious fundamentalism is based on religious prejudices and fanaticism defying the essential teachings of multiple religions. If we consider the potential teachings of all the religions, we could see many commonalities that offer hope in a divided and traumatized world. This paper seeks to explain how religions can become a force for peaceful co-existence rather than causing division and war. Unfortunately, religious differences in India cause more harm and disharmony. Sometimes even some avoidable conflicts are sparked off by religious differences between people who at some point lived in harmony with each other. This is all because of fundamentalistic attitudes of believers of each religion. Therefore, religious fundamentalism is neither acceptable nor healthy for development and growth. Moreover, it contradicts the very principles of religious sobriety. Perhaps one can interpret the spirit of fundamentalism existed in all the religions.

Therefore, the solution is not to deny religious pluralism but to encourage religious tolerance without which India will continue to experience bloodshed and division on the basis of religion. India is torn apart because of the antagonistic, competitive and rivalry in the name of religion. Instead of promoting harmony this existence of multiple religions creates disharmony and a sense of rejection. India as a secular country is losing its credibility as the growing religious extremism continues to increase violence against religious minorities. Therefore, all religious groups have the responsibility to desist from spreading communal violence by building and restoring mutual trust, peace and reconciliation among people of all faiths. All religions and religious institutions should embrace all faiths with openness and provide a way to coming together thereby discovering unity in God may promote unity and oneness among all. In addition, one needs to be reminded that all religions have to be recognized for its spiritual efficacy and profound social concerns that reform any society. If it is the motto of all the religions in India, our country would not be prey to the segregation, killing and hatred anymore. All religions should embrace one another as brothers and sisters.

17

Significance of Karbala Tragedy: A Shia Perspective

Aphenbou Abonmai

Introduction

The martyrdom of Imam Husayn ibn Ali is one of the most important events in the history of Islam. The event of Husayn's martyrdom is also known as Karbala Tragedy or Karbala Massacre as this unfortunate event occurred at a place called Karbala, near Kufa, Iraq. The martyrdom of Husayn has special significance for Shia Muslims because, in their understanding, it is not merely a historical event, of what happened at Karbala in the seventh century, but something that has eternal significance, in the sense that its significance is relevant even today. Hence, an attempt is made here to understand how Shia Muslims look at the whole issue of Karbala tragedy, and how, in their understanding, this event was a culmination of the differences that have divided the *umma* (Muslim community) starting from the crisis of succession that they faced right after the death of the Prophet. The word 'Shiah' is an Arabic word which simply means party, and it is used to refer to those Muslims who believe and support the idea that succession to Prophet Muhammad should be only from the progeny of Ali and Fatima. They constitute one of the two major sects in Islam today.

Leadership Crisis after the Death of Prophet Muhammad

The crisis of succession after the death of Prophet Muhammad is a very important issue that continues to divide Muslims even today. This issue is foundational to understanding many problems within Islam, including what happened at Karbala. After ten years of leading and guiding the nascent Muslim *ummah,* Prophet Muhammad died in 632 CE. After his death, even before the dead body was buried, while the family members of the Prophet and his relatives, including his cousin and son-in-law Ali, were busy arranging and preparing for the burial, the Ansars[1] were already meeting in the *saqifa* of the Banu Sa'ida to decide the successor. Hearing that the Ansars were about to elect caliph, Abu Bakr and Umar and other Muhajiruns[2] also rushed to the *saqifa.*[3] Here big debate ensued between the Ansars and Muhajirun as both the groups claimed their own rights to caliphate. After much debate and negotiation, Abu Bakr was elected as the first caliph in this *saqifa*. Now, it is clear that Abu Bakr was elected as the successor in haste. That was the beginning of the whole issue of succession because, though some people thought that "neither he [Prophet] nor his followers had made any plans for the furtherance of the government of Islam after his death,"[4] which later became the position of the Sunni Muslims, for some, the Prophet had already made it clear that his cousin and son-in-law Ali ibn Abu Talib would be his successor.

The usual reference for this position is the event of Ghadir Khumm where Prophet Muhammad said that for those people who consider him as their master, Ali is also their master. But not all Muslims consider this as the appointment of Ali as the successor of the Prophet. Mahmoud Ayoub writes about a historical account attributed to Abd Allah b. Muslim b. Qutaybah al-Dinawari, where, upon the death of the Prophet, Abd Allah b. al-Abbas, Prophet's uncle, went to Abu Bakr and Umar and asked if they have any knowledge about what the Prophet said about succession, to which both confessed their ignorance. Then he went to Ali and asked him to stretch out his hand so that he may pledge his allegiance, saying that if he, as Prophet's uncle, pledge his allegiance to him, everyone will follow suit. But Ali responded, "Will anyone quarrel with us concerning this matter?"[5] This whole episode, in one hand, clearly points to the fact that the Prophet did not name anyone as his successor in any indisputable way. On the other hand, Ali's response is very interesting. His short response

---

1 Ansars refer to those Medinians who supported the Prophet when he migrated to the city. So they were also called Supporters.

2 Muhajiruns refer to those people who migrated to Medina along with the Prophet in 622 CE.

3 Laura Veccia Vaglieri, "The Patriarchal and Umayyad Caliphates," in *The Cambridge History of Islam: Vol. I: The Central Islamic Lands*, edited by P. M. Holt, Ann K. S. Lambton and Bernard Lewis (London: The Cambridge University Press, 1970), 57.

4 L. Bevan Jones, *The People of the Mosque: An Introduction to the Study of Islam with Special Reference to India* (Calcutta: Baptist Mission Press, 1959), 32.

5 Mahmoud M. Ayoub, *The Crisis of Muslim History: Religion and Politics in Early Islam* (Oxford: Oneworld Publications, 2006), 8-9.

clearly reveals his perspective on the whole issue of succession. What Ali said could be understood to mean that Ali was certain of who will succeed the Prophet, and that his position as the successor is clear enough, in his opinion, that anyone need not raise any objection about it. This is also the position that Shia Muslims hold when it comes to the issue of succession. From their perspective, the issue of succession was clear from the time the Prophet was alive, that Ali will succeed the Prophet. They also believe that Ali was always clear of his own position in this matter.

Uthman's Caliphate: The Beginning of Deviation

Abu Bakr became the first caliph of the *umma*. His caliphate was from 632-634 CE. Then Umar ibn al-Khattab became the second caliph, from 634-644 CE. In 644 Uthman ibn Affan became the third caliph till he was murdered in 656. The caliphate of Uthman is important vis-à-vis the attitude of the Shias towards the Umayyad dynasty. This does not mean that they consider the first two caliphates as legitimate. For them all the three caliphates were illegitimate, and usurpation of power from the Alids. But when it comes to Uthman, there were many issues that marked his caliphate as the beginning of corruption and of straying away from the Islamic values and principles. It can be mentioned that he was from an aristocratic origin, of the Umayyad clan, a leading clan of the Quraysh that enjoyed power and prestige in the pre-Islamic society. Moreover, for many years, the leader of the clan, Abu Sufyan, relentlessly opposed Prophet Muhammad and his newfound faith.[6] After Uthman became the caliph, he rekindled the old spirit of tribalism. Earlier in the life of the *ummah,* Prophet Muhammad, with the message of equality and social justice, did not allow any favouritism or preference towards any clan or tribe. But the repressed desire for power, position and wealth, and the mindset that Quraysh tribe was born to rule, were all resurrected with the caliphate of Uthman.

He changed the title of the caliph, 'Vicegerent of the Vicegerent of the Messenger of God' with the new title, 'Vicegerent of God' with the belief that his authority was God-given. With that conviction, he felt he had every right and power to do what he wills and did not allow any criticism or interference in what he does.[7] Both Abu Bakr and Umar were humble in the fact that they did not consider themselves to be equal in rank and status with the Prophet. Thus, Abu Bakr sat a step lower than the prophet, and Umar even lower than Abu Bakr. But Uthman sat at the topmost seat where the Prophet used to sit.

6 Carl Brockelmann, *History of the Islamic Peoples* (London: Routledge & Kegan Paul Ltd., 1949), 63.

7 Wilferd Madelung, *The Succession to Muhammad: A Study of the Early Caliphate* (New York: University of Cambridge Press, 1997), 80-81.

Seeing this, someone was reported to have said, "Today evil was born."[8] The unabashed favouritism that Uthman showed to his close kin from the beginning of his caliphate is also an established historical fact that not even Sunnis deny.[9] He also brought back those who were disgraced by Prophet Muhammad for opposing Islam, like his uncle al-Hakam b. Abi al-As. During his caliphate, many of his officials became exceedingly wealthy, built luxurious buildings, owned many slaves and amassed great wealth.[10] Observing all these, historian al-Masudi wrote: "This was not the case during the time of Umar b. Al-Khattab. Rather, it was then a clear and straight path."[11] The words of Masudi clearly point to the fact that the time of Uthman marked the beginning of corruption and deviation from the straight path, the Islamic principles of life. This is not to say that there was nothing wrong during the first two caliphates. But, the first two caliphs did their best to walk and lead the *ummah* according the teachings of the Qur'an and of the Sunna of the Prophet. So, seeing the beginning of deviation, many Muslims to look to Ali as the only hope, to guide and lead them in the right path. It can be noted that Uthman's caliphate intensified the differences and division among the Muslims created by the succession crisis at the beginning.

Muawiyah's Opposition to Ali and the Civil War

When Uthman was murdered in 656, the Muhajiruns and Ansars took Talhah and Zubayr, and went to Ali's house. They said to him that they will not leave without giving their allegiance to him as caliph. But, Ali insisted that if it has to be done then it should be done openly in the mosque with the approval of the Muslims and not secretly in his house. So, they went to the mosque, and Muhajiruns and the Ansars gave their allegiance to Ali, and all those who were present in the mosque including Talhah and Zubayr.[12] After Ali took the office of caliphate, he brought changes in the administration. Ali was a man who of uprightness, who wanted to do things strictly according to the

8 Ayoub, *The Crisis of Muslim History*, 51.

9 For example, soon after he became caliph, he appointed Ali b. Adi b. Rabi'a as governor of Mecca. Next year he sacked Umayr b. Sa'd al-Ansari and gave all the provinces under him (Hims, Qinnasrin and Upper Mesopotamia) to Muawiya his close kin, and governor of Syria. The governorship of Egypt was also given to his own foster-brother Abd Allah b. Sa'd b. Abi Sarh of Amir Quraysh. From Madelung, *The Succession to Muhammad*, 81 & 86.

10 Ayoub, *The Crisis of Muslim History*, 53 & 55.

11 As quoted in Ayoub, *The Crisis of Muslim History*, 53.

12 *The History of al-Tabari: Vol. XVI: The Community Divided,* translated and annotated by Adrian Brockett (Albany: State University of New York Press, 1997), 2. Tabari also mentions one tradition that records Talhah as the first person to give allegiance in the Mosque on that day.

Qur'anic values and principles of justice. As such, he did not want to keep those people who were appointed by Uthman, because his appointments were motivated by favouritism based on blood relation rather than on the basis of candidate's moral and spiritual qualifications. So, he replaced the governors of Basra, Egypt, and Yemen. When he tried to replace the governor of Mecca, the people refused to accept his directive, and they refused to give their allegiance to Ali.[13]

Another city that refused to pledge their allegiance to Ali was Damascus. Muawiyah believed that he was appointed as the governor of Syria by Umar, and Uthman confirmed his governorship. Therefore, Muawiyah refused to pledge allegiance to Ali. Moreover, Muawiyah cooked up a rumour in Syria, and made people to believe that Ali was responsible for the murder of Uthman and that he was sheltering the murderers.[14] This made the Syrians stronger in their opposition to Ali and also stronger in their support for Mauwiyah. With the knowledge that Syrians and Meccans were staunchly in support of him, Muawiyah asserted more and more for his bid to the caliphate, using retaliation for Uthman's blood as his biggest reason to rebel against Ali's caliphate. After all the negotiations failed to reconcile and bring understanding between Ali and Muawiyah, the Battle of Siffin was fought. This was known as the First *Fitnah* (Civil War). Fighting reached its climax on July 28, 657 CE. But, the next day Muawiyah sent his deputy to ask for truce, to which Ali accepted.[15]

Both Ali and Muawiyah and their respective parties agreed to let the Book of God and the Sunna of the Prophet decide their case. They agreed to choose two arbiters, one each from both the parties. Muawiyah chose Amr b. al-As to represent his party and Ali's group chose Abu Musa al-Ashari. These two arbiters met in Dawmat al-Jandal. After weeks of negotiations, they came to the conclusion that both Ali and Muawiyah should be removed and someone who was not part to any party in the conflict be made caliph. With that decision, they came to announce their verdict to the people who were anxiously waiting for them.[16] Abu Musa spoke first, saying:

> People, we have considered the affairs of this community and we do not think that there is anything that is more beneficial for it or more conducive to resolving its difficulties than that upon which I and Amr have agreed. That is, that we should depose Ali and Muawiyah and that this community should confront the issue and appoint over themselves from among themselves whomever it is that they want.

---

13 Madelung, *The Succession to Muhammad*, 151-152, & 155.

14 Ayoub, *The Crisis of Muslim History*, 98-101.

15 Ayoub, *The Crisis of Muslim History*, 121, 125.

16 Ayoub, *The Crisis of Muslim History,* 129-130.

> I have accepted the deposition of Ali and Muawiyah, and now you confront the issue and give power over you to whomever you think is fitting for this matter.[17]

Then Amr stood up and said:

> This fellow has spoken as you have heard and declared the deposition of the one whom he represents. Similarly, I declare that he is deposed, and I confirm my support for my candidate Muawiyah. He is the next-of-kin to Uthman b, Affan and the one who seeks vengeance for his blood. Of all the people, he has most right to take his place.[18]

This whole episode was nothing but betrayal of Ali and of the whole people of the house of the Prophet. This also showed the height of insincerity and un-Islamic character on the part of Muawiyah and his party. Muhammad Chamseddine says that this event sowed the seed of assassination that came to be fulfilled in the year 661 CE.[19]

The Immediate Events Leading to the Karbala

After Ali was assassinated in 661, Muawiyah usurped the caliphate from Hasan ibn Ali and became the caliph. And before he died, he appointed his own son, Yazid ibn Muawiyah, as caliph. But, majority of Muslims regarded Yazid as unfit to be the caliph of the *umma*.[20] Therefore the sons of the previous caliphs, Abd Allah b. Az-Zubayr, Abd Allah b. Umar and Abd ar-Rahman b. Abu Bakr, let alone Husayn ibn Ali, did not pledge allegiance to Yazid. This was a great challenge for Yazid. He needed their support to consolidate his caliphate. S. Husain M. Jafri expresses that the support of Husayn was even more significant being the only surviving grandson of the Prophet.[21] So, Yazid tried to gain the support of these people. It is learnt that Yazid ordered al-Walid b. Utba, the governor of Medina, to secure Husayn's allegiance forcefully, and if at all impossible then to behead him. But, Husayn was very clear of his stand that he will never lend his support to a person like Yazid. By refusing to support Yazid, Husayn also realized that he could no longer stay in Medina safely. So, he took

---

17 *The History of al-Tabari: Vol. XVII: The First Civil War*, translated and annotated by G. R. Hawting (Albany: State University New York Press, 1996), 109.

18 *The History of al-Tabari: Vol. XVII*, 109.

19 Ayatollah Muhammad Mahdi Chamseddine, *Hussain's Revolution: Its Cause and Implications* (n.p.: The Mainstay Foundation, 2015), 58-59.

20 Ayoub, *The Crisis of Muslim History*, 154.

21 S. Husain M. Jafri, *Origins and Early Development of Shi'a Islam* (London: Longman, 1978), 175.

his whole family and left Medina by night, and went to Mecca.[22] When Husayn was in Mecca, he received many letters and messages from his supporters in Kufa urging him to come to Kufa and become their leader. One of the letters was signed by leaders like Sulayman ibn. Surad al-Khuza'i, al-Musayyab ibn. Najaba, Rifa'a ibn Shaddad, Habib ib. Al-Muzahir, and Muslim ibn Awsaja. These people had been following the Alids from the very beginning and have proven their loyalty.[23] But as a prudent man, Husayn did not just go to Kufa himself, but first sent his trusted cousin Muslim ibn Aqeel to ascertain the situation in Kufa. When Muslim reached Kufa, many people came to him and expressed their allegiance to Imam Husayn. The number of people who swore allegiance to Imam differs; some put at eighteen thousand, some at twenty-five thousand and some even at forty thousand. After witnessing the support of the Kufans for Husayn, Muslim sent a trusted leader of Shias in Kufa along with a letter to Husayn saying that the Kufans were really in support of him, and wanted him to be their leader. So, he requested him to come to Kufa as soon as he received the letter.[24]

Meanwhile, the supporters of Yazid knew very well about the arrival of Muslim and all the developments that were taking place among the supporters of Husayn. When Yazid was informed about the development, he sacked the present governor of Kufa, Numan ibn Bashir, and appointed Abdullah ibn Ziyad in his place.[25] Seeing the situation in Kufa, when the new governor came to the city, he came in disguise: black turban with a covered face, and he brought only a few horsemen. When he arrived in Kufa, the Kufans who were waiting for Husayn, thinking of Ibn Ziyad as Husayn, welcomed him with a shout: "Hail to you, O son of the Prophet; we have been waiting for you." But when they reached the Mosque, to the dismay of the Kufans, Ibn Ziyad uncovered his veil and gave an intimidating speech declaring reward for the supporters of the Caliph and death and untold punishment for Husayn's supporters. The Kufans were stricken by fear and completely lost heart, and withdrew their support to Husayn and his movement.[26] Abdullah started his crackdown on all the dissidents, killed Muslim ibn Aqeel and other leaders, and uprising against Yazid was quelled overnight.[27]

22 Yasin T. al-Jibouri, *Kerbala and Beyond* (Qum: Ansariyan Publications, 1999), 33-34.

23 Jafri, *Origins and Early Development of Shi'a Islam*, 177-178.

24 al-Jibouri, *Kerbala and Beyond*, 33-38.

25 Musharraf Hussain al-Azhari, *The Tragedy of Karbala: The Prophet's Grandson's Struggle Against and Oppressive Tyrant* (Bobbersmill: The Invitation Publications, 2008), 11.

26 Jafri, *Origins and Early Development of Shi'a Islam*, 183.

27 al-Azhari, *The Tragedy of Karbala*, 11.

Events at Karbala

As for Husayn, after receiving the letter, he left Mecca and started his journey towards Kufa along with family members and some well-wishers. Hurr ibn Yazid al-Riyahi was ordered by the governor to stop Husayn and his followers at a deserted place and where there is no water.[28] So they were stopped at the area called al-Taff, which later came to be known as Karbala. From the seventh day of Muharram, Husayn and his supporters were denied access to water. But how can they survive without water in that scorching desert? The enemies saw that Husayn was accompanied by women and children, even infants. But there was not even a slice of humanity in the hearts of Yazid and his force. As they could no longer bear the thirst, and the cries of the children asking for water, on the night of eighth day, al-Abbas b. Ali b. Abu Talib along with few other soldiers, went to draw water from the river Euphrates. They were able to fetch water after much strife with the enemies guarding the water.[29]

On ninth day of Muharram, Zubayr b. Al-Qayn and Habib b. Muzahir, along with about twenty horsemen, came towards the camp of Husayn and his supporters with the message from the governor that either Husayn give his allegiance or they will be attacked. After asking them to wait for the response till the morning of tenth Muharram, they let them return without any confrontation. That night, seeing that the battle was inevitable in the morning, and that many of them have already suffered enough for his sake, and that there were people with him who have already lost their family members, Husayn asked his followers to go home. He told them that the darkness of the night will be their cover and they will not be spotted by the enemies. But no one was willing to forsake Imam Husayn. They said:

> What would people say? They would say that we deserted our shaykh, our leader, our cousins, and the best of uncles; that we had not shot any arrows alongside them; that we had not thrust any spears alongside them; that we had not struck any swords alongside them; that we do not know what they did. No, by God! We will not do that. Rather, we will offer for your safety our lives, property, and families. We will fight with you until you reach your destination. How abominable is life after you![30]

This is one beautiful incident where the courage and generosity of Husayn as well as the commitment and devotion his followers had for him manifested.

28 *The History of al-Tabari: Vol. XIX: The Caliphate of Yazid b. Mu'awiyah*, translated and annotated by I. K. A. Howard (Albany: State University of New York Press, 1990), 102.

29 al-Jibouri, *Kerbala and Beyond*, 50 & 52.

30 *The History of al-Tabari: Vol. XIX*, 116.

That night they prayed to God for the battle that they will be fighting the next morning. The next morning also they performed the morning prayer. After the prayer, Husayn got his thirty-two horsemen and forty foot soldiers positioned for the battle. Amidst the cries of women and children, the battle was fought, and went on till midday. By this time most of the followers of Husayn were already martyred but the battle lingered on because no one was willing to actually kill Imam Husayn. From the reports of Abu Mikhnaf, al-Tabari writes that Imam was already wounded but everyone felt uneasy to really put an end to Imam's life. So, they expected and waited for each other to do the job. Then Shamir b. Dhi al-Jawshan shouted to the soldiers, "Shame on you! Why are you waiting for the man? Kill him, may your mothers be deprived of you!" After that they started to attack Husayn. Zurah b. Sharik al-Tamimi struck a blow, and Husayn was falling and tumbling. Then Sinan b. Anas b. Amr al-Nakha'i speared him, and cut off his head. Husayn's head, along with women and children were taken to Yazid in Damascus.[31] Only Zayn al-Abidin, who could not fight as he was so sick, survived, and all other men were martyred.

Shia Understanding of Husayn's Revolution and Sacrifice

Imam Husayn's courage and his ultimate sacrifice have deep meaning and significance for the Shia Muslims. His revolution and sacrifice have social, religious, theological, and political significance. Husayn's sacrifice is also significant as it gives them identity, as a source of inspiration and an example for all the coming generations of the Shias.

A Rebellion against Social Injustice

One of the most important significance of Karbala lies in the social context in which it took place. In other words, the significance of Karbala is fully manifested when the social context in which it took place is understood. In the first place, it can be mentioned that Muawiyah used "tactics of terror, murder, and starvation"[32] against those who do not agree with him as a way of securing their allegiance. One of his commanding officers, Sufyan ibn Awf Al-Ghamidi, narrated what was commanded to him by Muawiyah:

> Muawiyah summoned me one day and said, 'I will send with you army vast in numbers...Head towards the Euphrates until you reach the town of Hit. Place the town under siege. If you find any soldiers, attack them... These raids will terrify the people of Iraq... Kill whoever you find who does not share your opinions. Bring any

31 *The History of al-Tabari: Vol. XIX,* 140, 160-161.

32 Chamseddine, *Hussain's Revolution*, 62.

town on the way to ruin. Take the villagers' property, as that is more torturous than death.[33]

As part of his terror, murder and starvation tactics, he cut off the Shias from the public treasury. He destroyed the houses of those people suspected to be leaning towards Ali's path, and "Whenever they heard of a newborn named Ali, they would kill him."[34] Another problem was what can be termed as racism. The general attitude of the Umayyids was that Quraysh were born to be rulers, and the non-Arabs were considered as second-class citizens, and put at the lowest rung of the society. Moreover, the Umayyids did not tolerate any opinion that does not agree with theirs. People who differed in opinion from that of the Umayyids were in danger of being eliminated and confiscation of property.[35]

There was also a kind of resurrection of the spirit of tribalism. When we go back to pre-Islamic Arabia, we see that it was a tribal society where the spirit of tribalism was very strong. There were constant fights among the tribes leading to what Karen Armstrong calls "a murderous cycle of vendetta and counter-vendetta."[36] In the midst of this, Prophet Muhammad preached the message of equality, justice and peace. His preaching led to a new religion called 'Islam' which means 'submission', implying that those who follow Islam, called Muslims, have submitted their entire being to Allah, and to obeying his commandments. One of the most important aspects of obeying Allah's commandments is to behave to other human beings with justice, equity and compassion.[37] Prophet Muhammad spent his whole life trying to instil these ideas into the hearts and minds of the people through his teachings as well as by living out his teachings. The Prophet was able to stop the spirit of tribalism within the Muslim community during his lifetime, but then it was rekindled from the time of Uthman's Caliphate and the practice was continued during the time of both Mauwiya and Yazid.[38] Thus, Imam Husayn's revolution was a revolution to bring back the Islamic values of compassion, equality, justice and peace in the society. It was a struggle to re-establish an authentic Islamic society where people who are weak and vulnerable are treated with respect, equality and compassion.

---

33 Ibn Hilal Al-Thaqafi, Ibrahim ibn Muhammad, *Al-Ghaaraat*, 1:25, 349, as quoted in Chamseddine's *Hussain's Revolution*, 62-63.

34 Mohammed Ali Albodairi, *Understanding Karbala* (n.p.: The Mainstay Foundation, 2017), 100.

35 al-Jibouri, *Kerbala and Beyond*, 34.

36 Karen Armstrong, *Islam: A Short History* (London: Weidenfeld & Nicolson, 2001), 3.

37 Armstrong, *Islam,* 5.

38 Chamseddine, *Hussain's Revolution*, 50 & 80.

Religious Awakening

In order to better understand the significance of Karbala in terms of protection of Islam, a brief mention of the Shia understanding of the concept of Imamate is crucial. One important understanding of Imamate among the Shia Muslims is that Imam is a protector of Islam. In the midst of his arguments that Prophet Muhammad would not leave this world without choosing his successor,[39] Ayatollah Jafar Sobhani writes "it is not conceivable that a person should take great pains to construct some great building, and then leave it completely *unprotected*, appointing no *watchmen,* or *supervisors* to maintain and *preserve* it."[40] Imam is given the responsibility to protect and preserve the true religion as revealed through and taught by Prophet Muhammad. And this responsibility is the "first and foremost priority of Imam Hussain."[41] For the Shia Muslims, what Imam Husayn did was faithfully and courageously carrying out his responsibility of safeguarding Islamic faith which has deviated from its true teachings under the corrupt rule of Umayyad dynasty. Umayyad rulers used religion as a tool to justify their oppressive and corrupt regime by subscribing to the theology of predestination. With the theology of predestination, the Umayyad rulers were able to convince the people that it was God who predestined them to rule the people and whatever was happening in the society at that time was the will of God. This understanding was successful in painting the efforts of those who tried to revolt against their oppressive rule as people who are working against the will of God. He also commanded that preachers should curse Ali, renounce and slander his family from the pulpit. But he gifted and showered his favours to those people who narrated the virtues of Uthman and praise him in public.[42] In other words, many Muslims of this period were not able to differentiate between what is right and wrong. Many people were brainwashed to accept the deviated version of Islam as the right one, and reject the true version the Alids were trying to present to them. Their sense of judgement was numbed, and their eyes blinded by their desire for material wealth and power that Muawiyah offered.

Imam Husayn stood up to reform and save Islam from this deplorable condition. But one question that can be asked is, was Imam Husayn successful in his attempt to reform and save Islam? For some the martyrdom of Imam Husayn can be considered as a complete failure. But for Shias, it was not a

39 It is the position of the Shi'i Muslisms that Prophet elected Imam Ali ibn Abu Talib as his successor though Sunni Muslims think otherwise.

40 Ayatollah Jafar Sobhani, *Doctrines of Shi'i Islam: A Compendium of Imami Beliefs and Practices*, translated by Reza Shah-Kazemi (New York: I. B. Tauris & Co. Ltd., 2001), 99. Emphasis added.

41 Albodairi, *Understanding Karbala*, 43.

42 Chamseddine, *Hussain's Revolution,* 103-104, 113-115.

failure because his martyrdom achieved many important things. His martyrdom was "an act of revelation, exposing repression and oppression, corruption and tyranny. Hussein's martyrdom was no longer an end but a beginning."[43] It was the beginning because his martyrdom created movement, vision, and hope. It revived the "striving spirit of the Muslim nation – the spirit of ambition and aspiration that had long been dormant."[44] It awakened the Muslims from their spiritual slumber, and unveiled the scale from people's eyes to see the oppression and tyranny of the Umayyads, and helped them see which version of Islam was truly right. Karbala brought them to their senses that they also should rise up against corruption and evil, and reminded them that they should not compromise their spiritual or Islamic principles for anything. This spiritual awakening led to many post-Karbala revolts in different places.

Redemptive Understanding of Karbala

The martyrdom of Imam Husayn at Karbala has a deep theological significance for the Shias. Mahmoud Ayoub writes that "the suffering of *Imam* Husayn has been taken by the Shi'i community to be a source of salvation through the interiorization and emulation of that suffering by the community and through the high favor of the *Imam* as an intercessor."[45] This shows the redemptive aspect of the Karbala tragedy, in that the Husayn's sacrificial suffering and death has opened a new aspect towards the Islamic understanding of redemptive suffering. Qur'an says:

> If a wound hath touched you, be sure a similar wound hath touched the others. Such days (of varying fortunes) We give to men and men by turns: that Allah may know those that believe, and that He may take to Himself from your ranks martyr-witnesses (to Truth). And Allah loveth not those that do wrong. Allah's object also is to purge those that are true in Faith and to deprive of blessing those that resist.[46]

This means that sufferings in life are part of trials for the believers, and a way of God purifying his people. One's response to sufferings in life reveals one's state of faith in God; if a person endures the sufferings, holding fast to his or her faith, then God will reward that person. Prophetic tradition also sees sufferings in a similar light. Calamities, misfortune and all kinds of

---

43 Lesley Hazleton, *After the Prophet: The Epic Story of the Shia-Sunni Split in Islam* (New York: Anchor Books, 2009), 183.

44 Chamseddine, *Hussain's Revolution,* 249.

45 Mahmoud Ayoub, *Redemptive Suffering in Islam: A Study of the Devotional Aspects of Ashura in Twelver Shi'ism* (The Hague: Mouton Publishers, 1978), 15.

46 Qur'an 3:140-41.

sufferings, even a single thorn that pricks one's foot, are all ways to cleanse sins that a person may have. For instance, responding to Abu Waqqas, Prophet Muhammad said, "the believer is inflicted with calamities until he is free from any sin clung to him."[47] To this already existing understanding of the connection between sufferings in life and salvation, a new understanding of redemption through intentional participation in the sufferings of the Karbala martyrs came up as a result of what happened at Karbala.

Political Implications of Karbala

Karbala tragedy is also politically connected. When the tragedy and martyrdom is read from the political perspective, it can be understood as a revolt against the principles of politics of power and despotism.[48] It can be mentioned that Shia Muslims never consider Umayyad rule as legitimate. Apart from being illegitimate, the government was also corrupt, intolerant and unjust. For the Shia Muslims, both Muawiyah and Yazid used brute force to secure the support of their subjects. Their policy was that of 'allegiance or death'. For instance, as mentioned earlier, Muawiyah gave order to one of his commanders saying, "kill whoever you find who does not share your opinion." His son Yazid also commanded al-Walid to secure Husayn's allegiance by force, and if refused, to behead him and bring his head to him to Damascus.[49] This is a clear situation of despotism, absolutism, and tyranny of the Umayyad rulers. They were intolerant of any opinion or voice that is against their wishes. Imam Husayn stood up against this tyrannical rule. His revolt was a revolt against the oppressors and a voice for the oppressed. But, it was neither only for his time nor for Islam alone. Husayn's revolt and sacrifice were for all the people, everywhere. What he did, he did it for all those who are oppressed throughout the history. He is believed to be present in all wars, struggles and battlefields, if it is done for freedom of people, for restoration of justice and to do away with corruption. Whenever people struggle for these issues, Imam Husayn is present. In this way, though Imam Husayn gave up his life at Karbala back in seventh century, he is resurrected in every generation.[50]

---

47 Muhsin Akbas, "Redemptive Suffering in Islamic Thought: A Critical Approach," *Deuifd* XXXI/2010: 194, https://www.academia.edu/879985/Redemptive_Suffering_in_Islamic_Thought_A_Critical _Approach (accessed on 26-08-2019).

48 Mansoor Akbar Kundi, "Political Lessons of Karbala," *The Dialogue* 3/2 (April-June 2008), 231, http://www.qurtuba.edu.pk/thedialogue/dialogue3_2.htm (accessed on 26-08-2019).

49 al-Jibouri, *Kerbala and Beyond*, 33.

50 Hazleton, *After the Prophet*, 183.

Karbala and Shia Identity

According to Yitzhak Nakash, "no other event in Islamic history has played so central a role in shaping Shi'i identity as the martyrdom of Husayn and his companions at Karbala."[51] The martyrdom of Imam Husayn and his companions at Karbala in 680 CE led Shias all over the world to commemorate this tragic event in the first ten days of Muharram every year. On the tenth day of Muharram, called Ashura, the day the martyrdom took place, Shias perform "rituals of remembrance"[52] where they do flagellation and public mourning procession. This Muharram observance and the rituals involve have come to form a unique Shia identity today. Writing about *matam* (mourning and repetitive breast-beating in order to show their lamentation for Husayn and his companions who were martyred at Karbala), David Pinault says that such practice was created by Shias and exclusively belongs to them. As such he says that it has been a practice that gives them a unique identity as Shia community.[53] Albodairi also says that Karbala solidifies the Shia identity. He says "the rituals of commemoration and supplication, and the visitation of sanctified graves and holy shrines, all imbedded a unique sense of identity in the Shia Muslim."[54] He also says that devotion to the descendants of Ali and Fatima is not just a matter of ritual but an identity. In this way Karbala tragedy shapes the identity of the Shia Muslims. This identity gives them a sense of unity and strength to face any degree of persecution, and has been successful in keeping the Shia faith alive till today.

Karbala: A Prototype of the Struggle against Evil

One of the reasons that Shias believe the revolt of Imam Husayn was successful in spite of the fact that Husayn was martyred along with his supporters in Karbala is that Karbala became an example for all the generations to come. Karbala became a prototype of revolution by generating many revolutions post-Karbala. The first was 'the Repenters' Revolt' that happened not long after the Karbala Tragedy because of those people who felt guilty for fighting against Prophet's grandson instead of standing by him and fighting for his cause. After seeing Yazid's army returned joyfully from Karbala, the Shias mourned, and reproached each other in guilt. They gathered around five leaders in Kufa, Suleiman ibn Sard al-Khuzaei, al-Musayyab ibn Najiya al-Firaari, Abdullah ibn Saad ibn Nufayl al-Azdi, Abdullah ibn Wael al-Tamimi, and

51 Yitzhak Nakash, *The Shi'is of Iraq* (Princeton: Princeton University Press, 1994), 142.

52 Nakash, *The Shi'is of Iraq*, 142.

53 David Pinault, "Shi'ism in South Asia," *The Muslim World* 3/4 (Jul-Oct 1997), 244-245, https://search-proquestcom.library.britishcouncil.org.in:4443/docview/216434051/42728 56E0A774E71PQ/1? accountid=14 5163 (accessed on 26-08-2019).

54 Albodairi, *Understanding Karbala*, 147.

Rafa'a ibn Shaddad al-Bajli, and started to think of ways to do something to compensate for their guilt. Suleiman became their leader, and they convinced Shias from other parts like Medina and Basra, and after four years of Husayn's revolution, rose in rebellion against the Umayyad dynasty. They met Umayyad army in Damascus and they were all killed.[55] Other rebellions like Rebellion in Medina, the Revolt of Mukhtar, the Revolt of Matraf, the Revolt of Ibn al-Ashath, the Zaidi Revolt, and the Revolt of Abi al-Saraya were also understood to be reactions to and inspired by the Massacre of Karbala. The inspiration of Karbala continues even into the twentieth century, like in the case of Iranian Revolution of 1979. Ali Shariati played an important role in awakening the consciousness of the people by making them realize the need to rise up against the oppressive Shah regime. During 1970s he gave lectures in Tehran and thousands of people from all walks of life thronged to his lecture halls. He made Karbala resurrected in the hearts and minds of the people, and instilled a new hope and power in them to rise up against the monarchical, authoritarian and pro-western Shah regime. Shariati transformed Karbala into "an eternal and transcendent phenomenon." Hazleton says that "as Shariati went on to take his listeners into the seventh century, inside Hussein's mind, he had no need to stress the parallel with what they themselves faced under the repressive regime of the Shah."[56] What happened at Karbala created a lasting impact on the mindset of the Shia Muslims, and became a prototype for future revolutions in the history of the Shia Muslims.

Reflection and Conclusion

In the understanding of Shia Muslims, Karbala becomes a symbol of struggle between good and evil; a struggle against injustice and corruption, and against every dehumanizing force or system in the society. For them, both Yazid and Husayn are not merely persons, but representations of two very different mindsets. The former represents carnality, the wild aspect of human nature, untamed and uncontrolled. It is a mindset that believes that fulfilling the "desires of the flesh, and the desires of the eyes and the pride of life" is the purpose of human existence. The latter is a different mindset where true meaning of life is found in submission to the will of God, which is also the true meaning of Islam. It is a mindset that puts values and principles above one's life, and the determination to protect those values and principles even at the cost of one's life.

Time and place may be different, but the situations under which Imam Husayn revolted, be it religious, political and social, remain the same in many ways, in many different parts of the world even today. Corruption, greed for

55 Chamseddine, *Hussain's Revolution*, 254-257.

56 Hazleton, *After the Prophet*, 182.

material wealth in the form of capitalism, despotism, nepotism, authoritarian governments around the world, muzzling the voice of opposition, oppression of the weak, the poor and the minorities, to name a few, are still rampant in the world even today. We see Yazids all around, and the Battle of Karbala being fought in many places around the world today.

Karbala can also be understood and related even to a personal level, to what is called 'the inner struggle' that takes place in every human person. From the Islamic understanding of jihad, this inner struggle is *jihad e akbar,* or greater jihad, implying that it is of greater importance to overcome the evil desires within our heart. If Karbala teaches us to fight the evils out there, in our society, then it surely teaches us to fight all the more the evils inside our hearts, and to overcome those evils in our hearts with goodness and love. Karbala is not only for Shias or Muslims because Karbala happens every day, if not without, then certainly within each person. As Ali Shariati says, Karbala is an "eternal and transcendental phenomenon."

18

Sankaradeva's *Eka-Saranam-Nama Dharma*: An Inclusivist Approach

Khaidem Ajit Kumar Singh

Introduction

The emergence of bhakti moment became an alternative from of religion to the common mass irrespective of region or language. Srimanta Sankaradeva was the pioneer of this movement. He guided the people in different socio-religious and political contexts. Bhakti became the vehicle through which common mass achieve *mukti*, as this was denied to them based on caste and gender. Sankaradeva propagated Bhakti as an approach of liberation. Bhakti movement is essentially accommodative; it was a source of uniting the people.

Social, Religious and Political Background of Assam in 14th CE

Social Background

Fifteen century Assam presented a varied collection of diverse shades and grades of culture, religion, race and political status. The social condition of the country was utterly depressing, degenerating and tending towards revolution. There was a wide gulf between the higher and lower castes, and the dominance of the Bramanas over the rest of the society was binding. This superiority complex was firmly established in all aspects of the society.[1] H.V. Shreenivasa mentions that,

1 P. Govinda Pillai, *The Bhakti Movement Renaissance or Revivalism?* (Greater Noida: AAKAR BOOK, 2017), 184-185.

> Persons of humble birth, who wished to wear chaddar or shawl, were obliged to fold it over the right, as the upper class did. The common people were not permitted to build houses of masonry, or with a round end… Musalmans, Morias, Doms and Haris forbidden to wear their hair long, and members of the two latter communities were further distinguished by having a fish and broom, respectively tattooed on their forehead.[2]

This is a witness to the domination of the high caste over the low caste.

Religious Background

Sankaradev was born to a Saivite family. His father Kusumavara worshipped Siva.[3] It was a flourishing religion at the time of Sankaradeva. Ramananda one of his biographer states: "people did not worship Krishna or performed the deeds sacred to Hari. They, on the other hand, would fain worship Bhairava and consider it to be the greatest of religions."[4] Here human sacrifice was offered to Siva. Kacari soldiers not satisfied with this sort of worship insisted that they be allowed to worship Siva according to their tribal custom.[5] This substantiates that Siva worship was quite common with the Assamese people.

In addition to the Saivism, there was a worship of Shakti throughout the medieval period and till the 18th century in Assam. Kamakshya was the most prominent shrine of the sect; the worship was connected the various rites. In the course of time, the concept of goddess developed. In this form, she was popularly known as Kesaikhati (eater of raw flesh) because of the annual human sacrifice at her temple at Sadiya called the Tamereswari Devi temple. It was during the time of Ahom dynasty, under the rule of Gadadhar Singh Vaishnavism attained remarkable dimensions. Vaishnava religion obtained a strong footing in the country. Probably Sankaradeva might have been influenced by the Ahom kings. Subsequently, Sankaradeva became the fountain head of the Bhagavati movement in Assam. This was during the Ahom King Suhungmung.[6] Vaishnava Gosains were respected. Ahom King and Ratnadhvaj King accepted Vaishnavism and granted endowments for the

---

2 H.V. Sreenivasa Murthy, *Vaiṣṇavism of Śaṃkaradeva and Rāmānuja A Comparative Study* (Delhi: Motilal Banarsidas, 1973), 31-32.

3 Maheswar Neog, *Early History of the Vaisnava Faith and Movement in Assam: Sankaradeva and his Times* (Delhi: Motilal Banarsidas, 1985), 81.

4 Neog, *Early History of the Vaisnava Faith and Movement in Assam: Sankaradeva and his Time,* 242.

5 Murthy, *Vaisnavism of Samkaradeva and* Ramanuja, 33.

6 Suhungmung the 14th number of Ahom king, Suhungmung (reign 1497-1539) (Swarganarayan, Dihingia Raja) was one of the most important Ahom kings, who ruled at the cusp of Assam's medieval history.

maintenance of Vaihsnava monasteries. Subsequently Vaishnavism received official recognition from Jayadhvaj King.[7]

Political Background

Political unity in Assam was at its lowest level in the beginning of the 12th century CE. Assam was ruled by Pala Dynasty[8] but it did not last long. As a result, various dynasties arose. Chutiya kings who ruled the country east of Subaansiri and Disang; Kacharis ruled the south bank of the Brahmaputra; and number of Bhuyans occupied the land west of the Kacharis.[9] They were brought to destruction by the invasion of Muslim sultans by Muhammad Bhaktiyar towards the end of the 12th century and followed by Ghiyas-ud-din in 1227 CE and he proceeded triumphantly as far as Sadiya where he was defeated and finally driven back to Bengal. Hussain Shah (1493-1513) invaded at the invitation of Bramana councillor of Nilambar, King of Kamata[10] and resulted to fall of his kingdom. Hence, the rule of the independent kings came to an end.

Another independent Ahom king subjugated the Nagas, Morans and Borahis, and established his influence over a considerable portion of eastern Assam. He extended his territory and maintained relationship through matrimonial alliance with Koch king in order to protect his kingdom. Fresh hostility broke out but later the relationship was restored by the Ahoms under Sukhampha (1552-1603). By the end of the 16th century, Koch kingdom declined due to repeated invasion of Muslim. At this critical time, Koch king sought the help from Ahom, to drive out the Muslims. Koch kingdom came to an end. Later Bara Bhuyan appears in the political scene; he encountered opposition from enemy. This hostility compelled them to change place frequently. They migrated and settled at Alipukhari at the time of Rajadhara.[11]

The next leader was Bhuyan, Kusumavara, the father of Sankaradeva. The period of Sankaradeva saw the disintegration and decay of the power of the

7 Edward Gait, *A History of Assam* (Gauhati: EBH Publishers, 2008), 287.

8 Pala dynasty, ruling dynasty in Bihar and Bengal, India, from the 8th to the 12th century. Its founder, Gopala, was a local chieftain who rose to power in the mid - 8th century during a period of anarchy. It was during the reign of Ramapala (1077–1120), the last important Pala king, did much to strengthen the dynasty in Bengal and expanded its power in Assam and Orissa; he is the hero of a Sanskrit historical poem, the Ramacarita of Sandhyakara. On his death, however, the dynasty was virtually eclipsed by the rising power of the Senas, though Pala kings continued to rule in southern Bihar for 40 years. The main capital of the Palas appears to have been Mudgagiri (now Munger) in eastern Bihar. *Pala dynasty: India Dynasty*, https://www. britannica.com/topic/Pala-dynasty (Accessed on 23/2019).

9 Murthy, *Vaiṣṇavism of Saṃkaradeva and Ramanuja*, 25-26.

10 Edward Gait, *A History of Assam*, 44.

11 Murthy, *Vaisnavism of Samkaradeva and Ramanuja*, 27-28.

Bhuyans. Sankaradeva assumed the charge of his office in his teenage but the constant Kachari friction, the pressure of the expanding Ahoms and death of his first wife, Suryavati, made him realize the futility of worldly power.[12] These are the two incidents that turned his life from the politics to devotion. He submitted to Ahom king along with his people and follow the order of the king. But, the task[13] given to his people brought anger and he escaped from the hand of Ahom. With this comes the end of the glory of Bara Bhuyans and Sankaradeva gave up the yoke of worldly bondage to search for the kingdom of God.

Arrival of Bhakti Movement in Assam

Bhakti movement scatter throughout Assam and other parts of India through the efforts of Nimbarka (11th century), Madhvacharya (13th century), Kabir (15th century) Chaitanya, Namdev (15-16th century) and other saints. Prior to the arrival of Bhakti movement in Assam, Saktism bordering on extreme Tranticism, was also widely prevalent. The followers of these cults were all found indulging in evil practices like animal and human sacrifices, magical rites, spells and the likes. The departure of Sankaradeva's wife cause Sankaradeva to make pilgrim for 12 years. After 12 years of pilgrimage in various parts of India, Sankaradeva experienced new faith in 15th century, which is known as the *Eka Sarana Nama Dharma* meaning devotion to one God.[14] In other word, it is generally called as Neo-Vaishnava. The arrival of Bhakti movement in Assam is based on the theme of *Eka Sarana Nama Dharma* where Sankaradeva brought both the concept of Shaktism and Vaishnavism as well as other faiths into one single framework. The Neo-Vaishnavism supports the concept of one Supreme God.

Life and Teachings of Sankaradeva

There is no consensus among historians regarding his birth and duration of life. One of the reliable biographers, Daitari Thakur assumes that Sankaradeva died in the evening of the second day of the bright half on the lunar month in the solar bhadra, 1490 Saka/1568 CE.[15] However, he is silent about the date of

---

12 Neog, *Early History of the Vaisnava Faith and Movement in Assam: Sankaradeva and his Times*, 68.

13 The king asked them to help him in catching wild elephants, including Samkaradeva and his followers. Elephant stamped Samkaradeva's people. This enraged the shot-tempered king, who ordered to behead all members of the offending party. Samkaradeva, however, made good escape; his followers, Madhavadeva and Hari, his son-in-law, made captives. Madhavadeva was released, but hari had to pay his head as penalty. Murthy, *Vaisnavism of Samkaradeva and Ramanuja*, 28.

14 Satyendranath N. Sarma, *The Neo-Vaishnavite Movement and the Sattra Institution of Assam* (Guwahati: Lawyer's Book Stall, 1966), 25.

15 Neog, *Early History of the Vaisnava Faith and Movement in Assam: Sankaradeva and his Times*, 98.

the Sankaradev's birth and the years of his life. Ramananda gives, thursday, the 7th Bhadra, as the time of Sankaradeva's demise, and the midnight of the second bright day in the month of Phalguna as the time of his birth, but he did not mention the year. Maheswar Neog, H.V. Sreenivasa Murty and others have given the most plausible date of his birth—Asvina, 1371 Saka.

He was born in the Bhuyan family at Alipukhuri, a place about sixteen miles from the town of Nowgong. His father, Kusumavara was the chief of the Siromoni Bara Bhuyan and his mother was Satyasandha (they were the devotee of Siva) who died three days after his birth. He was brought up by his grandmother Buri Gosain Khersuti. They were very much delighted to see the marks of greatness in the horoscope and declared:

> In merit he is like Narayana; in gravity like the ocean:
> In Valour like Aditya and in virtue like God Maheswara.[16]

Sankaradeva lived a life of ease and luxury up to 12th year. He was very fond of sports and cared very little about others. Therefore his grandmother was unhappy with him and said, "I am with all the members of our family, proud of having so good natured a child in you. The only painful feature in you is that you are not disposed to read. All your ancestors were renowned scholars. You too should keep the prestige and tradition of your four fathers."[17] But Sankaradeva replied with a grave face: "Send me to school and I will show you whether I can learn or not."[18] Though he went to school he was not interested in learning.

By the time he left the schools at the age of 17 or 18, he learned Sanskrit, *Vedas, Upanishad* and the *Puranas*. Among the *Puranas*, he was deeply impress with *Bhagavada Purana.* Critical study of the *Bhagavada Purana* made Sankaradeva adhere Vaishnava. At the age of twenty one (1470) or twenty two Sankaradeva married Suryavati, daughter of Harivaragiri Kayastha. But, she died soon after giving birth to a girl child. With a wounded heart he prepared for pilgrimage[19] to overcome the pain. Returning from the pilgrimage after

16 Murthy, *Vaisnavism of Samkaradeva and Ramanuja,* 46.

17 Murthy, *Vaiṣṇavism of Śaṃkaradeva and Rāmānuja,* 47.

18 Murthy, *Vaiṣṇavism of Śaṃkaradeva and Rāmānuja,* 47.

19 Some extent it is certain that Sankara set out his pilgrimage in 1481 when he was thirty two years of age (Maheswar Neog, *Early History of the Vaiṣṇava Faith and Movement in Assam: Śaṅkaradeva and his Times*, 102) but Kakati gives 1483 as the date of his pilgrimage (Banikanta Kakati, ed. *Vaisnavite myths and legends*, 37). He travelled for his pilgrimage for three years. During his pilgrimage, he became acquainted with great vaisnava renascent movement of other parts of India which supplied the necessary ideals and inspirations to him as the initiator of Assam. Sarma, *The Neo-Vaisnavite Movement and the Satra Institution of Assam*, 15.

12 years he began his mission for the public.[20] His mission spread throughout Assam, specially, Koch kingdom.[21] Sankaradeva spent his last days in Koch-Bihar and passed away on thursday, the 7th or the 21st Bhadra (September,), 1569 CE.[22]

His method of teachings was based on Bhakti. He teaches an alternative way of life to the people. His teachings includes devotion to one God which brings the freedom to all. Untouchability, superstitious, ignorance, gender inequality, and social evil were denounced by him.[23] Sankaradeva teaches monotheistic religion and one supreme God. Therefore, his creed is known as *Eka Sarana Nama Dharma*. In *Eka Sarana Nama Dharma*, there is only one God—Vasudeva Krishna—and there is none else other than the One. The worship of other gods and goddesses are strictly prohibited. According to Sankaradeva, the Supreme God is Krishna, Who is the saviour of all.[24] His main teachings can be summarised in the following points:

i. God is one, God is omnipotent and all people are same, there is no distinction in the caste or social status, be it small or bigger in the society and humanity is above all.
ii. All the existence of creatures are the part of God, therefore one should worship them as a part of God.
iii. One should surrender to God.

---

20 People attending them were given opportunities to raise question and even dispute with him. Sankaradeva patiently replied to them whether they were his followers or professed opponents. Sankaradeva gained many followers in this way. Though many of them belonged to the middle rung of caste hierarchy, occasionally some Brahmin and rich merchants, too, joint him. One of them was Bhavanada who was very rich and had contributed liberally to Sankaradeva for his congregations and other missionaries activities. Pillai, *The Bhakti Movement Renaissance or Revivalism?*, 179-180.

21 Named after the Koch tribe of Assam, Koch dynasty played an important role in forming the history of Assam during the medieval period. The beginning of Medieval Assam is marked by the rise of the Khen dynasty of the Kamata kingdom, established by Prithu in the western part of the old Kamarupa Kingdom, and the beginning of attacks by the Turks of Bengal. The Kamata kingdom, named after the capital at Kamatapur, was frequently attacked by the rulers of Bengal, and Alauddin Hussain Shah finally removed the last Khen king in 1498. But Hussein Shah and subsequent rulers could not consolidate their rule in the Kamata kingdom, mainly due to the revolt by the Bhuyan chieftains and other local groups. The Koch dynasty emerged as the dominant kingdom after the fall of the Khen dynasty in 1498 and Kamat Dynasty in 1515. http://www.assamtopix.com/2014/07/rule-of-koch-dynasty-in-assam.html, (Accessed on 28/ 07/18).

22 Maheswar Neog, *Early History of the Vaiṣṇava Faith and Movement in Assam: Sankaradeva and his Times*, 120.

23 *Vaishnavism in Assam*, https://asomsattramahasabha.org/articles/LIFE%20OF%20SANKARDEVA.pdf (Accessed on 24/08/2019).

24 H.V. Sreenivasa Murthy, *The Lasting Values of Sankaradeva's Teachings*, (Accessed on 23/ 08/ 2019).

iv. Uttering God's name can give one's freedom from all the sorrows.
v. Non-violence is the only way to peace.
vi. The arts, culture, literature are the ways to worship God and enjoying happiness in this materialistic world and, above all.
vii. One should perform his/her duties without any result.[25]

His teachings brought about changes in the Assamese society. Due to his contribution, he was acknowledged as the Father of the Assamese. The impact of his teaching was on social equality, peaceful coexistence with other communities, bhakti lifestyle, and love and compassion for one another.

His Understanding of Bhakti

The particular form of Vaishnavism evolved by Sankaradeva is known as *Eka Sarana Nama Dharma.*[26] It enjoined the worship of one god, that is, Vishnu in his many incarnation. Chiefly as Krishna and Rama, and interdicted its votaries from the worship of any other deities, because as the *Bhagavata Puranas* urges, it is enough to water the roots of a tree by branches and foliage get their sap or give food to the *pranas* by which limbs get their nourishment. Or, as the Bhagavata gita demands, one should take sole refuge in the *Bhagavata*, the powerful Lord, who saves one from the faults of omission of all the duties. Sankaradeva says that bhakti includes the eight-fold different forms of *kritana* (saying praises of the Lord), *sravana* (listening to the praise of the Lord), *acharna* or *puja* (worshiping to an idol with flowers etc.), and so on. Sankaradeva's *dharma mahapurushiya* is a worship of the *mahapurusha*—the Supreme Person, who is lord over the primal *prakriti* and *purusha.*[27]

Eka Sarana Nama Dharma Approach of Inclusivism

Sankaradeva's approach is inclusive in nature. Sankaradeva advocated pure bhakti. He says that eternal *Braman* cannot be worship through any medium, because, *Braman* is above all the qualities of the world. The worship can be done only through love or devotion and an inner relationship between god and human. A real devotee (*Bhakta*) does not seek salvation (*mukti*), although it could be attained through bhakti. Bhakti is the means for the liberation from both the political, socio economy and worldly bondage towards the spiritual paths.

Concept of *Eka Sarana Nama Dharma*

Sankaradeva propagation of *Eka Sarana Nama Dharma* preaches devotion of one God by uttering their own choice of particular names (Vishnu or Krishna).

25 Hari Charan Das, "Knowledge Management System of Srimants Sankardeva and His Research Methods," *Global Research Methodology Journal* (May-July, 2011), 5-6.

26 *Eka sarana nama dharma* means the ultimate refuge in one God.

27 Murthy, *Vaisnavism of Samkaradeva and Ramanuja,* 35.

Sankaradeva simplifies the form of worship by uttering one name of deity. He also don't acknowledge the name of Radha and Krishna. He noted four important elements of Neo Vaishnavism: (i) God (ii), Guru (iii) the fraternity of Bhakats and (iv) Namm.[28] The concept *Eka Sarana Nama Dharma* gives space for both Hindu and the non-Hindu. Sankaradeva further argues that since Lord Vishnu is all in One, therefore, it is not necessary to worship other manifestation of various God and Goddesses. He preaches *Eka Sarana Nama Dharma* "the religion of taking refuge with the One God only."[29]

Eka Sarana Nama Dharma and Social Inclusivity

He is also known as a social reformer. In the midst of subjugation based on caste, gender, and untouchability Neo-Vaishnavite brings freedom in the societal life. Sankaradeva does not draw distinction by caste, gender, and others. His main objective was to reform the society from violence, oppression, exploitation and ignorance. To propagates liberty for victim of social stigma and bondage. The revolutionary activities undertaken by Sankaradeva removed caste disparity from Brahmaputra valley. His concept *Eka Sarana Nama Dharma* is thus inclusive in nature; it unites people.

In 1468 century CE, he established a Kirtanghar (prayer house) at Tembuwani. The prayer house/hall becomes the gathering centre for the national life of Assam over time. This innovative social institution encompassed different aspects like religion, culture, and social issues.[30] People of all castes sat together in the Kirtanghar. Kirtanghar became an ambience of peace and unity irrespective of differences. His main idea was to reconstruct the society by providing an alternative approach through bhakti. As a result, people come together, respect and recognize as that all are part of God's creation. Thus, his method of inclusivistic in the context of diversity in faith and culture.

Religious Liberation

The arrival of Sankaradeva brought about changes in the lives of the people. Sankaradeva affirmed repeatedly that there was no need of animal sacrifice in the worship of lord Krishna. He prohibited sacrificing animals. In his writing,

28 Shekhar Chakraborty, "Uniqueness of Sankaradeva's Neo Vaisnavite Movement: A Socio Cultural Renaissance in Assam," in *An International Multidisciplinary Research e-Journal* 1 (December), 3.

29 Suniti Kumar Chatterji, "The Eka Sarana Dharma of Sankaradeva: The Greatest Expression of Assamese Spiritual Outlook," in *Eka Sarana Dharma of Srimanta Sankardeva,* edited by Paran Goswami. https://www.scribd.com/document/235298877/Eka-Sarana-Dharma-of-Srimanta-Sankardeva (Accessed on 31/08/2019).

30 Sanjib Kumar Borkakoti, *Janajatiya Mising Kristi aru Asomor vaishnava sanskritir majat binimaya,* edited by Pranab Kumar Barua, (Nagaon: January, 2005), (Accessed on 24/08/2019).

he says that the sacrifices of animals will have its effect on one's *karma*. He developed simple form of worship of lord Krishna based on Shravana-Kirtana, listening and chanting the name of God.

Eka Sarana Nama Dharma became very popular for its simplicity. As a result, Shakti form of worship declined. Neo-Vashnavite adheres to the concept of brotherhood and inclusive nature of religious pantheons.[31] Sankaradeva's work brought about tremendous impact towards the upliftment of the backward classes and minimization of the rigidity of caste distinctions. He accepted all people irrespective of tribes, caste, classes and religion in his new movement.[32] This movement brought total transformation and freedom from religious stigmatization.

Sankaradeva brought the message of love and release of the soul. He states that through bhakti an individual's voice could be heard by God, if only it rose from the pure and sincere heart. His religious activities formed the basis for the growth of culture and literature, both rich and varied. The common people in from every walks of life embrace a simplified and democratised Hinduism irrespective of caste colour, gender and age.[33]

Eka Sarana Nama Dharma and Gender

Sankaradeva was not merely a religious preacher. He stand as a social reformer. His concept of *Eka Sarana Nama Dharm* never denies or satirizes any gender. Sankaradeva redeemed woman from that degraded state and elevated her to equal status with man in the performance of the religion of devotion.[34] Women position were in the terrible circumstances where they became an object for lust. Sankaradeva pave the path of liberation in terms of gender in his reform movement; he allowed both the man and women in his Bhakti. Women were also initiated for arranging the elements of worship and the rituals. He sees both the man and women as Krishna and Radha, Rama and Sita. He said that the role of the women is at par with the men in many of the Satras[35] where they

31 Rinku Borah, "The Neo Vaishnavism of Srimanta Sankaradeva: A great Socio – Cultural Revolution in Assam," *MSSV Journal of Humanities and Social Sciences* 1/1 (June 2006), 2.

32 Borah, "The Neo Vaishnavism of Srimanta Sankaradeva," 4-5.

33 Parashmani Das, *Biswa Darwarat Srimanta Sankardeva*, edited by W. L. Smith & Prabhat C. Das (Guwahati: BLJ Publication, 2013), 188.

34 Sanjib Kumar Borkakoti, *Srimanta Sankaradeva as a Feminist* http://atributetosankaradeva.org/Sankaradeva_feminism.pdf (Accessed on 25/08/2019).

35 Satras is the monastery of Vaishnavit. In 15th century the first Satra was founded in Majuli. Since then sixty five Satras have come up for the propagation of ethics and socio-cultural ideals. However, at present there are only twenty two Satras in Majuli. The others had to be shifted to safer places due to the devastation of flood and erosion. *Satras of Assam*, https://tourismcorporation.assam.gov.in/portlet-sub-innerpage/satras-of-assam-0 (Accessed on 24/ 08/2019).

are given an equal footage. The prayer hall of Sankaradeva brings about liberty. The Neo-Vaisnavite movement conveys Bhakti of gender equality, justice and liberation from gender stigmatization and patriarchical domination.[36]

Bhakti as a Means to Acquire the Higher Realm

Sankaradeva was a champion of revolution. In Assam, Sankaradeva preaches the Bhakti cult of love and tolerance and devotion towards the Almighty God. As a pilgrim, Sankaradeva travelled all over India; he upholds the unity of Hindu culture. He travelled all over Assam preaching his new gospel. As a result, Sankaradeva became one of the most famous authoritaty of Nirguna sect.[37] The prayer hall (Namghar) became the centre of their prayer. It was open for the every one irrespective of caste and creed. The prayer hall brings about spiritual upliftment towards the higher realm. The gathering of multi community boost unity.[38] Sankaradeva concept of *Eka Sarana Nama Dharma* becomes the source for devotion in God. He believes that every creature is a part of God. Therefore, his bhakti movement incorporated music, songs and poems in praise of One God.

Concluding Remark

The inclusive nature of Sankaradeva's Neo-Vaishnavism based on *Eka Sarana Nama Dharma*, categorically construct an approach of inclusivity equality, equity and justice irrespective of caste, tribes, class, gender and religion. He asserted that bhakti is an approach to unite the people and the same bhakti can bring liberation. His concept of *Eka Sarana Namadharma* is to teach everyone to live together, focusing and surrender on one God towards the elevation of one's soul to a higher level. It enables liberation from all forms of bondages. This Neo-Vaishnavism with the core teaching of *Eka Sarana Nama Dharma* releases the chain of distinction and ushers in inclusivity.

---

36 Padmakshi Kakoti and Pradip Jyoti Mahanta, "Understanding Women in the Religious Institutions: A Study With Reference To the Sattras of Assam." *IOSR Journal of Humanities and Social Science* 1/5 (Sep.-Oct. 2012), 20-22.

37 Rajnandini Das, "Sankaradeva and Kabirdas: A Short Comparative Analysis of Their Bhakti" *The International Journal of Humanities & Social Studies* 4/9 (September, 2016), 70.

38 Mehjabeen S. Rahman, "Role of Satra & Namghar in the Evolution of Genesis of Assamese Identity," *International Journal of Social Sciences and Management* 2 (April, 2015), 111-112.

19

Theory of Religious Belief: Disbelieving to Believe

K.G. Pousonglung

There are numbers of religion that are practiced and believed full heartedly all around the world. There are religion that believed and worship in human with extraordinarily humanitarian quality. There are religion that believed and worshiped in the nature; there are religion that believed and worship in the divine that had created and sustained this nature. From time immemorial, humankind attempted to define religion out of which several theories were formulated. Several approaches have been applied, yet all seem to answer just a piece of it. There has not been any successful theory or approach to understand religion or for that, God in its entirety. This writings do not intend or even attempt to claim a success story with regard to religion and God. But, what the following discussion does is doubt everything that could possibility be doubted. The article brings out the paradoxical nature of religion as its field to investigate. There are paradoxes in religion—such as origin and history, incomprehensible yet comprehensible notion of God/s, many Gods yet same or similar religious teachings—that can never be reconciled and consequently which has become the epicentre for religious differences and highlights the irony of religious claim. In the light of this discussion, the paper attempts to identify paradoxes and re-examine them with the sceptic lens.

The History of the Study of Religion

Human history is the record of the events from the past. History is beyond written records. The existence of human being precedes history. There is of course, with the advancement and achievement in the field of science and technology a broader horizon is unfolding. History inform us the developmental stages of human activities, the changes and progress. The history of the study of religion similarly is the unfolding of religious events and also how human perceived religion. According to Joseph Kitagawa, study of religion is the study of the nature and expressions of the religious experience of humankind as that experience is manifested in history.[1] The objective in doing the history of the study of religion is to strive to grasp a given reality in its own terms, in its own uniqueness, and in its own context.[2] This can involve identifying religious elements, compiling and explaining of the facts that are gathered. So the interest here is not the science, but the development of that science for studying those facts and the approaches that are applied.

The study of religion is not a modern phenomenon. Eric J. Sharpe believed that the origin of the study of religion lies in the period of classical antiquity, when cultural contacts became more extensive and people began to experience the presence of other religions.[3] Such interaction shows that religious systems not only posit differences but also exhibit pointed similarities. Reflection on the nature of the gods was thus stimulated. The comparison with different civilizations gave the expatriate Greek mind a horizon unknown in the Greek homeland, and one that, indeed, was not to be known there for considerable time.[4] About the same time the Indian sub-continent was witnessing a shift from the ritualistic Vedic religion to a more philosophically oriented approach to religion. As the Greek speculation played along the nature of gods, the Upaṇṣadic rationality was deliberating on the relation of Brahman and Ātman.

Similar mode of enquiry continued in the religion of the Indian sub-continent until it had taken firm ground in determining their stand as a separate religious community basing on their philosophical speculation. But unfortunately in the West, such free thinking came into attack from the church. Now the attention was soon absorbed in dogmatic questions and the rebuttal

---

1 Joachim Wach, *Essays in the History of Religions*, edited by Joshep M. Kitagawa and Gregory D. Alles (New York: Macmillan Publishing Company, 1988), xii.

2 Jerald C. Brauer, *The History of Religions: Essays in Methodology*, edited by Mircea Eliade and Joseph M. Kitagawa (Chicago: The University of Chicago Press, 1962), viii.

3 Eric J. Sharpe, *Comparative Religion: A History*, 2nd ed. (London: Gerald Duckworth and Company Ltd., 1986), 2.

4 Jan de Vries, *The Study of Religion: A Historical Approach*, translated by Kees W. Bolle (New York: Harcourt, Brace and World, Inc., 1967), 4.

of heretical opinions.[5] And similar phenomenon of theistic revivalism came to play in the form of *Bhakti* movement in India. *Bhakti* movement in itself was a philosophically theistic religion, but the concomitant jealous attitude resulted in communal and doctrinal conflict. There has been an attempt by different sects to place their God above all other Gods. The hierarchical nature of Hinduism had never cease to exist till date. This resulted in the assertion of the attitude of religious supremacy. Consequently religion becoming the victim of hostility and persecution. The brutality that were carried out in the name of religion is horrifying. The Christian Crusades against Islam and in turn, the pressure of Muslim rulers upon Christian nations. Even the acclaimed tolerant religion are not an exception. The persecution of Buddhist by Confucianism in China, Hindu against Christianity and Islam and Buddhist against Islam.[6]

The period following the Reformation from the 16th to the 19th century C.E. was the century of Enlightenment which changed the intellectual outlook. The scope of religious study spread further beyond the Christian fold. It was a period of revival of the classical scholarship.[7] The 19th century witnessed the herculean paradigm in the way people understood the natural world in particular and religion in general. Charles Darwin's (1809-1882) *On the Origin of the Species* (1859) challenges the religious narratives of the world and its inhabitants. A new era of scientific and rational enquiry into the nature of religion was dawning. At this point, it would be entirely wrong to credit the Reformation or Charles Darwin for this scientific enquiry methodology into the study of religion. As noted earlier, prior to the Christian era, many fashionable modern concepts, such as the socio-political function of religion and the origin of religious beliefs in psychological needs was already in practiced. Greek ethnographic historians, such as Herodotus[8] (485 BCE), provided an ancient anticipation of the anthropological approach to the study of religion.[9] The uniqueness of this century was its inclination towards the evolutionary approach in the study of religions.

---

5 Vries, *The Study of Religion: A Historical Approach*, 14-16.

6 Heller, "The History of Religions as a Preparation for the Co-operation of Religions," *The History of Religions: Essays in Methodology*, 132-133.

7 Jacques Waardenburg, *Classical Approaches to the Study of Religion*, vol. 1 (The Hague: Mouton and Co., 1973), 7.

8 Prior to Herodotus, there was no writer who had ever made a systematic, thorough study of the past or tries to explain the cause-and-effect of events. His work *The Histories* gives an account of the Greco-Persian Wars. After him, such historical analysis became an indispensable part of intellectual and political life. "Herodotus," https://www.history.com/topics/ancient-history/herodotus (12/7/2019).

9 Seymour Cain, "Study of Religion: Methodological Issues," *The Encyclopaedia of Religion*, vol. 14, edited by Mircea Eliade and et.al. (New York: Macmillan Publishing

Religion, today is widely discussed and also has become an object of study rather than an object of belief or faith.[10] There are various approaches to the study of religions owing to its complex nature. Whatever the approaches be, they seek to trace the origin of religion and their existential nature. Approaches like anthropological approach and sociological approach looked for the *a priori* of the religion while philosophical approach and psychological approaches not only discuss the origin but also studies the nature of human minds and thoughts. In the phenomenological approach researcher study the phenomena, events and nature and characteristics of religion. All these approaches are the result of the polemic, apologetic and accumulative attitude of the researchers. It would not be wrong to assert that without sceptical temperament towards religion, the world would have not witnessed such development in the field of religious studies. Also one cannot deny the shifting of the attitude from polemic to accumulative.

The Paradox of Religion

Any books on religion, unhesitatingly declared the difficulties and complexities in defining religion at the outset. And truly it is so. There is not one single definition that could content religion exhaustively. There are numerous definitions from different approaches so also from different scholars even if they advocate the same approach.[11] Additionally there is also another problems in the study of religion. In the study of religion it is important to bracket one's belief and religious environment. But, by nature human are predisposed and prejudicially inclined to view other religion from his or her own religiously seasoned environment. Finding the facts and analysing religion is therefore difficult unless it is solely of one's own faith. This makes it difficult to differentiate the origin and the history of religion.

Origin and History of Religion

Origin of religion means the *a priori* of religion. While history or history of religion contains the narration of the origin along with the successive narration

---

Company, 1987): 67- 68.

10 Seth D. Kunin, *Religion: The Modern Theories* (Baltimore and London: The Johns Hopkins University Press, 2003), 3.

11 For example, William James defines religion as "the feelings, acts, and experience of individual men in their solitude, so far as they apprehend themselves to stand in relation to whatever they may consider the divine." William James, *The Varieties of Religious Experience*, 5th impression (Np: The Fontana Library Theology and Philosophy, 1971), 50. Whereas Sigmund Freud, understood religion as an "obsessive action" or just an "illusion". They both approach religion from psychological point of view. Sigmund Freud, *Introductory Lectures on Psychoanalysis*, translated and edited by James Strachey (New York; London: W.W. Norton & Company, 1966), 258; Sigmund Freud, *The Origins of Religion*, vol. 13 (London: Penguin Books, 1990), 31-33.

of the event in the aftermath of that origin. Origin of religion is shrouded in mysteries of the myths and folklores. This does not mean that myth are to be neglected or despised. There is a residue of reality hidden in the myth. As Raimundo Panikkar (1918-2010) writes, "Myth gives us a reference point that orients us in reality."[12] History is and must be based on the scientific archaeological evidences and authentic texts and also other reliable sources. The distinctive nature between these two is diminishing. The historical reality of religion is disappearing in the mirage of myth. Myth, Ernst Cassirer (1874-1945) writes, is the epic element in primitive religious life; rite is the dramatic element. We must begin with studying the latter in order to understand the former. Taken in themselves the mythical stories of gods or heroes cannot reveal to us the secret of religion, because they are nothing but the interpretations of rites.[13] But unfortunately, myth had become the centre stage of any given religion.

The term 'origin' can be heretical and confusing to some religious group. These religions believed that their religion existed eternity to eternity. The Hindus called their religion *Sanatana Dharma,* which literally means 'eternal religion'. There are religious communities each proclaiming a faith with a long and impressive, even brilliant, past and with the continuing creative allegiance of mighty civilizations. This is known in theory; the knowledge is today supplemented in practice by personal contact and widespread social intermingling.[14] No matter how defused and infused the religion is with the accumulation of various elements from other faiths, the claim of 'eternal religion' survived the corruption.

From the modern approaches to the study of religions, the term 'origin' as understood by the traditional believers has come under attack. Some of these modern approaches to the study of religions defies the older concept of 'origin'. Herbert Spencer (1820-1903) believes that religion evolved into a complex modern theological system from a simple religion just as society evolved from primitive to the civilized.[15] From the critical analysis of such statement, one can infer that there must be a point where the rudimentary of religion existed. There is a problem with such assumption. For if religion was a 'divine providence', such evolution is unwelcoming. Moreover it demean the 'divine providence'. The evolution, therefore, as Wilfred Cantwell Smith (1916-2000) rightly puts

12 R. Panikkar, *Myth, Faith and Hermeneutics: Cross-Cultural Studies* (New York: Paulist Press, 1979), 20.

13 Vries, *The Study of Religion: A Historical Approach*, 210; Ernst Cassirer, *The Myth of the State* (London: Yale University Press, 1946), 28.

14 Wilfred Cantwell Smith, *The Meaning and End of Religion* (Minneapolis: Fortress Press, 1991), 2.

15 Garry Trompf, *In Search of Origins* (New Delhi: Sterling Publishers Private Limited, 1990), 21.

it, is "mentally making religion into a thing, gradually coming to conceive it as an objective systematic entity."[16] Approaches to religious studies locate the origin of religion differently. Anthropological approach is firmly based in the empirical ethnographic data.[17] It view religion in a successive history. Religion or for that matter God or belief in supernatural being is illusively derived from fear or dream. This similar observation is affirmed also in psychological approach. Sociological approach on the other hand view religion as a social construed. Such religion which has grown from their response to natural world has evolved to a ritualistic and complex religion. And history tells us that the religion which had originated has evolved, reformed and revived given to the context of the society need. Religion in that sense is no more a constant. And therefore the claim of religious superiority is meaningless and has no scientific and historical authenticity.

Historically, religion has its beginning and so its origin. Religiously it don't. Human are religious being, however it may be with God or without God. They had no choice of not to be religious. Whether one like it or not, one is confronted with the idea of created being and the burden of indebtedness continue to sustain life-long. On the hand, historically the religion originates from various factors. And this factors are one way or the other related to human intellect or unfortunate ability to reason. It was the radical ability to imagine beyond oneself that give rise to religion. Herbert Spencer believes that religion derived from the propitiation of the other-self of distinguished ancestors.[18] For William James religion is the product of "sick soul."[19] No matter what, the theory of the origin of religion, historically takes back to wild imagination. But, ironically the religious origin of religion place the creation, moral and ethical values all on the God or the creator God.

The Incomprehensible Yet Comprehensible God

From the observation of current religious scenario, the claim of religion as a human construct seems to be reasonably plausible. Religion contrary to its teaching of peace and love has violent aspects. Every tribe, every community and every nations has their own religion or same religion with varying practices. And all of them claim their version of religion to be the only

16 Smith, *The Meaning and End of Religion*, 51.

17 Kunin, *Religion: The Modern Theories*, 150.

18 E.O. James, *Comparative Religion* (London: University paperbacks, Methuen and Co. Ltd., 1961), 37.

19 Since the "sick soul unlike the healthy mindedness, must be twice-born, the divided self-reunified and renewed through a process of conversion to achieve happiness. For the sick soul, there are two lives, the natural and the spiritual and one must be lost to achieve the other. William James, *The Varieties of Religious Experience*, 5th impression (n.p: The Fontana Library Theology and Philosophy, 1971), 172.

Truth. But, the fact is many of us who claim our belonging to a faith based group have not practically perceived God (which some say is impossible) or comprehend what God really is? The knowledge of God contained by an individual is traditional, self-assumption or implanted and is incomplete. Very few possess genuine heart which searches God and hence very few finds It (to the possible extent of human comprehension). The rest they claim to find It, yet have not found It. Some would say, I did not find God but God found me. Some still would say there is no God, and if there is it is you and me. In fact God has a unique way of manifesting Itself to humankind. Therefore, one cannot deny others claim of having encountered God. But, the question must be open to which God are they talking about? Are they talking about the same God or different God? If they are talking about the same God why are they preaching different messages? Are scriptures really from God? Why are there numerous religious texts? Did God revealed one thing to other and another to other? Is there many Gods or God? There are many more other questions that continues to trouble us. And the only answer that we may get or give is "of course not" and "I don't know". Yet we continue to stress the supremacy of our own God (as if we own It).

Religion and violence has a long history. The reason being that every religious groups wanted their God to be the Supreme or the only One. At this point it is essential to understand what religion means and what does it teaches. Religion is a set of moral, ethical and spiritual rules that binds the community in peace and harmony. Religion teaches love, compassion, charity and all the goodness human can contribute. Garry Trompf writes,

> Many will want to affirm that religion is about 'belief' – belief in a God or divine beings, or belief as trust in such spiritual power(s), or belief in certain fundamental truth... To pray, to meditate, to experience an altered state of consciousness, to be made aware of the supernormal by special experience, any one or all of these motions will be considered essential, and among those who put it this way, most will doubtless insist that religion which is mere assent to stated propositions is lifeless. Another group again, mostly made up of those who do not perceive themselves to be part of any religion, is likely to describe it in terms of its externals or paraphernalia – of churches and temples, habits and saffron robes, popes and Dalai Lamas, hierarchies and castes, even of political clout or persecuted minorities.[20]

20 Trompf, *In Search of Origins*, 3.

Well, the latter is practically true and that is what religion had become today. The world today believes in complexities and sophisticate-ness. And that has come to apply even to the so called God given religion or eternal religion. The want for sophisticate religion had driven human away from the simple truth of religion, i.e., "Love".

The truth is, whatever one say about God or religion, they can never exhaust God in one's expression. It is impossible to comprehend God. Because if God can be comprehended, than God is no more God. But, this is the paradox in our religion today. We know we cannot comprehend God yet we comprehend God's insecurity (from us human). We know God is omnipotent, yet we become protector of our God. We know God wants peace, yet we continue to spread hatred. Unfortunately, we do not know God, but we act as if we know. Nicolas Berdyaev (1874-1948) is right in saying that, "Truth is a fullness which is not bestowed in its consummated completeness. Fanaticism has always been the result of taking part for the whole and men have been unwilling to admit a movement towards completeness."[21] This is dangerous and the danger is what we are witnessing today in our society. And there is greater danger in not realizing the beauty of plurality – plurality of God.

Many Gods Yet Identical Religious Teachings

All the Gods taught human to love each other and to love the flora and fauna. And this love cannot surface until we realise that the God who manifested to the Israelites is not the God who manifested to Muhammad, It is neither Krishna nor Gautama Buddha. It was Yahweh not Allah and neither Krishna nor Gautama Buddha. Also the same, Krishna is not Yahweh but He was *Murlidhar* Krishna who came to protect the righteous and teach love and duty to the world. The same is with the prophets Muhammad, Gautama Buddha and others who had come to spread love, harmony and equality in the chaotic situations of the time. There cannot be a God but Gods. They are not the same they are all separated by time and space. Jesus was born in Bethlehem, Muhammad in Mecca Saudi Arabia, Krishna in Mathura, Vardhamana in Vaishali, Gautama Buddha in Lumbini at different time and different geographical location. So is the same with other God(s) and deified spiritual leaders.

As far as the fight for superiority is concern it is human made. Gods cannot be compared or contrasted, They are what They are. God of the Israelites is the Supreme God of the Israelites, God of the Hinduism is the Supreme God of the Hindus, God of the Muslims is the Supreme God of the Muslims, etc.

21 Nicolas Berdyaev, *Truth and Revelation*, translated by R.M. French (New York: Harper and Brothers Publishers, 1953), 22. Nicolas was a Russian religious and political philosopher and a Christian existentialist. "Nikolai Berdyaev," https://www.newworldencyclopedia.org/entry/Nikolai_Berdyaev (14/07/2019).

Universalising of any of these Gods will result in fatal consequences as the world had already witnessed and witnessing.

Christians claim that Jesus is the only way (John 14:6) and salvation can be received only through him (Acts 4:12). Muslims claim only the Qur'an to be the only revealed truth and believing in Prophet Muhammad, the last prophet as Absolute. Hindus would say that one may attain salvation through *karma marga, Jñāna marga, bhakti marga* and *raja marga*. Well Hinduism gives choices yet without liberty in praxis. If Hinduism stands for what it is than it would have been the most desirable and universal religion. Vivekananda (1863-1902) said, "Hinduism teaches not only tolerance but acceptance", well the truth now stand in contrast. Not only Hinduism all the religious institute had forsaken the simple truth – Love. The core of every teachings of Gods and spiritual teachers had been "love", "compassion", and "acceptance" and not simply tolerance.

But now all the religion, leaving that simple truth, are in the race of supremacy. This race for supremacy leads to communal clashes and ultimately resulting in world-wide phenomena. To this end it is interesting to note what Vivekananda said,

> We find that all religions teach the eternity of the soul, as well as that its lustre has been dimmed, but that its primitive purity is to be regained by the knowledge of God. What is the idea of God in these different religions? The primary idea of God was very vague. The most ancient nations had different deities – sun, earth, fire, water. Among the ancient Jews we find numbers of these gods ferociously fighting with each other. Then we find Elohim whom the Jews and the Babylonians worshipped. We next find one God standing supreme. But the idea differed according to different tribes. They each asserted that their God was the greatest. And they tried to prove it by fighting. The one that could do the best fighting proved thereby that its God was the greatest. Those races were more or less savage. But gradually better and better ideas took place of old ones. All those old ideas are gone or going into the lumber room. All those religions were the outgrowth of centuries; not one fell from the skies. Each had to work out bit by bit.[22]

All religion begins from a primordial stage. As the society progressed religion also progressed along with it. But, looking into the present scenario of religion it is difficult to say if we had really left our savage nature behind. Because what we see today is no more different than our past uncivilized world.

---

22 *What Religion is: In the Words of Swami Vevekananda*, edited by Swami Vidyatmananda (Kolkata: Advaita Ashrama, 2006), 5.

There is no hesitation in killing and persecuting for the sake of one's religion. In the surface people talk about unity and oneness of God, yet underneath there is a dark shadow continuing its age old fight for supremacy.

The whole point is, it is better to have unity in diversity than unity in disguise. Where in the pretext of equality and brotherhood we deliberate our talks to win over and denigrate others. Even if one is willing to stand for the concept of one Universal God that would be with the cost of compromising ones faith. Compromising cannot be the solution to the existing problem of God and religion. It has to be more than that and also more than tolerance. Vivekananda said,

> Not only toleration, for so-called toleration is often blasphemy, and I do not believe in it. I believe in acceptance. Why should I tolerate? Toleration means that I think that you are wrong and I am just allowing you to live.[23]

Evidently it is what we come to see in the so called religious reconciliation events. Tolerance can only be the beginning but not the end in the struggle for universal religious peace. For religious plurality is real. And S.J. Samartha (1920-2001) rightly states, that "To ignore it (religious plurality) and behave as if it does not exist may amount to self-deception."[24]

> We see that the apparent contradictions and perplexities in every religion mark but different stages of growth. The end of all religions is the realizing of God in the soul. That is the one universal religion.[25] Vivekananda said,

> Hundreds of attempts have been made in India, in Alexandria, in Europe, in China, in Japan, in Tibet and lastly in America, to formulate a harmonious religious creed, to make all religions come together in love. They have all failed, because they did not adopt any practical plan. That plan alone is practical which does not destroy the individuality of any man in religion, and at the same time shows him a point of union with all others. But so far all the plans of religious harmony that have been tried, while proposing to take in all the various views of religion have, in practice, tried to bind them all down to a few doctrines, and so have produced more new sects, fighting, struggling and pushing against each other.[26]

23 *What Religion is: In the Words of Swami Vivekananda*, 24.

24 S. J. Samartha, *One Christ Many Religions: Toward a Revised Christology* (Bangalore: BTESSC, 2014), 168.

25 *What Religion is: In the Words of Swami Vivekananda*, 3.

26 *What Religion is: In the Words of Swami Vivekananda*, 31, 32.

This inability to synchronize or produce a universal creed toward religious harmony may be due to our sub-conscious religious supremacy. No matter what it is, today the world of religion had come to a state from where there is no turning back or compromising. It does not mean that our religious clashes had to continue due to the uncompromising nature. The point here is, we need not compromise our faith but accept the truth of diversity, the beauty of many-ness of God.

If we are to do away with religious clashes and disharmony it is time we start accepting the truth of "Many Gods" and start respecting without compromising. The God I worship cannot be the God of my friend, for my expectation and assumption of God is different from my friend's. But, that does not sanction the right to dominate or destroy the existence of other God. For my God have not taught me to do so. And I believe neither other God(s). The reason why God reveal Its existence is to say that God loves us. In spite of Its ability to stay un-manifested It had manifested to prove Its love in person, to die for us, to fight for us. And this is the example that we as human need to learn, to love. Not in the disguise of unity but in the truth of diversity. It is better to have unity in diversity than unity in disguise. And if God is God, than God knows well how the perceptive ability of the creature, i.e. human.

Sceptically Religious: Disbelieve to Believe

Today religion had acquired a negative connotation. Religion is no more a matter of faith alone, but it had become a matter of dignity, identity and privileges. Therefore, it would not be wrong to say that today religion has lost the transcendental meaning and had accumulated a mundane interpretation to itself. And because of which religion today has become a medium of satisfying a whimsical desire for superiority and subjugation. Today God or religion has become a machine that manufactures human necessities. It is because there are very few who really have the knowledge of religious significance. And there are even fewer people who are interested in knowing it. Richard Dawkins in his book *The God Delusion* criticises religious group of indoctrinating children, which is not true. But, he is right in saying that children are forbidden to raise questions or doubts about religion. Therefore children grew up following only '*dos and don'ts*' whereas completely ignoring the '*whys*' of religion or one's faith. In reality there is no place in religion for doubters.

We are taught to believe in religion, religious teachings, priests, God or any other religious elements without questioning. Belief is the foundation of all religions. Without belief there is no religion. Even the scientific approaches to the study of religion are based on belief. According to anthropological approach the *a priori* of religion is the *belief* in the spirit (E.B. Taylor). For psychological approach it is the *belief* in just an 'obsessional neurosis'

(Sigmund Freud). Similarly, philosophical approach, and other approaches has their own *belief* for the origin of religion. The beginning of *belief* is believing. This makes the entire process of faith practice sometimes illogical and ridicules. Believers had no scope of authenticating the religious prescriptions. This lack of liberty for authenticating one's own belief led to religious illiterateness. And then one ends up following or believing in religion or god because others do. This process of believing does not give a long term convincing feelings and explanation of one's query. Consequently, when the doubts arises, faith in religion or god fades away. The foundation of faith on belief is just like building a castle on the sand, it can easily be knocked down.

But, what if faith is established on the foundation of doubts, doubting every religious proposition. Religion, as it is today is under the control of human. Take for example what we believe today is the interpretation of yesterday's events. The theology we have is the product of interpretation and interpretation is inevitably fallible. Religion, therefore beyond the life of religious founder or initiator is highly prone to whimsical interpretation (not denying that there are faithful one who committedly carried out their obligation. Of course there faithfulness can also be doubted for the sake of authenticating). The interpreted Gods cannot be trusted. Such Gods must be viewed with a sceptic lens. Of course, believers are also sceptic. They are sceptic about God, they are sceptic about religion and they are sceptic about anything that is related to God and religion. But, then their doubts or scepticism are not about their God or religion or anything that is related to their religion. Their doubts are about others' God, others' religion and anything that is relating to other's God and religion. Such doubts do not strengthen belief but infused hatred and prejudices for other. Therefore, doubt must be genuine and it must be about one's own belief, one's own God and one's own religion or anything that is related to one's own religion.

In reality, the origin of religion itself was based on doubt. Now some may say it was curiosity rather than doubt. Well it is right! But again, isn't curiosity a result of sceptical attitude toward the given circumstances? It is indeed difficult to distinguished doubt and curiosity, for they are two sides of a same coin. And it is doubt that raises curiosity. Without a serious doubt religion would have not evolved to such sophisticated and complex body of ritualism and dogmatism. But, there is a drawback in an unsystematic doubting. The process of doubting should not be sporadic, it must be coherently continuous and persistent. An unsystematic and inconsistent doubt or lack of doubt upon some religious phenomena can lead to disastrous interpretation of any religious events. And there are people who had taken advantage of such circumstances. They present religion in the way human desire and not in the way religion ought to be. Thanks to such classy and intricate placating of religion, today God no more is confined to what God is, but God has come to mean what human desires God to be. The problem was that people stopped doubting and were too busy making sense of what they see of religion for their selfish personal gain.

Contemporary religions, therefore, serve a mundane affairs rather than the divine. Religion today is not seen for the quality, but seen for the quantity it can provide. Religion has been objectified, it is no more what Rudolf Otto called a *mysterium*. Religion ought to be a mystery, it is a mystery, God is a mystery and God cannot be objectifies and in the same way religion cannot be objectified. If religion is objectified it is no longer a religion, but it had become what Sigmund Freud called *wish fulfilment* and Carl Jung believed it to be the activity of the *collective unconscious mind.* And if religion is what they say it is, then religion is just a trend, a crowd psyche.[27] But, religion is not a crowd or an objectified system like that of an Indian Constitution or any jurisprudences. Religion is a very divinely subjective inner experience of something that is mysterious and most importantly inexpressible and indescribable. And so, every bit and pieces of religious activities or what people or religious group claim to be religious or even God must be seriously doubted and must be viewed through the prism of scepticism.

Conclusion

The scientific approaches to the study of religion has contributed much to the understanding of religion in a systematic and historical way. As it is evident that there has not been any definitions of religion that could give an all-round understanding of what religion really is. From the study of the history of religion it is also evident that religion or the study of religion had undergone several phases of changes, changes that had kept the religion alive for this generation and may be for the next generations to come. No matter whatever changes had taken place the central image of religion, i.e., God or divine, as William James called it had never diminished. But, it is unfortunate that various distorted picture of this central image had taken the centre stage of today's religion. And therefore, there is a need to re-evaluate and rethink on the method that are applied to study religion.

In the study of religion and particularly the methodology that are applied in the process must strengthen the belief in religion. And in order for the strengthening of belief to happen one must be able to critique any illogical and doubtful representation of religion or God. By doing so one is not distorting the image, but rather restoring the distorting image of religion. A true quality of a

27 Crowd psyche is a behavioural changes that are developed as a result of the crowd. In the crowd psyche individual or the crowd lack judgemental ability and are in the pursuance of the crowd momentum. Under such circumstances, what the crowd feel right—with the lack of responsibility—come to considered right no matter what the cost be.

religious being is his/her ability to doubt and question every bits and pieces of his/her own faith. This is of course not an easy process. And as such, faith do not come that easy too. But the belief is that, the faith that is established after a good critique and sceptical analysis cannot be distorted nor corrupted, since it had already neutralized the its vulnerability.

20

The Dance of Śiva (*Tandava*) as the Source of Creation and Existence

Soloman. S

Introduction

Hinduism is one of the oldest religions in the world; it continues to be a living religion. It is no exaggeration to suggest that the bulk of the mythology found in the Hindu epics and Purānas is about Brahma, Visnu, and Siva. The Trimurti of Brahma, Visnu and Siva first appear in Indian literature in the *Maitri Upanisad.*[1] In the trinity of the divine manifestation—Brahma, Vishnu and Siva—Lord Shiva is the one who destroys that which is old and impure in order to make room for a new creation which is pure and divine. Lord Siva annihilates egos, attachments and ignorance. Many fear Lord Shiva's destructive capacity, though it is destruction for the purpose of regeneration. Without death, life cannot begin anew. Without the annihilation of old habits, attachments and ego, we cannot progress toward the goal of God realization. Unless our vessel has been emptied of all that is old, negative and impure, it cannot be filled with divine qualities.[2]

---

1 G. M. Bailey, "Trifunctional elements in the mythology of the Hindu Trimurti," *Numen* 26/2 (December, 1979), 152.

2 Chidanand Saraswat, "Shiva as Destroyer," *Dialogue & Alliance* 19/2 (Fall/Winter, 2005/2006), 79.

Siva's dances are the source of creation, destruction, and liberation. His *Roudra Tandava* is the dance of destruction and the *Ananda Tandava* is the dance of bliss. Many believe and fear Lord Siva's dance of destruction. But does not realise that it empties the cup of attachment so that we may be re-filled with true awareness, true knowledge, and true Divine light. Thus, it is not destruction for destruction's sake. It is destruction for the sake of re-creation. In this light, we can see the dance of Siva as the source of Creation and Existence.

Śiva

God Śiva is all in all, one without second, the Supreme Being and only Absolute Reality. He is *Pati*, our Lord, Immanent and transcendent. To create, preserve, destroy, conceal and reveal are his five powers.[3] The word Śiva, has been derived from the Tamil root word Śivan (*Shevapu* & *ondru*) meaning the red one. So is the word Shambhu, an epithet of Śiva, from *chembu* or *shembu* meaning copper or the red metal.[4] He is one of the major Gods of later Hindu pantheon, forming with Brahmā and Viṣṇu—the great triad of Hindu deities. The word Śiva occurs in the *Rig-Veda*, not as the name of the god, but in a context where it only means auspicious. Śiva as the name of god doesn't appear prominently before 200 BCE.[5]

Among the many deities of Hindu thought and practice, Siva presents a complex character fraught with seeming contradictions. In the few hymns of the Rig Veda dedicated to Rudra (or Rudra-Siva), the deity emerges as both a great healer and a fearsome destroyer. The poets of the Rig Veda implore him, "Do not slay our men in thy wrath,"[6] and, at the same time, ask for his blessing "that everything in this our village may be prosperous and free from disease."[7] The early medieval Purănas develop such contrasts in his character even further. Śiva, a loving husband to his spouse, Parvatï or Urna, is also drawn to the life of ascetic contemplation. In his wrath, this "erotic ascetic" clashes with that other great deity of the Hindu pantheon, Visnu; decapitates his own father-in-law; burns three demonic cities; beheads the creator-god, Brahma;

3 Satguru Sivaya Subramuniyaswami, *Dancing with Siva* (New Delhi: Munshiram Manharlal Publishers, 1996), 49.

4 Jayaram V, *Lord Shiva in Ancient Historic Traditions*, https://www.hinduwebsite.com/img/hinduwebs ite-logo.png, (26.7.2019).

5 Benjamin Wlaker, *An Encyclopedia Survey of* Hinduism (New Delhi: Munshiram Manoharlal Publishers), 406.

6 Rig Veda 1.114.8, Quoted in Anne E. Monius "Siva as Heroic Father: Theology and Hagiography in Medieval South India Anne E. Monius," *Harvard Theological Review* (April, 2004), 169.

7 Rig Veda 1.114.1, Quoted in Anne E. Monius, "Siva as Heroic Father: Theology and Hagiography in Medieval South India Anne E. Monius," 169.

and kills the demon king of Lanka, Rävana. At the same time, he lovingly allows his head to break the fall of the River Ganga to earth and consumes the poisonous by products of the churning of the milk ocean to save the gods. All of Siva's activity in the world, whether ferocious or compassionate is couched theologically, from the Purānas onward, in terms of *lila*: the divine "play" or "sport" that is without cause or reason, done solely for the enjoyment of the lord.

Modern Hindu poster or calendar art preserves something of these contradictory characteristics as well: Siva is most often depicted as a great practitioner of yoga, seated cross-legged on a mat of tiger skin; his matted locks, mark of the ascetic, sport venomous serpents, and in one hand he grips his trident weapon. Yet the River Ganga evidence of his compassionate concern for the well-being of the earth, also courses through his hair, and often his beloved wife, Parvatï, daughter of the mighty Himalayan range sits or stands by his side. All of these mythological narratives and features of Śiva are known to those early poets of the Tamil-speaking Śaiva tradition whose works are anthologized in the canonical Tirumurai.[8]

The Saiva Tradition

Some scholars maintain that the worship of Śiva goes back many thousands of years in the subcontinent of the Indus valley civilization, where steatite seals have been found suggestive of a deity akin to Śiva. The famous "Pasupati" seal shows a seated, perhaps ithyphallic, horned figure surrounded by animals. Sir John Marshall has claimed that this is a prototype of Śiva as the yogin and Pasupati, the Lord of animals. But, is not clear from the seals that this is a proto-Śiva figure and Asko Parpola[9] has convincingly suggested that the seal is in fact a seated bull, almost identical to figures of seated bulls found on early Elamite seals of ca. 3000–2750 BCE. There are early textual references to Rudra, arguably a forerunner of Śiva, one of whose epithets is "auspicious" (Śiva), in the Rig Veda. Here three hymns are addressed to Rudra, the 'roarer.' He is clothed in an animal skin, brown, with a black belly and a red back. Even at this time he is an ambiguous deity who is like a ferocious beast destroying families and livestock, yet who is also a benevolent healer of disease (Rig Veda 2.33, 1.43; 1.114).[10]

It is not only with the Śvetāśvatara Upaniṣad, composed some time prior to the Bhagavad Gītā, that a theism focused upon Rudra-Śiva begins to

8 Monius, "Siva as Heroic Father: Theology and Hagiography in Medieval South India Anne E. Monius," 169-170.

9 Asko Parpola is a Finnish Indologist and Sindhologist, He specializes in the Indus script.

10 Gavin Flood, ed., *The Blackwell Companion to Hinduism* (Oxford: Blackwell publishing, 2003), 204-205.

emerge in the literature. The formation of Saiva traditions as we understand them begins to occur during the period from 200 BCE to 100 CE. Apart from the Śvetāśvatara, we have references to a Śaiva devotee, a Śiva-bhāgavata, in the grammarian Patanjali's commentary on the Pāṇini grammar (Pāṇ, 5.2.76).

During the Gupta dynasty (ca. 320–50 CE) the Purāṇas developed along with Smārta brahmin forms of worship. The Saiva Purāṇas, most notably the Linga and Śiva Purana, contain standard material on genealogy, caste responsibilities, and cosmology, along with specifically Śaiva topics of installing the symbol (linga) of Śiva in temples, descriptions of the forms of Śiva and material on early Śaiva sects. The Puranas mentions four sects in particular, these are the Pāśupata, Lākuliśa, Śaiva, and Kāpalika sects. A picture therefore emerges of a puranic Śaiva tradition.[11]

The Manifestations of Śiva

Śiva's manifestation are complex and contradictory, for he is all encompassing reality who revolves all polarities in his being. His auspicious and terrible aspects are all mirrors of the same primary self. Śiva is the God who must not be named, for to name is to limit and curtail; yet his many names together constitute the sum of his unknowable mysteries. The many realities of the multifaceted Śiva are encompassed by the aspects described in his different manifestations.[12]

Rudra

In the Vedas, Śiva appears as Rudra, the howler. He is the embodiment of the 'Great father', of the thunderbolt. Harbinger of both rain and prosperity, he is entirely fearful in his terrible beauty. Rudra is he whose name is not uttered, the wild God of the Rig Veda, the First one. In his manifestation as the lord of thunderbolts, he encompasses Agni, the elements of fire. Like Agni, he both sustains and destroys life.[13]

Mahādev

Śiva is also called Mahādev or the Great God. He transcends any notion we could form of the divine. He wields dangerous weapons and he blesses at the same time, for he has many hands. He lives outside human imagination, on the fringe of society, high up on the mountains. Even if he agrees to behave as a family-man, he remains a stumbling stone. He does not care about ritual purity, he walks around naked or clad in a tiger-skin; snakes and skulls hang

11 Flood, ed., *The Blackwell Companion to Hinduism*, 205.

12 Namita Gokhale, *The Book of Shiva* (New Delhi: Penguin Books, 2001), 15.

13 Gokhale, *The Book of Shiva*, 15-16.

around his neck and when he comes down from his mountain, he prefers to hang around the cremation grounds.[14]

Similarly there are 1008 names which describes the manifestation and attributes of Śiva, of which some can be found below: Achaleshavar: immovable Lord; Adinath: Primeval master; Aghora: non-terrifying, pleasing; Ghora: Fearsome; Nageshvar: Lord of serpents; and Nataraja: Lord of dance.[15] Out of these manifestations, Naṭrāja is the central theme of this research. The Lord of dance, who sustains, creates and liberates the universe through his dance.

Iconography of Naṭrāja: The King of Dancers

Dancing Śiva is the form of the Hindu god Śiva best known in the West, and indeed seems to be the most popular visual representation of Hinduism for the modern world. Although there is a wide variety of Dancing Śivas, dating back to at least the fifth century CE, what has become so familiar to us is one particular form, known as Naṭrāja, 'King of Dancers.' This image achieved canonical form in Cōḻa bronzes of the tenth century CE and then continued to be reproduced in metal, stone, and other substances up to the present. The Cōḻa Naṭrāja is often said to be the supreme statement of Hindu art.[16]

The root idea behind the dances of Śiva is the manifestation of Primal rhythmic energy. Amongst the greatest of the names of Śiva is Nataraja, Lord of Dancers, or King of Actors.[17] Naṭrāja dances with his right foot supported by a crouching figure and his left foot elegantly raised. Of his four arms, one swings downwards, pointing to the raised foot; another with palm held up signals, 'Do not fear!' In his other hands he holds aloft a drum and a flame. The river Ganga sits in his hair. A cobra uncoils from his lower right forearm, and the crescent moon and a skull are on his crest. He dances within an arch of flames. This dance is called the Dance of Bliss (*ānandatāṇḍava*).[18]

Ānandatāṇḍava

The central episode of *Ānandatāṇḍava* concerns the visit of Śiva as a beggar to certain sages to test their marriage ascetics, who lived in pine forest. He is accompanied by Viṣṇu, who is told to assume the form of an entrancing and beautiful woman by Śiva and Śiva goes as a handsome beggar. Together they

14 Winand M. Callewaert, *Gods and Temples in South India* (New Delhi: Manohar Publications, 1995), 46-47.

15 Gokhale, The Book of Shiva, 3-4.

16 David Smith, *The Dance of Śiva, Religion, art and poetry in South India* (Cambridge: Cambridge University Press, 1996), 1.

17 Ananda K. Coomaraswamy, *The Dance of Shiva* (New York: The Noonday Press, 1957), 66.

18 Smith, *The Dance of Śiva, Religion, art and poetry in South India*, 1.

arouse the lusts of the sages and their wives. The sages are enamoured of Mohinī, Viṣṇu as the enchantress, and their wives enamoured of Bhikṣāṭana—the wandering beggar. The older sages, angered at the intrusion and disruption, produce means of attack from their sacrificial fire: tiger, deer, axe, mantras, and dwarf which were of no avail as Śiva takes them as his attributes. He then dances the *Ānandatāṇḍava* for the first time.[19]

The uplifted left leg is revealing grace, which releases the mature soul from bondage. The lower left hand gestures towards the holy foot in assurance that Śiva's grace is the refuge for everyone—the way of liberation. Naṭrāja's dance is not just a symbol. It is taking place within each one of us, at the atomic level, this very moment. The *Āgamas* proclaim, "The birth of the world, its maintenance, its destruction, the soul's obscuration and liberation are the five acts of His dance."[20]

The crouching figure on whom Śiva is seen to be dancing is a demon dwarf Muyalakan, who was sent to fight him and Śiva crushed the demon under his foot and danced on the trampled body of the demon. Thus, the evil force was crushed and the balance of the rhythm of life was maintained by Śiva through his dance. The demon on whom Nataraja danced is also known as *Apasnara Purusha*. This is the aspect of ignorance in a person arising out of forgetfulness. When he is obtained and there is release for the bondage of the world.

Tandava: The Celestial Dance

The Tandava or celestial dance of Lord Śiva is extremely thrilling and charming. It is exquisitely graceful in pose and rhythm and intensely piercing in effect. Nritya or Tandava is an inseparable, sacred movement of the various limbs of the body in accordance with the inner divine Bhava. Nritya is a divine science. The Adigurus for this celestial Nritya were Lord Śiva, Krishna and Mother Kali. In Nritya, the six Bhavas, viz., Srishti, Samhara, Vidya, Avidya, Gati and Agati are demonstrated.

The dance of Lord Śiva is for the welfare of the world. The object of His dance is to free the souls from the fetters of Maya, from the three bonds of Anava (ego), Karma (action) and Maya (illusion). He is not the destroyer but He is the regenerator. He is the Mangala Data and Ananda Data, bestower of auspiciousness and bliss. He is more easily pleased than Lord Hari, He grants boons quickly, for a little Tapas or a little recitation of His five letters.[21]

19 Smith, *The Dance of Śiva, Religion, art and poetry in South India*, 31-33.

20 Subramuniyaswami, *Dancing with Siva*, 41.

21 The five letter word is Namassivaya, which represents Jiva or the individual soul. The Panchakshara Namassivaya forms the body of Lord Siva. The hand that wears fire is 'Na'. The foot that presses the demon Muyalaka is 'Ma'. The hand that holds Damaru is 'Si'. The right and left hand that move about are 'Va'. The hand that shows Abhaya is 'Ya'. Sri

Nataraja: The Protector

A Rakshasa worshipped Brahma and asked Him to grant him the power to destroy the whole world. Brahma was partially unwilling to grant him this boon. He consented in a half-hearted manner and asked him to wait. The Devas, hearing this, were terribly frightened and went to Śiva and told Him everything. Śiva danced in order to delay the granting of this boon by Brahma, to distract him and thus save the world.[22]

Nataraja: The Liberator

Nataraja means the lord of the stage. The idea is that the world is a stage. The place of the dance, the theatre is *thillaivanam*, i.e., the body (of the individual as well as the cosmos) spoken as *vanam* or forest on account of the multitude of its components. The platform on that theatre is the cremation ground, i.e., the place where all the passions and the names and forms that constitute the vision of the world have been burnt away; pure consciousness devoid of attachment to anything outside and devoid of illusion. The Nataraja teaches that *maya* (illusion) should be crushed down; that the world should become subject to us and not we to the world; that the deer like mind should be left behind, and *ahankar* (egoism) be destroyed; that a person should ascend to the region of pure, unconditioned consciousness free from passion and free from deception, and enjoy the calmness which is his birth right, and bliss, the light and the truth that form the self. Viewed in the light of this inner meaning, the Nataraja is no more a meaningless idol, a piece of stone or copper, but a symbol of the highest teaching, an object that can inspire and elevate.[23]

Conclusion

Śiva is the King of Dance, or the King of Dancers. He is the Cosmic Dancer. Perhaps Hinduism's richest and most eloquent symbol, Naṭarāja represents Śiva, the Primal Soul, Parameśvara, as the power, energy and life of all that exists. This is Śiva's intricate state of Being in manifestation. The dance of Śiva—Lord of Dancers—is the dance of the entire cosmos, the rhythmic movements in all. All that is, whether sentient or insentient, pulsates in His body. Naṭarāja is art and spirituality in perfect oneness, chosen to depict the Divine because in dance that which is created is inseparable from its creator, just as the universe and soul cannot be separated from God. Naṭarāja is also

---

Swami Sivananda, *Lord Siva and His Worship* (Tehri-Garhwal: The Divine Life Society, 1996), 447. Also see, Sri Swami Sivananda, *Lord Siva and His Worship* (Tehri-Garhwal: The Divine Life Society, 1996), 38.

22 Sri Swami Sivananda, *Lord Siva and His Worship*, 61.

23 Krishna Saigal, *Gods and Goddesses in Hinduism* (Delhi: Kalpaz Publications, 2007), 267-268.

stillness and motion formed together. The stillness speaks of the peace and poise that lies within us all, at the center. The intense motion depicted by His hair flying wildly in all directions, is an intimation of the fury and ferocity, the violent vigor, which fills this universe wherein we dwell. The implication of these opposites is that God contains and allows them both, that there is divine purpose at work in our life, whether we find ourselves engaged in its beauty or its "madness." Dance and dancer are one; not an atom moves on any plane of existence but by His Will. Thus, this elegant symbol embodies emancipation, creation and sustenance in unity of all the cosmos.

Contributors

The Revd. Dr. Eric J. Lott, born in UK in 1934, is an authority on Indian Religious Tradition. He taught Religions at Andhra Christian Theological College, Hyderabad and United Theological College, Bangalore for over three decades. He has authored many scholarly books including *Vedantic Approaches to God*; *Vision, Tradition, Interpretation*; and the recently published *Embodied God in Indian Eco-Vision: Engaging with Sri Ramanuja's Theology*. Presently he is living in UK.

Rev. Dr. Israel Selvanayagam, a presbyter of the Church of South India, has taught Religions, Mission and Interreligious Relations in several institutions both in India and the West. He has authored and published extensively in the field of religion and interreligious relations. Currently, he is a minister with the Methodist Church, based in Evesham, England.

Rev. Dr. Santanu K. Patro is presently the Registrar of the Senate of Serampore University. He specializes in Hindu Religious Tradition. His Doctoral research focussed on the study of Black Kali from Feminist Perspective. He was formerly teaching at Gurukul Lutheran Theological College, Chennai, in the Department of Religion.

Dr. Jetti A. Oliver is the Chancellor of Sam Haggingbottom University of Agriculture, Technology and Sciences (SHUATS), Allahabad. He is the Chairperson of Telugu Theological Literature Board (TTLB), and a dedicated leader in National Council of Churches in India and the Churches in Telangana and Andhra Pradesh since several decades.

Rev. Dr. Prof. Arun Gopal was the Founder-Director of the C.S.I. Synod Department of Christian Education and a former Professor of Christian Education, Pacific Theological College, Suva, Fiji Islands. He is a retired Presbyter of the C.S.I. Madras Diocese.

Rev. Dr. Rodinmawia Ralte was formerly the Associate Professor of Religion and Philosophy at Bishop's College, Kolkata and also the Associate Professor of Religion at the North India Institute of Post Graduate Theological Studies (NIIPGTS), Kolkata. He also taught at the Academy of Integrated Christian Studies (AICS), Aizawl, Mizoram for several years. He is presently serving as a Pastor under the Baptist Church of Mizoram. He has authored several books and numerous articles.

Rev. Dr. V. Kanagu Nelson is a Professor in Religion Department in Tamil Nadu Theological Seminary. He is an active advocator of interfaith program.

Dr. S. S. Waheeddulla Hussaini Quadri Multani received M.A. (Islamic Studies), M.Com, and Ph.D degrees from Osmania University, Hyderabad and Maulvi Kamil from Jamia Nizamia, Hyderabad. He worked as a Guest Faculty in the Department of Islamic Studies in MANUU, Hyderabad. Presently, he is associated with Henry Martyn Institute, Hyderabad as a senior faculty. He is also an associate editor of the Journal of the Henry Martyn Institute.

Rev. Satvasheel Pandhare completed Bachelor of Commerce Degree from the University of Pune. She is an ordained minister of the Church of North India since 2000 and has served in the Diocese of Pune and Kolhapur. She served as Principal of The United Seminary of Maharasthra, Pune. She completed her Bachelor of Divinity from United Theological Seminary of Maharashtra and Master of Theology from Bishop's College, Kolkata. Presently, she is pursuing Doctoral Studies in the Department of Religion.

Pranay Bin is pursuing Doctor of Theology in the Department of Religions at Advanced Institute for Research on Religion and Culture (ARRC), Hyderabad, under the Senate of Serampore College (University).

Gifta Angeline Kumar is pursuing Doctor of Theology in the Department of Religions at South Asia Theological Research Institute (SATHRI) Kolkata, under the Senate of Serampore College (University).

Aorenla Longchar is pursuing Doctor of Theology in the Department of Religions at Advanced Institute for Research on Religion and Culture (ARRC), Hyderabad, under the Senate of Serampore College (University).

Pamhor Thumra is pursuing Doctor of Theology in the Department of Religions at Advanced Institute for Research on Religion and Culture (ARRC), Hyderabad, under the Senate of Serampore College (University).

Otoka S is pursuing Doctor of Theology in the Department of Religions at Advanced Institute for Research on Religion and Culture (ARRC), Hyderabad, under the Senate of Serampore College (University).

Baila Chanekessvalu is an ordained minister from the Church of South India. Presently, he is teaching in Karnataka Theological College, Mangalore.

Jeevan Kumar Ravela was a research student at United Theological College, Bangalore. At present, he is teaching at Andhra Christian Theological College, Hyderabad in the Department of Old Testament.

Aphenbou Abonmai is pursuing Master of Theology in the Department of Religions at Advanced Institute for Research on Religion and Culture (ARRC), Hyderabad, under the Senate of Serampore College (University).

Khaidem Ajit Kumar Singh is pursuing Master of Theology in the Department of Religions at Advanced Institute for Research on Religion and Culture (ARRC), Hyderabad, under the Senate of Serampore College (University).

K. G. Pousonglung is pursuing Master of Theology in the Department of Religions at Advanced Institute for Research on Religion and Culture (ARRC), Hyderabad, under the Senate of Serampore College (University).

Soloman. S is pursuing Master of Theology in the Department of Religions in Advanced Institute for Research on Religion and Culture (ARRC), Hyderabad, under the Senate of Serampore College (University).

Swami Raju Tadivaka's Literary Contributions

Books

1. ***Na Prabhuvu-Nenu: Sajeeva Sakshayam*** (My Lord and I: Living Testimony), 3rd Revised Edition, Hyderabad, Swami Publications, (2003, 2004, 2006, 2011), 2018, pp. i-viii, 1-136.
2. ***Bharatavanilo Adhunika Chaitanya Udyamalu*** (Modern Renaissant Movements in India), Hyderabad, Telugu Theological Literary Board, 2004, 2014, pp. i-xii, 1-404.
3. ***The Study of Religion: Methods and Perspectives***, Bangalore, Board of Theological Education of Senate of Serampore/South Asia Theological Research Institute, 2004, i-viii, 1-188.
4. Seventy three pages appendix in ***Manamathamulu Mukhya Lakshnamulu*** of Dr. Eric J. Lott, Hyderabad, TTLB, (2005, 2012), 2016 249-324.
5. ***Vira Cult in Folk Religion of Guntur District: A Dalit Perspective***, New Delhi, ISPCK, 2005, pp. i-xv, 1-377.
6. ***Bahulamata Bharatadesamulo Kristhava Sakshyam***, Hyderabad, TTLB, 2006, Reprinted 2013, pp. i-x, 1-203.
7. ***Christian Responses to Plurality of Religion***, Bangalore, BTESSC/SATHRI, 2006, pp. i-viii, 1-134.
8. ***Parishodhana mariyu Rachana Padhtulu*** (Research and Writing Methods), Byderabad, TTLB, 2007, pp. i-viii, 1-60.
9. ***Vivekananduni Naveena Vedantam*** (Neo – Vedanta of Vivekananda), Hyderabad, TTLB, 2009.
10. ***Chennakesava Cult and Dalits,*** Bangalore, BTESSC/SATHRI, 2010, pp. i-viii, 1-134.

11. ***Manava Arogyam mariyu Kristhava Daivasashra Prathyutharam*** (Human Health and Christian Theological Response), Hyderabad, TTLB, 2010, pp. i-x, 1-112.
12. ***My Lord and I: A Living Testimony***, Swami Publications, Hyderabad, 2012, pp. 1-131.
13. ***Ahunika Tharaniki Telugulo Bible Bhashyam*** (Bible Commentary in Telugu to Modern Generation), TTLB/APCC, Hyderabad, 2013, Revised print June, 2015, Andhra Evangelical Lutheran Church, Guntur, November 2015; Revised 2018, pp. i-xi; 1-1765.
14. ***Christian Theological Responses: Contemporary Contextual Concerns***, New Delhi, Christian World Imprints, 2014. pp. i-xviii+182, Index, 23 cm (Hardcover), ISBN 13-978-81-925121-9-8. Paper Back 2018.
15. ***Bharatiya Tatvasashtra Punadulu*** (Indian Philosophical Foundations) Telugu, TTLB, Hyderabad, 2016, pp. i-vii and 1-209.
16. ***Eco-Concerns in Indian Religious Traditions: Inter-Faith Cooperation Towards Healthy Environment,*** New Delhi, Christian World Imprints, 2018, pp. i-xxiv; 1-231.

Articles

1. **"The Study of Religion: Methods and Perspectives – A Synopsis"** in ***The SATHRI Journal of Contextual Theology***, ed. Dr. Samson Prabhakar, Vol. 1, Number 1, Bangalore, Board of Theological Education of Senate of Serampore College, January, 2006, pp. 205f.
2. **"Re-Visioning Theologies: A Multi-Faith Perspective"** in ***The SATHRI Journal of Contextual Theology***, ed. Dr. Samson Prabhakar, Vol. 2, Number 1, Bangalore, Board of Theological Education of Senate of Serampore College, May, 2008, pp. 137-149.
3. **"Nannu Bratakaneeyaru! Nannu Edaganeeyaru" (Let me Live! Let me Grow-an ecological homiletics),** in ***Samaikya***, ed. B. Sunil Vara Kumar, Hyderbad, Andhra Christian Theological College Publications, 2008, pp. 38-40.
4. **"Inter-Religious Dialogue on 'Peace"** in ***Samaikya***, ed. T. Swami Raju,, Hyderbad, Andhra Christian Theological College Publications, 2009, pp. 23-26. (This paper is presented in an Inter-Religious Dialogue arranged by Islamic Research and Educational Foundation on November 29th 2008 at Hockey Grounds, Vijayanagar Colony, Hyderabad).
5. **"Inclusive Pluralistic Spirituality for Harmonious Inter-Faith Relations"** in ***Many Ways of Pluralism,*** ed. V.J. John, Essays in honor

of Kalarikkal Poulse Aleaz (Festschrift), ISPCK & Bishop's College, Kolkata, 2010, pp. 129-142.

6. **"Quest of More Inclusive Pluralistic Spirituality"** in ***Samaikya,*** ed. V. Manikya Rao, Hyderabad, Andhra Christian Theological College Magazine, 2010, pp. 31-36.
7. **"Christu Jayanthi: Paryavaranaparirakshna"** in ***Upadesamalika***, ed. Rev. K.L. Richardson, Andhra Christian Theological College, Hyderabad, Advent, 2010. pp. 9-13.
8. **"Interfaith Cooperation and Political Context"** in ***Journal of The Henry Martyn Institute***" Vol. 29, January – June 2010, pp. 11-17.
9. **"Youth! Know Your Strength"** in ***Samaikya,*** ed. S. Vijayakumari, Hyderabad, Andhra Christian Theological College Magazine, April, 2011, pp. 41-42.
10. **"Lord's Resurrection Witness"** in ***Upadesamalika***, ed. Rev. K.L. Richardson, Andhra Christian Theological College, Hyderabad, Lent, 2011. pp. 51-56.
11. **"Christian Ecumenical Journey: Towards Inclusive Ecumenism"** in ***Samaikya***, ed. T. Mathews Emmanuel, Hyderabad, Andhra Christian Theological College, April 2013, pp. 26-31.
12. **"Subaltern Movements: Insights for Inter-Faith Dialogue"** in *The Yobel Spring*, Festschrift to Rev. Dr. Chilkuri Vasantha Rao on his 50th birthday, eds. Praveen PS. Perumalla, Royce M. Victor & Naveen Rao, ISPCK/ ACTC, New Delhi, 2013.
13. **"Eco-Justice: Contemporary Global Concern"** in *Equipping the Church: Social Justice and Eco-concern"* published in the booklet prepared for One Day Women Meet in connection to Golden Jubilee of Andhra Christian Theological College, ACTC, Hyderabad, 27-02-2014, pp. 14-2.
14. **"Paryavarana Adhyathmikata – Aavasyakatha: Samakaaleena Samaja Bhadhyata"** in *Samaikya*, Goldern Jubilee Edition with the theme "Social Justice & Eco-Spirituality" ed. P. Praveen Prabhu Sudheer, Hyderabad, Andhra Christian Theological College, June 2014, pp. 39-44.
15. **"Paryavarana Parirakshanalo Sthreela Badyata",** in *Devuni Shrustini Kapadutalo Sthreela Bhadyata*, Published in the booklet prepared for One Day National level Women Meet held on February 17th 2015 in ACTC, Hyderabad, pp. 17-19; and two songs composed on women published in the same booklet "**Beti Bachavo – Beti –Padavo**" p. 5, and "**Aadapillante alusenduku?**", p. 9.

16. **"Eco-sophy and Eco-spirituality"** in *Samaikya*, ed. K.L. Richardson, Hyderabad, Andhra Christian Theological College, April, 2015, pp. 29-32.
17. **"Globalization: Challenges to Contemporary Social Life"** in *Hyderabad Journal of Theology*, ed. T. Swami Raju,, Vol.1, Issue No. 1, Hyderbad, Andhra Christian Theological College, April, 2015.
18. **"Spirituality of Vaishnavism"** in *Spirituality: Towards a Comprehensive Perspective,* eds. P. Mohan Larbeer and Santanu K. Patro, BTESSC, Bangalore, 2016. pp. 165-176.
19. **"Eco-Worship"**, in *Morning Devotions of Serampore College Convocation – 2016*, ACTC, Hyderabad, February, 2016, pp. 9-12.
20. **Abhadratalo Sthree...Sanga Parichryalo Savallu"** (Unprotected Women—Challenges in Church Ministry) in *Okkaruju Sthreela Sadassu* (One Day Women Meet), Andhra Christian Theological College, Hyderabad, Monday, March 7th, 2016, pp.10-13; theme songs – song no.1 "Christava Sangama – Christu nava vaduvu sangama", p. 4; song no. 7 "Bheti Bachavo – Bheti Padavo", p. 8.
21. **"Sthree-Purusha Samanatvam: Marala Kattudamu Randi"** (Women-Men Equality: Come Let us build Together) in *Enimidava Jatiya Okkaruju Sthreela Mahasaha* (8th National Level One Day Women's Conference), Andhra Christian Theological College – Institute For Women & Gender Studies, Hyderabad, February 24th 2017, pp. 16-19.
22. Tadivaka Swami Raju, "Palnati Yuddhamu - Nayakurali Nagamma Patra", in *Madyayuga Andhradesa charitralo Palnadu – Nayakuralu Nagamma,* Aacharya Rami Reddi Chandrashekara Reddy (ed.), Akhila Bharata Redla Samkshema Samakhya, Srisailam, 2015, pp. 92-100.
23. Tadivaka Swami Raju, "Martin Luther Sanga Samskarana mariyu Samsmarana", *Samaikya*, K.L. Richardson (ed), Andhra Christian Theological College, Hyderabad, 2017, pp. 1-3.
24. Tadivaka Swami Raju, "Aadhunika Kalamulo Aadarsha Mahila" *Maarutunna Kalamulo Kraisthava Mahila,* Ninth one day National Women Meet, Institute for Women and Gender Studies, Andhra Christian Theological College, Hyderabad, Tuesday, 13 February, 2018, pp. 19-23.
25. Tadivaka Swami Raju, "William Carey: Father of Modern Renaissance in India" in ***Samaikya***, (ACTC College Magazine), ed., N. V. Grace Bhanu, Hyderabad, Andhra Christian Theological College, April 2018, pp. 1-4.
26. Tadivaka Swami Raju, "Dalitula Chaitanyamulo Dalita Sahityamu Paatra", *Dalita Jaagrutilo Dalita Sahityamu*, A. John Prabhakar (ed.), Andhra Christian Theological College, Hyderabad, 2018, pp. 1-10.

27. "Personal Reflection on Church History Series", in *'We' Magazine*, Bilingual Monthly, (ed.) P. A Sudhakar, Vol. 13, Issue 3, New Mind Publications, Hyderabad, September 2018, p. 9.
28. "Inter-Faith Cooperation to Safeguard Healthy Environment" in ***Journal of the Henry Martyn Institute,*** Vol.37, Number 2, July-December 2018; pp. 39-54.
29. "Re-Visioning Luther's Reformation and It's Impact on Indian Renaissance" in ***Re-imagining Reformation: Essays in Honor of P.G. George***; eds. Y.T. Vinayaraj, Dexter Maben, Woba James, ISPCK, New Delhi, 2017, pp. 335-361.
30. Ch. Vasantha Rao and T. Swami Raju, "Interfaith Cooperation and Political Context" in *Awakening to the Immensity of the Mystery: Theory and Practice in Inter-Religious Relations"* ed. Packiam T. Swmuel, ISPCK/ HMI, New Delhi, 2019.